Bible Proofs for Catholic Truths

Also by Dave Armstrong
from Sophia Institute Press®:

A Biblical Defense of Catholicism

The Catholic Verses

The One-Minute Apologist

Dave Armstrong

Bible Proofs for Catholic Truths

A Source Book for Apologists and Inquirers

SOPHIA INSTITUTE PRESS®
Manchester, New Hampshire

All biblical citations from the Authorised Version
(King James Version), 1611, unless otherwise noted.

Additional biblical citations from the Revised Standard Version
of the Bible (© 1971 by Division of Christian Education of the National
Council of the Churches of Christ in the United States of America).

For related reading on the author's blog, see:

The Bible, Church, Tradition, and Canon
http://socrates58.blogspot.com/2006/11/bible-church-tradition-canon-index.html

The Bible: Sola Scriptura
http://socrates58.blogspot.com/2006/11/bible-sola-scriptura-index-page.html

Salvation, Justification, & "Faith Alone"
http://socrates58.blogspot.com/2006/11/salvation-justification-faith-alone.html

Printed in the United States of America

Cover design by Theodore Schluenderfritz

Sophia Institute Press®
Box 5248, Manchester, NH 03108
www.sophiainstitute.com

Library of Congress Cataloging-in-Publication Data

Armstrong, Dave, 1958-
    Bible proofs for Catholic truths : a source book for apologists and inquirers / Dave Armstrong.
        p. cm.
    ISBN 978-1-933184-57-9 (pbk. : alk. paper)
    1. Catholic Church — Apologetic works. 2. Catholic Church —
Doctrines. 3. Bible — Quotations. 4. Bible — Criticism, interpretation,
etc. I. Title.
    BX1752.A763 2009
    230'.2 — dc22

                                                              2009020398

To St. Paul:
the model for all evangelists and apologists,
and St. Peter:
the model for popes and all other leaders of the Church.

Contents

Chapter Two
The Authority of the Catholic Church

Chapter Three
The Authority of Popes

Chapter Four

The Theology of Salvation

Chapter Five

Purgatory

Chapter Six

The Holy Eucharist and the Sacrifice of the Mass

Chapter Eleven

Penance, Redemptive Suffering, and Atonement on Behalf of Others

Chapter Twelve

Angels and the Communion of Saints

Chapter Thirteen

The Blessed Virgin Mary

Chapter Fourteen

Marriage and Sexuality

Chapter Fifteen

Abortion

Introduction

The aim of this book is very simple, and it reflects much of the emphasis in my Catholic apologetic efforts for the last eighteen years. I want to provide the biblical rationale for Catholic beliefs. The subject matter is as endless as the riches, wisdom, and depths of the Bible itself.

My immediate goal is to simply present categorized Bible passages. My own commentary will be kept to a minimum and used only in instances where I am straightforwardly reiterating what Holy Scripture itself states, noting relevant contextual considerations, Greek or Hebrew meanings of words (as explicated by linguistic scholars), or scriptural cross-references.

I have, of course, selected the passages and classified them. Insofar as I did that, I was engaging in "systematic theology." Human input (something beyond God's own words) is necessary as soon as one goes beyond simply placing a Bible on a table in front of someone and saying, "Read all of this: it completely supports what Catholics teach."

In all reasonable argumentation whatever, selective presentation takes place, and in systematic theology, it is necessary to locate the relevant biblical texts and to collect them for the purpose of illustrating that "the Bible teaches thus and so about *this* particular topic." And that involves judgment, which in turn includes a bias.

In that sense, this book is not *just* the Bible. My input and editing and orthodox Catholic presuppositions are present. But the central, essential *focus* is "just the Bible." Holy, Sacred Scripture is thoroughly "Catholic," as I hope to demonstrate in great detail. Praise God for his wonderful, materially sufficient revelation and his aid in helping us to understand and live by it.

Some Catholic teachings are less well attested by direct scriptural indications than others. Yet I believe that those doctrines are also "soaked" in the *spirit* of the Bible. The comprehensive selection of texts herein repeatedly demonstrates this, in my opinion. A multitude of pointers can be as compelling as a single unambiguous signpost, to show us our way. Readers are free to decide the relative strength of individual textual evidence.

Reading these extracts in their full context is even more rewarding and illuminating. The Bible is a harmonious whole, "living and active," and should be interpreted as such, rather than picked apart into fragments. For the purpose of systematic doctrinal study, however, it is quite helpful to categorize texts. Moreover, Catholics emphasize that the Bible is organically related to the tradition and the Church in which it is received and interpreted. If this book helps readers to move beyond arguments into a deeper appreciation of the Word of God, in which lies our salvation, I will be more than happy.

For my purposes in this work, I've chosen the Authorized (King James) Version of the Bible, due to its familiarity among Protestants. Its lofty, poetic prose is deeply embedded in the heritage of English literature and thinking, and Catholic readers will also find it inspiring. In cases of archaic expression, I have clarified in parentheses with the Revised Standard Version — one of the most accurate and beloved modern translations.

Lastly, Catholics and Protestants notoriously disagree as to which books constitute the biblical canon. The number of the inspired books accepted by the universal Church prior to the onset of Protestantism was disputed by Martin Luther and other non-Catholic Christians, and seven books were eventually omitted altogether in most Protestant editions of the Bible, or included separately as sub-canonical "apocryphal" texts. Some of these refer directly to distinctively Catholic doctrines (most notably, purgatory). I've included relatively few citations from these "disputed" books, but for the Catholic, they are Scripture too and ought not be excluded. If the non-Catholic reader wishes to pass over them, more than ample texts remain as "evidences."

Bible Proofs for Catholic Truths

Chapter One

The Authority of Apostolic Tradition

Authoritative sacred tradition

Matthew 23:1-3: Then spake Jesus to the multitude, and to his disciples, [2] Saying, The scribes and the Pharisees sit in Moses' seat: [3] All therefore whatsoever they bid you observe, that observe and do; but do not ye after their works: for they say, and do not. (RSV: "they preach, but do not practice")

1 Corinthians 11:2: . . . keep the ordinances, as I delivered them to you. (RSV: "maintain the traditions even as I have delivered them to you")

1 Corinthians 11:23: For I have received of the Lord that which also I delivered unto you . . .

1 Corinthians 15:3: For I delivered unto you first of all that which I also received, how that Christ died for our sins according to the scriptures;

Colossians 2:8: Beware lest any man spoil you through philosophy and vain deceit, after the tradition of men, after the rudiments of the world, and not after Christ.

2 Thessalonians 2:15: Therefore, brethren, stand fast, and hold the traditions which ye have been taught, whether by word, or our epistle. (RSV: "either by word of mouth, or by letter")

2 Thessalonians 3:6: Now we command you, brethren, in the name of our Lord Jesus Christ, that ye withdraw yourselves from every brother that walketh disorderly, and not after the tradition which he received of us.

2 Thessalonians 3:14: And if any man obey not our word by this epistle, note that man, and have no company with him, that he may be ashamed.

In 2 Thessalonians in RSV, "gospel" is mentioned twice (1:8 and 2:14), "tradition" twice (2:15 and 3:6), but neither "Scripture" nor "Scriptures" appears. "Word of the Lord" appears once (3:1), but it appears not to refer to the Bible.

2 Timothy 2:2: And the things that thou hast heard of me among many witnesses, the same commit thou to faithful men, who shall be able to teach others also.

Authoritative oral tradition / "word of God"

Matthew 13:22: He also that received seed among the thorns is he that heareth the word; and the care of this world, and the deceitfulness of riches, choke the word, and he becometh unfruitful. (other instances of "the word" in RSV: Matt. 13:19-21, 23; Mark 2:2; 4:14-20, 33; Luke 1:2; 8:12-13, 15; John 1:1, 14 [of Jesus]; John 14:24; Acts 6:4; 8:4; 11:19; 14:25; 16:6; Gal. 6:6; Eph.. 5:26; Col.. 4:3; 1 Pet. 3:1)

Luke 5:1: And it came to pass, that, as the people pressed upon him to hear the word of God, he stood by the lake of Gennesaret, (other instances of "word of God" in RSV: Luke 3:2; 8:11, 21; John 17:8; Acts 6:2; 13:5, 7, 44, 48; 17:13; 18:11; Rom.. 9:6; 1 Cor. 14:36; Eph. 6:17; Phil. 1:14; Col. 1:25; 1 Tim. 4:5; 2 Tim. 2:9; Titus 2:5; Heb. 6:5; 13:7; 1 John 2:14; Rev. 1:9; 20:4)

Luke 11:28: But he said, Yea rather, blessed are they that hear the word of God, and keep it.

Acts 4:4: . . . many of them which heard the word believed . . . (cf. Acts 2:41)

Acts 4:31: . . . they were all filled with the Holy Ghost, and they spake the word of God with boldness.

Acts 6:7: And the word of God increased; and the number of the disciples multiplied in Jerusalem greatly; and a great company of the priests were obedient to the faith. (cf. 12:24)

Acts 8:14: . . . Samaria had received the word of God . . . (cf. 11:1)

Acts 8:25: And they, when they had testified and preached the word of the Lord, returned to Jerusalem, and preached the gospel in many villages of the Samaritans. (other instances of "word of the Lord" in RSV: Acts 15:35-36; 16:32; 19:10, 20; 1 Thess. 1:8; 4:15; 2 Thess. 3:1)

Acts 10:36-44: The word which God sent unto the children of Israel, preaching peace by Jesus Christ: (he is Lord of all:)
[37] That word, I say, ye know, which was published throughout all Judaea, and began from Galilee, after the baptism which John preached; [38] How God anointed Jesus of Nazareth with the Holy Ghost and with power: who went about doing good, and healing all that were oppressed of the devil; for God was with him. [39] And we are witnesses of all things which he did both in the land of the Jews, and in Jerusalem; whom they slew and hanged on a tree: [40] Him God raised up the third day, and shewed him openly; [41] Not to all the people, but unto witnesses chosen before of God, even to us, who did eat and drink with him after he rose from the dead. [42] And he commanded us to preach unto the people, and to testify that it is he which was ordained of God to be the Judge of quick and dead. [43] To him give all the prophets witness, that through his name whosoever believeth in him shall receive remission of sins. [44] While Peter yet spake these words, the Holy Ghost fell on all them which heard the word.

Acts 13:46: Then Paul and Barnabas waxed bold, and said, It was necessary that the word of God should first have been spoken to you: but seeing ye put it from you, and judge yourselves unworthy of everlasting life, lo, we turn to the Gentiles.

Acts 13:49: And the word of the Lord was published throughout all the region.

Acts 14:3: Long time therefore abode they speaking boldly in the Lord, which gave testimony unto the word of his grace, and granted signs and wonders to be done by their hands. (cf. Acts 20:32 in RSV: "word of his grace")

Acts 15:7: And when there had been much disputing, Peter rose up, and said unto them, Men and brethren, ye know how that a good while ago God made choice among us, that the Gentiles by my mouth should hear the word of the gospel, and believe.

Acts 15:27: We have sent therefore Judas and Silas, who shall also tell you the same things by mouth. (RSV: "by word of mouth")

Acts 17:11: These were more noble than those in Thessalonica, in that they received the word with all readiness of mind, and searched the scriptures daily, whether those things were so.

Romans 10:8: . . . The word is nigh thee, even in thy mouth, and in thy heart: that is, the word of faith, which we preach; (RSV: "The word is near you, on your lips and in your heart")

Romans 16:25: Now to him that is of power to stablish you according to my gospel, and the preaching of Jesus Christ, according to the revelation of the mystery, which was kept secret since the world began,

1 Corinthians 1:18: For the preaching of the cross is to them that perish foolishness; but unto us which are saved it is the power of God. (RSV: "the word of the cross")

1 Corinthians 14:29-30: Let the prophets speak two or three, and let the other judge. [30] If any thing be revealed to another that sitteth by, let the first hold his peace. (RSV: "If a revelation is made to another sitting by, let the first be silent")

2 Corinthians 3:6: Who also hath made us able ministers of the new testament; not of the letter, but of the spirit: for the letter killeth, but the spirit giveth life. (RSV: "ministers of a new covenant, not in a written code but in the Spirit; for the written code kills")

Ephesians 1:13: In whom ye also trusted, after that ye heard the word of truth, the gospel of your salvation: in whom also after that ye believed, ye were sealed with that holy Spirit of promise, (cf. 2 Tim. 2:15 in RSV: "word of truth")

Philippians 2:16: Holding forth the word of life; that I may rejoice in the day of Christ, that I have not run in vain, neither laboured in vain. (cf. 1 John 1:1 in RSV: "word of life")

Philippians 4:9: Those things, which ye have both learned, and received, and heard, and seen in me, do: and the God of peace shall be with you.

Colossians 1:5-6: For the hope which is laid up for you in heaven, whereof ye heard before in the word of the truth of the gospel;
[6] Which is come unto you, as it is in all the world; and bringeth forth fruit, as it doth also in you, since the day ye heard of it, and knew the grace of God in truth:

Colossians 3:16: Let the word of Christ dwell in you richly in all wisdom; teaching and admonishing one another in psalms and hymns and spiritual songs, singing with grace in your hearts to the Lord.

1 Thessalonians 1:6: And ye became followers of us, and of the Lord, having received the word in much affliction, with joy of the Holy Ghost:

1 Thessalonians 2:13: For this cause also thank we God without ceasing, because, when ye received the word of God which ye heard of us, ye received it not as the word of men, but as it is in truth, the word of God, which effectually worketh also in you that believe.

In 1 Thessalonians in RSV, "Scripture" or "Scriptures" never appear. There are five appearances of "word," "word of the Lord," or "word of God" (1:6, 8; 2:13 [twice]; 4:15), but in each instance it is clearly in the sense of oral proclamation, not Scripture.

2 Thessalonians 2:15: Therefore, brethren, stand fast, and hold the traditions which ye have been taught, whether by word, or our epistle.

2 Timothy 1:13-14: Hold fast the form of sound words, which thou hast heard of me, in faith and love which is in Christ Jesus.

[14] That good thing which was committed unto thee keep by the Holy Ghost which dwelleth in us. (RSV: "Follow the pattern of the sound words which you have heard from me . . . guard the truth which has been entrusted to you")

2 Timothy 2:2: And the things that thou hast heard of me among many witnesses, the same commit thou to faithful men, who shall be able to teach others also. (RSV: "what you have heard from me")

2 Timothy 4:2: Preach the word; be instant in season, out of season; reprove, rebuke, exhort with all longsuffering and doctrine.

Hebrews 2:1-4: Therefore we ought to give the more earnest heed to the things which we have heard, lest at any time we should let them slip. [2] For if the word spoken by angels was stedfast, and every transgression and disobedience received a just recompence of reward; [3] How shall we escape, if we neglect so great salvation; which at the first began to be spoken by the Lord, and was confirmed unto us by them that heard him; [4] God also bearing them witness, both with signs and wonders, and with divers miracles, and gifts of the Holy Ghost, according to his own will?

Hebrews 4:12: For the word of God is quick, and powerful, and sharper than any two-edged sword, piercing even to the dividing asunder of soul and spirit, and of the joints and marrow, and is a discerner of the thoughts and intents of the heart.

Hebrews 5:13: For every one that useth milk is unskilful in the word of righteousness: for he is a babe.

Hebrews 13:7: Remember them which have the rule over you, who have spoken unto you the word of God: whose faith follow, considering the end of their conversation. (RSV: "consider the outcome of their life, and imitate their faith")

James 1:18: Of his own will begat he us with the word of truth, that we should be a kind of firstfruits of his creatures.

James 1:22-23: But be ye doers of the word, and not hearers only, deceiving your own selves. [23] For if any be a hearer of the word, and not a doer, he is like unto a man beholding his natural face in a glass:

1 Peter 1:23: Being born again, not of corruptible seed, but of incorruptible, by the word of God, which liveth and abideth for ever.

1 Peter 1:25: But the word of the Lord endureth for ever. And this is the word which by the gospel is preached unto you.

1 Peter 2:8: And a stone of stumbling, and a rock of offence, even to them which stumble at the word, being disobedient: whereunto also they were appointed.

2 Peter 1:19, 21: We have also a more sure word of prophecy; whereunto ye do well that ye take heed, as unto a light that shineth in a dark place, until the day dawn, and the day star arise in your hearts . . . [21] For the prophecy came not in old time by the will of man: but holy men of God spake as they were moved by the Holy Ghost.

1 John 1:5: This then is the message which we have heard of him, and declare unto you, that God is light, and in him is no darkness at all.

1 John 2:7: Brethren, I write no new commandment unto you, but an old commandment which ye had from the beginning. The old commandment is the word which ye have heard from the beginning.

1 John 2:24: Let that therefore abide in you, which ye have heard from the beginning. If that which ye have heard from the beginning shall remain in you, ye also shall continue in the Son, and in the Father.

1 John 3:11: For this is the message that ye heard from the beginning, that we should love one another.

2 John 1:6: And this is love, that we walk after his commandments. This is the commandment, That, as ye have heard from the beginning, ye should walk in it.

Revelation 1:2: Who bare record of the word of God, and of the testimony of Jesus Christ, and of all things that he saw. (RSV: "bore witness to the word of God")

Revelation 3:3: Remember therefore how thou hast received and heard, and hold fast, and repent . . .

Revelation 3:10: Because thou hast kept the word of my patience, I also will keep thee from the hour of temptation, which shall come upon all the world, to try them that dwell upon the earth.

Revelation 6:9: And when he had opened the fifth seal, I saw under the altar the souls of them that were slain for the word of God, and for the testimony which they held . . .

Authoritative oral teaching
not recorded in scripture

Matthew 13:3: And he spake many things unto them in parables.

Matthew 28: . . . Teaching them to observe all things whatsoever I have commanded you: and, lo, I am with you alway, even unto the end of the world. Amen.

Mark 4:2: And he taught them many things by parables . . .

Mark 4:33: And with many such parables spake he the word unto them, as they were able to hear it.

Mark 6:34: And Jesus, when he came out, saw much people, and was moved with compassion toward them, because they were as sheep not having a shepherd: and he began to teach them many things.

Luke 11:53: And as he said these things unto them, the scribes and the Pharisees began to urge him vehemently, and to provoke him to speak of many things:

Luke 24:15-16, 25-27: And it came to pass, that, while they communed together and reasoned, Jesus himself drew near, and went with them. [16] But their eyes were holden that they should not know him . . . [25] Then he said unto them, O fools, and slow of heart to believe all that the prophets have spoken:

[26] Ought not Christ to have suffered these things, and to enter into his glory? [27] And beginning at Moses and all the prophets, he expounded unto them in all the scriptures the things concerning himself. (RSV: "But their eyes were kept from recognizing him . . . he interpreted to them . . .")

John 16:12: I have yet many things to say unto you, but ye cannot bear them now.

John 20:30: And many other signs truly did Jesus in the presence of his disciples, which are not written in this book: (cf. John 21:25 in RSV: "many other things which Jesus did")

Acts 1:2-3: Until the day in which he was taken up, after that he, through the Holy Ghost, had given commandments unto the apostles whom he had chosen: [3] To whom also he shewed himself alive after his passion by many infallible proofs, being seen of them forty days, and speaking of the things pertaining to the kingdom of God:

New Testament citations of older nonbiblical oral traditions

Matthew 2:23: And he came and dwelt in a city called Nazareth: that it might be fulfilled which was spoken by the prophets, He shall be called a Nazarene.

This notion cannot be found in the Old Testament, yet it was passed down "by the prophets." Thus, a prophecy, which is considered to be "God's Word," was passed down orally, rather than through Scripture.

Matthew 7:12: Therefore all things whatsoever ye would that men should do to you, do ye even so to them: for this is the law and the prophets.

Matthew 23:2: . . . The scribes and the Pharisees sit in Moses' seat:

The phrase or idea of Moses' seat cannot be found anywhere in the Old Testament. It is found in the (originally oral) Mishna, where a sort of "teaching succession" from Moses on down is taught.

1 Corinthians 10:4: And did all drink the same spiritual drink: for they drank of that spiritual Rock that followed them: and that Rock was Christ.

The Old Testament says nothing about such miraculous movement, in the related passages about Moses striking the rock to produce water (Exod. 17:1-7; Num. 20:2-13). But rabbinic tradition does.

2 Timothy 3:8: Now as Jannes and Jambres withstood Moses, so do these also resist the truth: men of corrupt minds, reprobate concerning the faith.

These two men cannot be found in the related Old Testament passage (Exod. 7:8 ff.), or anywhere else in the Old Testament.

James 5:17: Elias was a man subject to like passions as we are, and he prayed earnestly that it might not rain: and it rained not on the earth by the space of three years and six months.

The reference to a lack of rain for three years is absent from the relevant Old Testament passage in 1 Kings 17.

1 Peter 3:19: By which also he went and preached unto the spirits in prison;

This is drawn from the Jewish apocalyptic book 1 Enoch (12-16).

Jude 9: Yet Michael the archangel, when contending with the devil he disputed about the body of Moses, durst not bring against him a railing accusation, but said, The Lord rebuke thee.

Jude 14-15: And Enoch also, the seventh from Adam, prophesied of these, saying, Behold, the Lord cometh with ten thousands of his saints, [15] To execute judgment upon all, and to convince all that are ungodly among them of all their ungodly deeds which they have ungodly committed, and of all their hard speeches which ungodly sinners have spoken against him.

This is a direct quotation of 1 Enoch 1:9.

"The Faith" is synonymous
with sacred tradition

Acts 6:7: And the word of God increased; and the number of the disciples multiplied in Jerusalem greatly; and a great company of the priests were obedient to the faith.

Acts 13:8: But Elymas the sorcerer (for so is his name by interpretation) withstood them, seeking to turn away the deputy from the faith.

Acts 14:22: . . . Confirming the souls of the disciples, and exhorting them to continue in the faith, and that we must through much tribulation enter into the kingdom of God.

Acts 16:5: And so were the churches established in the faith, and increased in number daily.

Galatians 1:23: But they had heard only, That he which persecuted us in times past now preacheth the faith which once he destroyed.

Ephesians 4:13: . . . Till we all come in the unity of the faith, and of the knowledge of the Son of God, unto a perfect man, unto the measure of the stature of the fulness of Christ:

Philippians 1:25, 27: And having this confidence, I know that I shall abide and continue with you all for your furtherance and joy of faith . . . [27] Only let your conversation be as it becometh the gospel of Christ: that whether I come and see you, or else be absent, I may hear of your affairs, that ye stand fast in one spirit, with one mind striving together for the faith of the gospel;

Colossians 1:23: If ye continue in the faith grounded and settled, and be not moved away from the hope of the gospel, which ye have heard, and which was preached to every creature which is under heaven; whereof I Paul am made a minister;

Colossians 2:7: Rooted and built up in him, and stablished in the faith, as ye have been taught, abounding therein with thanksgiving.

1 Timothy 1:2: Unto Timothy, my own son in the faith . . .

1 Timothy 3:9, 13: Holding the mystery of the faith in a pure conscience . . . [13] For they that have used the office of a deacon well purchase to themselves a good degree, and great boldness in the faith which is in Christ Jesus.

1 Timothy 4:1: Now the Spirit speaketh expressly, that in the latter times some shall depart from the faith, giving heed to seducing spirits, and doctrines of devils;

1 Timothy 4:6: If thou put the brethren in remembrance of these things, thou shalt be a good minister of Jesus Christ, nourished up in the words of faith and of good doctrine, whereunto thou hast attained.

1 Timothy 5:8: But if any provide not for his own, and specially for those of his own house, he hath denied the faith, and is worse than an infidel.

1 Timothy 6:10, 12: For the love of money is the root of all evil: which while some coveted after, they have erred from the faith, and pierced themselves through with many sorrows . . . [12] Fight the good fight of faith, lay hold on eternal life, whereunto thou art also called, and hast professed a good profession before many witnesses.

1 Timothy 6:21: . . . Which some professing have erred concerning the faith. Grace be with thee. Amen.

2 Timothy 4:7: I have fought a good fight, I have finished my course, I have kept the faith:

Titus 1:1: Paul, a servant of God, and an apostle of Jesus Christ, according to the faith of God's elect, and the acknowledging of the truth which is after godliness;

Titus 1:13: This witness is true. Wherefore rebuke them sharply, that they may be sound in the faith;

Titus 3:15: . . . Greet them that love us in the faith . . .

James 2:1: My brethren, have not the faith of our Lord Jesus Christ, the Lord of glory, with respect of persons. (RSV: "show no partiality as you hold the faith of our Lord")

Jude 3: . . . ye should earnestly contend for the faith which was once delivered unto the saints.

Revelation 14:12: Here is the patience of the saints: here are they that keep the commandments of God, and the faith of Jesus.

"The truth" is synonymous with sacred tradition

Luke 1:1-4: Forasmuch as many have taken in hand to set forth in order a declaration of those things which are most surely believed among us, [2] Even as they delivered them unto us, which from the beginning were eyewitnesses, and ministers of the word;

[3] It seemed good to me also, having had perfect understanding of all things from the very first, to write unto thee in order, most excellent Theophilus, [4] That thou mightest know the certainty of those things, wherein thou hast been instructed (RSV: "that you may know the truth concerning the things of which you have been informed").

John 1:17: For the law was given by Moses, but grace and truth came by Jesus Christ.

John 4:23: But the hour cometh, and now is, when the true worshippers shall worship the Father in spirit and in truth: for the Father seeketh such to worship him.

John 8:31-32: Then said Jesus to those Jews which believed on him, If ye continue in my word, then are ye my disciples indeed;

[32] And ye shall know the truth, and the truth shall make you free.

John 14:6: Jesus saith unto him, I am the way, the truth, and the life: no man cometh unto the Father, but by me.

John 15:26: But when the Comforter is come, whom I will send unto you from the Father, even the Spirit of truth, which proceedeth from the Father, he shall testify of me:

John 16:13: Howbeit when he, the Spirit of truth, is come, he will guide you into all truth: for he shall not speak of himself; but whatsoever he shall hear, that shall he speak: and he will shew you things to come.

John 17:17-19: Sanctify them through thy truth: thy word is truth. [18] As thou hast sent me into the world, even so have I also sent them into the world. [19] And for their sakes I sanctify myself, that they also might be sanctified through the truth.

John 18:37: Pilate therefore said unto him, Art thou a king then? Jesus answered, Thou sayest that I am a king. To this end was I born, and for this cause came I into the world, that I should bear witness unto the truth. Every one that is of the truth heareth my voice.

John 19:35: And he that saw it bare record, and his record is true: and he knoweth that he saith true, that ye might believe. (RSV: "He who saw it has borne witness — his testimony is true, and he knows that he tells the truth")

Romans 2:8: But unto them that are contentious, and do not obey the truth, but obey unrighteousness, indignation and wrath,

1 Corinthians 2:13: Which things also we speak, not in the words which man's wisdom teacheth, but which the Holy Ghost teacheth; comparing spiritual things with spiritual. (RSV: "And we impart this in words not taught by human wisdom but taught by the Spirit, interpreting spiritual truths to those who possess the Spirit")

2 Corinthians 4:2: But have renounced the hidden things of dishonesty, not walking in craftiness, nor handling the word of God deceitfully; but by manifestation of the truth commending ourselves to every man's conscience in the sight of God. (RSV: "We have renounced disgraceful, underhanded ways; we refuse to practice cunning or to tamper with God's word, but by the open statement of the truth we would commend ourselves")

2 Corinthians 11:10: . . . the truth of Christ is in me . . .

2 Corinthians 13:8: For we can do nothing against the truth, but for the truth. (RSV: "but only for the truth")

Galatians 5:7: Ye did run well; who did hinder you that ye should not obey the truth?

Ephesians 1:13: In whom ye also trusted, after that ye heard the word of truth, the gospel of your salvation: in whom also after that ye believed, ye were sealed with that holy Spirit of promise, (cf. 6:14)

Colossians 1:5: For the hope which is laid up for you in heaven, whereof ye heard before in the word of the truth of the gospel;

2 Thessalonians 2:10-13: And with all deceivableness of unrighteousness in them that perish; because they received not the love of the truth, that they might be saved. [11] And for this cause God shall send them strong delusion, that they should believe a lie: [12] That they all might be damned who believed not the truth, but had pleasure in unrighteousness.
[13] But we are bound to give thanks alway to God for you, brethren beloved of the Lord, because God hath from the beginning chosen you to salvation through sanctification of the Spirit and belief of the truth:

1 Timothy 2:4: Who will have all men to be saved, and to come unto the knowledge of the truth.

1 Timothy 3:15: But if I tarry long, that thou mayest know how thou oughtest to behave thyself in the house of God, which is the church of the living God, the pillar and ground of the truth. (RSV: "the pillar and bulwark of the truth")

1 Timothy 4:3: . . . them which believe and know the truth.

2 Timothy 1:13-14: Hold fast the form of sound words, which thou hast heard of me, in faith and love which is in Christ Jesus.
[14] That good thing which was committed unto thee keep by the Holy Ghost which dwelleth in us. (RSV: "Follow the pattern of the sound words which you have heard from me . . . guard the truth which has been entrusted to you")

2 Timothy 2:18: Who concerning the truth have erred, saying that the resurrection is past already; and overthrow the faith of some. (RSV: "who have swerved from the truth")

2 Timothy 2:25: In meekness instructing those that oppose themselves; if God peradventure will give them repentance to the acknowledging of the truth;

2 Timothy 3:7-8: Ever learning, and never able to come to the knowledge of the truth. [8] Now as Jannes and Jambres withstood Moses, so do these also resist the truth: men of corrupt minds, reprobate concerning the faith.

2 Timothy 4:4: And they shall turn away their ears from the truth, and shall be turned unto fables.

Titus 1:1: Paul, a servant of God, and an apostle of Jesus Christ, according to the faith of God's elect, and the acknowledging of the truth which is after godliness; (cf. 1:14)

Hebrews 10:26: For if we sin wilfully after that we have received the knowledge of the truth, there remaineth no more sacrifice for sins,

James 5:19: . . . if any of you do err from the truth . . .

1 Peter 1:22: Seeing ye have purified your souls in obeying the truth through the Spirit . . .

2 Peter 1:12: Wherefore I will not be negligent to put you always in remembrance of these things, though ye know them, and be established in the present truth.

1 John 1:6: If we say that we have fellowship with him, and walk in darkness, we lie, and do not the truth:

1 John 2:21: I have not written unto you because ye know not the truth, but because ye know it, and that no lie is of the truth.

1 John 3:19: And hereby we know that we are of the truth, and shall assure our hearts before him.

1 John 4:6: We are of God: he that knoweth God heareth us; he that is not of God heareth not us. Hereby know we the spirit of truth, and the spirit of error.

1 John 5:7-8: For there are three that bear record in heaven, the Father, the Word, and the Holy Ghost: and these three are one. [8] And there are three that bear witness in earth, the spirit, and the water, and the blood: and these three agree in one. (RSV: "[7] And the Spirit is the witness, because the Spirit is the truth")

2 John 1:1-4: The elder unto the elect lady and her children, whom I love in the truth; and not I only, but also all they that have known the truth; [2] For the truth's sake, which dwelleth in us, and shall be with us for ever. [3] Grace be with you, mercy, and peace, from God the Father, and from the Lord Jesus Christ, the Son of the Father, in truth and love. [4] I rejoiced greatly that I found of thy children walking in truth, as we have received a commandment from the Father (RSV: "following the truth, just as we have been commanded by the Father").

3 John 1:1, 3-4: The elder unto the well-beloved Gaius, whom I love in the truth . . . [3] For I rejoiced greatly, when the brethren came and testified of the truth that is in thee, even as thou walkest in the truth. [4] I have no greater joy than to hear that my children walk in truth.

3 John 1:8, 12: We therefore ought to receive such, that we might be fellow-helpers to the truth . . . Demetrius hath good report of all men, and of the truth itself: yea, and we also bear record; and ye know that our record is true.

"The commandment" is
synonymous with sacred tradition

Matthew 15:3, 6: . . . Why do ye also transgress the commandment of God by your tradition? . . . [6] . . . Thus have ye made the commandment of God of none effect by your tradition. (RSV: "for the sake of your tradition? . . . you have made void the word of God")

Mark 7:8, 13: For laying aside the commandment of God, ye hold the tradition of men . . . [13] Making the word of God of none effect through your tradition, which ye have delivered . . . (RSV: "You leave the commandment of God, and hold fast the tradition of men . . . thus making void the word of God")

1 Timothy 6:14: . . . keep this commandment without spot . . . .

2 Peter 2:21: For it had been better for them not to have known the way of righteousness, than, after they have known it, to turn from the holy commandment delivered unto them.

2 Peter 3:1-2: This second epistle, beloved, I now write unto you; in both which I stir up your pure minds by way of remembrance.
[2] That ye may be mindful of the words which were spoken before by the holy prophets, and of the commandment of us the apostles of the Lord and Saviour:

1 John 2:3-8: And hereby we do know that we know him, if we keep his commandments. [4] He that saith, I know him, and keepeth not his commandments, is a liar, and the truth is not in him. [5] But whoso keepeth his word, in him verily is the love of God perfected: hereby know we that we are in him.

[6] He that saith he abideth in him ought himself also so to walk, even as he walked. [7] Brethren, I write no new commandment unto you, but an old commandment which ye had from the beginning. The old commandment is the word which ye have heard from the beginning. [8] Again, a new commandment I write unto you, which thing is true in him and in you: because the darkness is past, and the true light now shineth.

1 John 3:23: And this is his commandment, That we should believe on the name of his Son Jesus Christ, and love one another, as he gave us commandment.

2 John 1:5-6: And now I beseech thee, lady, not as though I wrote a new commandment unto thee, but that which we had from the beginning, that we love one another. [6] And this is love, that we walk after his commandments. This is the commandment, That, as ye have heard from the beginning, ye should walk in it.

"The doctrine" is synonymous with sacred tradition

Romans 16:17: Now I beseech you, brethren, mark them which cause divisions and offences contrary to the doctrine which ye have learned; and avoid them.

1 Timothy 4:6: If thou put the brethren in remembrance of these things, thou shalt be a good minister of Jesus Christ, nourished up in the words of faith and of good doctrine, whereunto thou hast attained.

Titus 2:10: Not purloining, but shewing all good fidelity; that they may adorn the doctrine of God our Saviour in all things.

2 John 1:9: Whosoever transgresseth, and abideth not in the doctrine of Christ, hath not God. He that abideth in the doctrine of Christ, he hath both the Father and the Son. (cf. also, "the Way" in RSV: Acts 9:2; 22:4; 24:14, 22)

"Teaching" is synonymous with sacred tradition

Acts 2:41-42: Then they that gladly received his word were baptized: and the same day there were added unto them about three thousand souls. [42] And they continued stedfastly in the apostles' doctrine and fellowship, and in breaking of bread, and in prayers. (RSV: "apostles' teaching")

Romans 6:17: But God be thanked, that ye were the servants of sin, but ye have obeyed from the heart that form of doctrine which was delivered you. (RSV: "the standard of teaching to which you were committed")

1 Timothy 4:16: Take heed unto thyself, and unto the doctrine; continue in them: for in doing this thou shalt both save thyself, and them that hear thee. (RSV: "Take heed to yourself and to your teaching; hold to that, for by so doing you will save both yourself and your hearers")

1 Timothy 6:1: . . . that the name of God and his doctrine be not blasphemed. (RSV: "the teaching may not be defamed")

"Gospel" or "good news" is
synonymous with sacred tradition

Matthew 4:23: . . . the gospel of the kingdom . . . (same words in RSV also in Matt. 9:35; 24:14)

Matthew 11:5: . . . the poor have the gospel preached to them. (cf. Luke 7:22. "Good news" in this sense appears in RSV in: Luke 1:19; 2:10; Acts 10:36; 13:32; 14:15; Rom. 10:15; Heb. 4:2, 6; 1 Pet. 1:12, 25)

Matthew 26:13: . . . this gospel . . . (same words also in RSV in Eph. 3:7; 2 Tim. 1:11)

Mark 1:1: . . . the gospel of Jesus Christ . . .

Mark 1:14: . . . the gospel of the kingdom of God. ("gospel of God" in RSV in Mark 1:14; Rom. 1:1; 15:16; 1 Thess. 2:2, 8-9; 1 Pet. 4:17)

Mark 1:15: . . . the gospel. (same words in RSV also in Mark 8:35; 10:29; 13:10; 14:9; 16:15; Luke 9:6; 20:1; Acts 8:25, 40; 14:7, 21; 15:7; 16:10; Rom. 1:15; 1:16; 10:16; 11:28; 15:20; 1 Cor. 1:17; 4:15; 9:14; 9:16; 9:18 [2]; 9:23; 2 Cor. 8:18; 10:16; Gal 1:7; 1:11; 2:2; 2:5; 2:7 [2]; 2:14; 3:8; 4:13; Eph. 3:6; 6:15; 6:19; Phil. 1:5, 7, 12, 16, 27; 2:22; 4:3, 15; Col. 1:5, 23; 1 Thess. 2:4; 2 Tim. 1:8, 10; 2 Tim. 2:9; Philem. 1:13; 1 Pet. 4:6)

Luke 3:18: And many other things in his exhortation preached he unto the people. (RSV: "So, with many other exhortations, he preached good news to the people")

Luke 4:18: The Spirit of the Lord is upon me, because he hath anointed me to preach the gospel to the poor . . . (RSV: "to preach good news")

Luke 4:43: And he said unto them, I must preach the kingdom of God to other cities also: for therefore am I sent. (RSV: "I must preach the good news of the kingdom of God")

 Luke 8:1: . . . preaching and shewing the glad tidings of the kingdom of God . . . (RSV: "preaching and bringing the good news of the kingdom of God"; "good news of the kingdom of God" appears also in RSV in Luke 16:16; Acts 8:12 ["about"])

Acts 8:35: Then Philip opened his mouth, and began at the same scripture, and preached unto him Jesus. (RSV: "he told him the good news of Jesus")

Acts 20:24: . . . to testify the gospel of the grace of God.

Romans 1:1-3: Paul, a servant of Jesus Christ, called to be an apostle, separated unto the gospel of God, [2] (Which he had promised afore by his prophets in the holy scriptures) [3] Concerning his Son Jesus Christ our Lord, which was made of the seed of David according to the flesh (RSV: "[3] the gospel concerning his Son").

Romans 1:9: . . . the gospel of his Son . . .

Romans 2:16: . . . my gospel. (same words also in RSV in Rom. 16:25; 2 Tim. 2:8)

Romans 15:19: . . . the gospel of Christ. (same words also in RSV in 1 Cor. 9:12; 2 Cor. 2:12; 9:13; 10:14; Phil. 1:27; 1 Thess. 3:2)

1 Corinthians 15:1: Moreover, brethren, I declare unto you the gospel which I preached unto you, which also ye have received, and wherein ye stand;

2 Corinthians 4:3: . . . our gospel . . . (same words also in RSV in 1 Thess. 1:5; 2 Thess. 2:14)

2 Corinthians 4:4: . . . the glorious gospel of Christ . . . (RSV: "gospel of the glory of Christ")

2 Corinthians 11:4: For if he that cometh preacheth another Jesus, whom we have not preached, or if ye receive another spirit, which ye have not received, or another gospel, which ye have not accepted, ye might well bear with him. (RSV: "a different gospel from the one you accepted, you submit to it readily enough"; "gospel" also in RSV in Gal 1:6; 1:7; 1:8; 1:9; 1:11)

2 Corinthians 11:7: . . . the gospel of God . . . (RSV: "God's gospel")

Galatians 1:6-12: I marvel that ye are so soon removed from him that called you into the grace of Christ unto another gospel:
[7] Which is not another; but there be some that trouble you, and would pervert the gospel of Christ. [8] But though we, or an angel from heaven, preach any other gospel unto you than that which we have preached unto you, let him be accursed.
[9] As we said before, so say I now again, If any man preach any other gospel unto you than that ye have received, let him be accursed. [10] For do I now persuade men, or God? or do I seek to please men? for if I yet pleased men, I should not be the servant of Christ. [11] But I certify you, brethren, that the gospel which was preached of me is not after man. [12] For I neither received it of man, neither was I taught it, but by the revelation of Jesus Christ.

Ephesians 1:13: In whom ye also trusted, after that ye heard the word of truth, the gospel of your salvation: in whom also after that ye believed, ye were sealed with that holy Spirit of promise,

Philippians 1:27: Only let your conversation be as it becometh the gospel of Christ: that whether I come and see you, or else be absent, I may hear of your affairs, that ye stand fast in one spirit, with one mind striving together for the faith of the gospel;

Colossians 1:23: If ye continue in the faith grounded and settled, and be not moved away from the hope of the gospel, which ye have heard, and which was preached to every creature which is under heaven; whereof I Paul am made a minister;

2 Thessalonians 1:8: . . . the gospel of our Lord Jesus Christ.

1 Timothy 1:11: According to the glorious gospel of the blessed God, which was committed to my trust.

Revelation 14:6: . . . the everlasting gospel . . .

"The message" is synonymous with sacred tradition

Mark 16:20: And they went forth, and preached everywhere, the Lord working with them, and confirming the word with signs following. Amen. (RSV: "confirmed the message")

Acts 11:14: Who shall tell thee words, whereby thou and all thy house shall be saved. (RSV: "he will declare to you a message")

Acts 13:26: . . . to you is the word of this salvation sent. (RSV: "the message of this salvation")

1 Corinthians 2:4: And my speech and my preaching was not with enticing words of man's wisdom, but in demonstration of the Spirit and of power: (RSV: "my message")

2 Corinthians 5:19: To wit, that God was in Christ, reconciling the world unto himself, not imputing their trespasses unto them; and hath committed unto us the word of reconciliation. (RSV: "message of reconciliation")

2 Timothy 4:15, 17: Of whom be thou ware also; for he hath greatly withstood our words . . . [17] . . . that by me the preaching might be fully known, and that all the Gentiles might hear . . . (RSV: "he strongly opposed our message . . . to proclaim the message fully")

Hebrews 4:2: For unto us was the gospel preached, as well as unto them: but the word preached did not profit them, not being mixed with faith in them that heard it. (RSV: "For good news came to us just as to them; but the message which they heard did not benefit them")

1 John 1:5: This then is the message which we have heard of him, and declare unto you, that God is light, and in him is no darkness at all. (cf. 3:11)

The new covenant is
synonymous with sacred tradition

Matthew 26:28: For this is my blood of the new testament, which is shed for many for the remission of sins.

Mark 14:24: And he said unto them, This is my blood of the new testament, which is shed for many.

Luke 22:20: Likewise also the cup after supper, saying, This cup is the new testament in my blood, which is shed for you.

1 Corinthians 11:25: After the same manner also he took the cup, when he had supped, saying, This cup is the new testament in my blood: this do ye, as oft as ye drink it, in remembrance of me.

2 Corinthians 3:6: Who also hath made us able ministers of the new testament; not of the letter, but of the spirit: for the letter killeth, but the spirit giveth life. (RSV: "ministers of a new covenant, not in a written code but in the Spirit; for the written code kills, but the Spirit gives life")

Hebrews 7:22: By so much was Jesus made a surety of a better testament. (RSV: "better covenant")

Hebrews 8:6-7: But now hath he obtained a more excellent ministry, by how much also he is the mediator of a better covenant, which was established upon better promises.

[7] For if that first covenant had been faultless, then should no place have been sought for the second. (cf. 8:8-10)

Hebrews 8:13: In that he saith, A new covenant, he hath made the first old. Now that which decayeth and waxeth old is ready to vanish away. (RSV: "In speaking of a new covenant he treats the first as obsolete")

Hebrews 9:15: And for this cause he is the mediator of the new testament, that by means of death, for the redemption of the transgressions that were under the first testament, they which are called might receive the promise of eternal inheritance. (RSV: "mediator of a new covenant; cf. 9:1, 18; 10:16)

Hebrews 12:24: . . . Jesus the mediator of the new covenant . . .

Authoritative interpretation / scripture is not always self-interpreting

Exodus 18:20: And thou shalt teach them ordinances and laws, and shalt shew them the way wherein they must walk, and the work that they must do. (RSV: "and you shall teach them the statutes and the decisions, and make them know the way in which they must walk and what they must do")

Leviticus 10:11: And that ye may teach the children of Israel all the statutes which the LORD hath spoken unto them by the hand of Moses.

Deuteronomy 33:10: They shall teach Jacob thy judgments, and Israel thy law: (RSV: "They shall teach Jacob thy ordinances")

2 Chronicles 17:7-9: Also in the third year of his reign he sent to his princes, even to Ben-hail, and to Obadiah, and to Zechariah, and to Nethaneel, and to Michaiah, to teach in the cities of Judah.

[8] And with them he sent Levites, even Shemaiah, and Nethaniah, and Zebadiah, and Asahel, and Shemiramoth, and Jehonathan, and Adonijah, and Tobijah, and Tob-adonijah, Levites; and with them Elishama and Jehoram, priests.

[9] And they taught in Judah, and had the book of the law of the LORD with them, and went about throughout all the cities of Judah, and taught the people.

2 Chronicles 35:3: And said unto the Levites that taught all Israel, which were holy unto the LORD . . .

Ezra 7:6, 10-11: This Ezra went up from Babylon; and he was a ready scribe in the law of Moses, which the LORD God of Israel had given: and the king granted him all his request, according to the hand of the LORD his God upon him . . . [10] For Ezra had prepared his heart to seek the law of the LORD, and to do it, and to teach in Israel statutes and judgments. [11] . . . Ezra the priest, the scribe, even a scribe of the words of the commandments of the LORD, and of his statutes to Israel.

Nehemiah 8:7-8, 12: Also Jeshua, and Bani, and Sherebiah, Jamin, Akkub, Shabbethai, Hodijah, Maaseiah, Kelita, Azariah, Jozabad, Hanan, Pelaiah, and the Levites, caused the people to understand the law: and the people stood in their place.
[8] So they read in the book in the law of God distinctly, and gave the sense, and caused them to understand the reading . . . [12] And all the people went their way to eat, and to drink, and to send portions, and to make great mirth, because they had understood the words that were declared unto them.

Proverbs 3:5: Trust in the LORD with all thine heart; and lean not unto thine own understanding.

Malachi 2:7-8: For the priest's lips should keep knowledge, and they should seek the law at his mouth: for he is the messenger of the LORD of hosts. [8] But ye are departed out of the way; ye have caused many to stumble at the law; ye have corrupted the covenant of Levi, saith the LORD of hosts. (RSV: "For the lips of a priest should guard knowledge, and men should seek instruction from his mouth")

Matthew 13:10-11: And the disciples came, and said unto him, Why speakest thou unto them in parables? [11] He answered and said unto them, Because it is given unto you to know the mysteries of the kingdom of heaven, but to them it is not given.

Mark 4:33-34: And with many such parables spake he the word unto them, as they were able to hear it. [34] But without a parable spake he not unto them: and when they were alone, he expounded all things to his disciples. (RSV: "privately to his own disciples he explained everything")

Luke 24:15-16, 25-27, 32: And it came to pass, that, while they communed together and reasoned, Jesus himself drew near, and went with them. [16] But their eyes were holden that they should not know him . . . [25] Then he said unto them, O fools, and slow of heart to believe all that the prophets have spoken:

[26] Ought not Christ to have suffered these things, and to enter into his glory? [27] And beginning at Moses and all the prophets, he expounded unto them in all the scriptures the things concerning himself . . . [32] And they said one to another, Did not our heart burn within us, while he talked with us by the way, and while he opened to us the scriptures? (RSV: "he interpreted to them in all the scriptures the things concerning himself")

Luke 24:45: Then opened he their understanding, that they might understand the scriptures. (RSV: "Then he opened their minds to understand")

John 6:60: Many therefore of his disciples, when they had heard this, said, This is an hard saying; who can hear it? (cf. Matt. 28:16-17)

In 6:66 we learn that this inability to understand (or accept) caused disciples to stop following Jesus. Therefore, if some of Jesus' very disciples couldn't understand what we have recorded in that chapter, isn't it plausible and to be expected that some reading it today would not understand, either? The same would apply, for that matter, to the entire gospel story of Jesus' life and death, because His own disciples usually didn't grasp what was going on. If they didn't get it, then why not many millions who read about the story, too?

Acts 8:27-35: And he arose and went: and, behold, a man of Ethiopia, an eunuch of great authority under Candace queen of the Ethiopians, who had the charge of all her treasure, and had come to Jerusalem for to worship, [28] Was returning, and sitting in his chariot read Esaias the prophet. [29] Then the Spirit said unto Philip, Go near, and join thyself to this chariot.

[30] And Philip ran thither to him, and heard him read the prophet Esaias, and said, Understandest thou what thou readest?

[31] And he said, How can I, except some man should guide me? And he desired Philip that he would come up and sit with him.

[32] The place of the scripture which he read was this, He was led as a sheep to the slaughter; and like a lamb dumb before his shearer, so opened he not his mouth: [33] In his humiliation his judgment was taken away: and who shall declare his generation? for his life is taken from the earth. [34] And the eunuch answered Philip, and said, I pray thee, of whom speaketh the prophet this? of himself, or of some other man? [35] Then Philip opened his mouth, and began at the same scripture, and preached unto him Jesus.

Galatians 6:6: Let him that is taught in the word communicate unto him that teacheth in all good things. (RSV: "Let him who is taught the word share all good things with him who teaches")

Colossians 1:25: Whereof I am made a minister, according to the dispensation of God which is given to me for you, to fulfil the word of God; (RSV: "to make the word of God fully known")

2 Peter 1:20: Knowing this first, that no prophecy of the scripture is of any private interpretation. (RSV: "of one's own interpretation")

2 Peter 3:15-17: And account that the longsuffering of our Lord is salvation; even as our beloved brother Paul also according to the wisdom given unto him hath written unto you;

[16] As also in all his epistles, speaking in them of these things; in which are some things hard to be understood, which they that are unlearned and unstable wrest, as they do also the other scriptures, unto their own destruction. [17] Ye therefore, beloved, seeing ye know these things before, beware lest ye also, being led away with the error of the wicked, fall from your own stedfastness. (RSV: "which the ignorant and unstable twist")

Doctrine develops over time

Deuteronomy 29:29: The secret things belong unto the LORD our God: but those things which are revealed belong unto us and to our children for ever, that we may do all the words of this law.

Psalm 25:4: Shew me thy ways, O LORD; teach me thy paths.

Psalm 25:12-14: What man is he that feareth the LORD? him shall he teach in the way that he shall choose.
[13] His soul shall dwell at ease; and his seed shall inherit the earth. [14] The secret of the LORD is with them that fear him; and he will shew them his covenant.

Psalm 86:11: Teach me thy way, O LORD; I will walk in thy truth: unite my heart to fear thy name.

Psalm 94:12: Blessed is the man whom thou chastenest, O LORD, and teachest him out of thy law;

Psalm 103:7: He made known his ways unto Moses, his acts unto the children of Israel.

Psalm 119:12: Blessed art thou, O LORD: teach me thy statutes.

Psalm 119:33: Teach me, O LORD, the way of thy statutes; and I shall keep it unto the end.

Psalm 119:64: The earth, O LORD, is full of thy mercy: teach me thy statutes.

Psalm 119:108: Accept, I beseech thee, the freewill offerings of my mouth, O LORD, and teach me thy judgments.

Proverbs 1:5: A wise man will hear, and will increase learning; and a man of understanding shall attain unto wise counsels:

Proverbs 3:32: For the froward is abomination to the LORD: but his secret is with the righteous.

Proverbs 9:9: Give instruction to a wise man, and he will be yet wiser: teach a just man, and he will increase in learning.

Isaiah 2:3: And many people shall go and say, Come ye, and let us go up to the mountain of the LORD, to the house of the God of Jacob; and he will teach us of his ways, and we will walk in his paths: for out of Zion shall go forth the law, and the word of the LORD from Jerusalem.

Isaiah 48:6: Thou hast heard, see all this; and will not ye declare it? I have shewed thee new things from this time, even hidden things, and thou didst not know them.

Jeremiah 3:15: And I will give you pastors according to mine heart, which shall feed you with knowledge and understanding.

Jeremiah 23:20: The anger of the LORD shall not return, until he have executed, and till he have performed the thoughts of his heart: in the latter days ye shall consider it perfectly. (RSV: "the intents of his mind. In the latter days you will understand it clearly"; cf. 30:24)

Jeremiah 31:31-34: Behold, the days come, saith the LORD, that I will make a new covenant with the house of Israel, and with the house of Judah: [32] Not according to the covenant that I made with their fathers in the day that I took them by the hand to bring them out of the land of

Egypt; which my covenant they brake, although I was an husband unto them, saith the LORD:

[33] But this shall be the covenant that I will make with the house of Israel; After those days, saith the LORD, I will put my law in their inward parts, and write it in their hearts; and will be their God, and they shall be my people. [34] And they shall teach no more every man his neighbour, and every man his brother, saying, Know the LORD: for they shall all know me, from the least of them unto the greatest of them, saith the LORD; for I will forgive their iniquity, and I will remember their sin no more. (cf. Heb. 8:8)

Jeremiah 33:3: Call unto me, and I will answer thee, and shew thee great and mighty things, which thou knowest not. (RSV: "great and hidden things")

Jeremiah 33:6: Behold, I will bring it health and cure, and I will cure them, and will reveal unto them the abundance of peace and truth.

Daniel 2:20-22: Daniel answered and said, Blessed be the name of God for ever and ever: for wisdom and might are his:

[21] And he changeth the times and the seasons: he removeth kings, and setteth up kings: he giveth wisdom unto the wise, and knowledge to them that know understanding: [22] He revealeth the deep and secret things: he knoweth what is in the darkness, and the light dwelleth with him.

Daniel 2:28-29: But there is a God in heaven that revealeth secrets, and maketh known to the king Nebuchadnezzar what shall be in the latter days. Thy dream, and the visions of thy head upon thy bed, are these; [29] As for thee, O king, thy thoughts came into thy mind upon thy bed, what should come to pass hereafter: and he that revealeth secrets maketh known to thee what shall come to pass.

Daniel 2:47: The king answered unto Daniel, and said, Of a truth it is, that your God is a God of gods, and a Lord of kings, and a revealer of secrets, seeing thou couldest reveal this secret.

Daniel 12:4: But thou, O Daniel, shut up the words, and seal the book, even to the time of the end: many shall run to and fro, and knowledge shall be increased.

Amos 3:7: Surely the Lord GOD will do nothing, but he revealeth his secret unto his servants the prophets.

Micah 4:2: And many nations shall come, and say, Come, and let us go up to the mountain of the LORD, and to the house of the God of Jacob; and he will teach us of his ways, and we will walk in his paths: for the law shall go forth of Zion, and the word of the LORD from Jerusalem.

Sirach 1:27: For the fear of the Lord is wisdom and instruction: and faith and meekness are his delight.

Sirach 3:19: Many are in high place, and of renown: but mysteries are revealed unto the meek.

Sirach 42:19: He declareth the things that are past, and for to come, and revealeth the steps of hidden things.

Matthew 5:17-18: Think not that I am come to destroy the law, or the prophets: I am not come to destroy, but to fulfil. [18] For verily I say unto you, Till heaven and earth pass, one jot or one tittle shall in no wise pass from the law, till all be fulfilled. (RSV: "until all is accomplished")

Matthew 9:16-17: No man putteth a piece of new cloth unto an old garment, for that which is put in to fill it up taketh from the garment, and the rent is made worse. [17] Neither do men put new wine into old bottles: else the bottles break, and the wine runneth out, and the bottles perish: but they put new wine into new bottles, and both are preserved. (cf. Mk 2:22; Luke 5:37-38)

Matthew 11:25: At that time Jesus answered and said, I thank thee, O Father, Lord of heaven and earth, because thou hast hid these things from the wise and prudent, and hast revealed them unto babes. (cf. Luke 10:21)

Matthew 13:24-32: Another parable put he forth unto them, saying, The kingdom of heaven is likened unto a man which sowed good seed in his field: [25] But while men slept, his enemy came and sowed tares among the wheat, and went his way. [26] But when the blade was sprung up, and brought forth fruit, then appeared the tares also. [27] So the servants of the house-holder came and said unto him, Sir, didst not thou sow good seed in thy field? from whence then hath it tares? [28] He said unto them, An enemy hath done this. The servants said unto him, Wilt thou then that we go and gather them up? [29] But he said, Nay; lest while ye gather up the tares, ye root up also the wheat with them. [30] Let both grow together until the harvest: and in the time of harvest I will say to the reapers, Gather ye together first the tares, and bind them in bundles to burn them: but gather the wheat into my barn. [31] Another parable put he forth unto them, saying, The kingdom of heaven is like to a grain of mustard seed, which a man took, and sowed in his field: [32] Which indeed is the least of all seeds: but when it is grown, it is the greatest among herbs, and becometh a tree, so that the birds of the air come and lodge in the branches thereof. (cf. Mark 4:30-32)

Matthew 13:35: That it might be fulfilled which was spoken by the prophet, saying, I will open my mouth in parables; I will utter things which have been kept secret from the foundation of the world.

Mark 1:14-15: Now after that John was put in prison, Jesus came into Galilee, preaching the gospel of the kingdom of God, [15] And saying, The time is fulfilled, and the kingdom of God is at hand: repent ye, and believe the gospel.

John 12:16: These things understood not his disciples at the first: but when Jesus was glorified, then remembered they that these things were written of him, and that they had done these things unto him.

John 14:26: But the Comforter, which is the Holy Ghost, whom the Father will send in my name, he shall teach you all things, and bring all things to your remembrance, whatsoever I have said unto you.

John 16:13: Howbeit when he, the Spirit of truth, is come, he will guide you into all truth: for he shall not speak of himself; but whatsoever he shall hear, that shall he speak: and he will shew you things to come.

Romans 3:31: Do we then make void the law through faith? God forbid: yea, we establish the law (RSV: "Do we then overthrow the law by this faith? By no means! On the contrary, we uphold the law")

Romans 4:11: And he received the sign of circumcision, a seal of the righteousness of the faith which he had yet being uncircumcised: that he might be the father of all them that believe, though they be not circumcised; that righteousness might be imputed unto them also:

Romans 11:33-34: O the depth of the riches both of the wisdom and knowledge of God! how unsearchable are his judgments, and his ways past finding out! [34] For who hath known the mind of the Lord? or who hath been his counseller? (cf. Isa. 40:28)

Romans 16:25-26: Now to him that is of power to stablish you according to my gospel, and the preaching of Jesus Christ, according to the revelation of the mystery, which was kept secret since the world began, [26] But now is made manifest, and by the scriptures of the prophets, according to the commandment of the everlasting God, made known to all nations for the obedience of faith:

1 Corinthians 2:7-16: But we speak the wisdom of God in a mystery, even the hidden wisdom, which God ordained before the world unto our glory: [8] Which none of the princes of this world knew: for had they known it, they would not have crucified the Lord of glory. [9] But as it is written, Eye hath not seen, nor ear heard, neither have entered into the heart of man, the things which God hath prepared for them that love him.

[10] But God hath revealed them unto us by his Spirit: for the Spirit searcheth all things, yea, the deep things of God.

[11] For what man knoweth the things of a man, save the spirit of man which is in him? even so the things of God knoweth no man, but the Spirit of God. [12] Now we have received, not the spirit of the world, but the spirit which is of God; that we might know the things that are freely given to us of God. [13] Which things also we speak, not in the words which man's wisdom teacheth, but which the Holy Ghost teacheth; comparing spiritual things with spiritual. [14] But the natural man receiveth not the things of the Spirit of God: for they are foolishness unto him: neither can he know them, because they are spiritually discerned. [15] But he that is spiritual judgeth all things, yet he himself is judged of no man. [16] For who hath known the mind of the Lord, that he may instruct him? But we have the mind of Christ.

1 Corinthians 13:9, 12: For we know in part, and we prophesy in part . . . [12] For now we see through a glass, darkly; but then face to face: now I know in part; but then shall I know even as also I am known. (RSV: "For our knowledge is imperfect and our prophecy is imperfect . . . For now we see in a mirror dimly, but then face to face. Now I know in part; then I shall understand fully, even as I have been fully understood")

2 Corinthians 3:5-6: . . . God; [6] Who also hath made us able ministers of the new testament; not of the letter, but of the spirit: for the letter killeth, but the spirit giveth life. (RSV: "ministers of a new covenant, not in a written code but in the Spirit")

Galatians 3:23-25: But before faith came, we were kept under the law, shut up unto the faith which should afterwards be revealed.

[24] Wherefore the law was our schoolmaster to bring us unto Christ, that we might be justified by faith. [25] But after that faith is come, we are no longer under a schoolmaster. (RSV: "we were confined under the law, kept under restraint until faith should be revealed. So that the law was our custodian until Christ came")

Galatians 4:1-4: Now I say, That the heir, as long as he is a child, differeth nothing from a servant, though he be lord of all;

[2] But is under tutors and governors until the time appointed of the father. [3] Even so we, when we were children, were in bondage under the elements of the world: [4] But when the fulness of the time was come, God sent forth his Son, made of a woman, made under the law,

Ephesians 1:9-10: Having made known unto us the mystery of his will, according to his good pleasure which he hath purposed in himself: [10] That in the dispensation of the fulness of times he might gather together in one all things in Christ, both which are in heaven, and which are on earth; even in him: (RSV: "For he has made known to us in all wisdom and insight the mystery of his will, according to his purpose which he set forth in Christ as a plan for the fulness of time, to unite all things in him, things in heaven and things on earth")

Ephesians 2:19-21: Now therefore ye are no more strangers and foreigners, but fellowcitizens with the saints, and of the household of God; [20] And are built upon the foundation of the apostles and prophets, Jesus Christ himself being the chief corner stone; [21] In whom all the building fitly framed together groweth unto an holy temple in the Lord: (RSV: "in whom the whole structure is joined together and grows into a holy temple in the Lord")

Ephesians 3:1-11: For this cause I Paul, the prisoner of Jesus Christ for you Gentiles, [2] If ye have heard of the dispensation of the grace of God which is given me to youward: [3] How that by revelation he made known unto me the mystery; (as I wrote afore in few words, [4] Whereby, when ye read, ye may understand my knowledge in the mystery of Christ) [5] Which in other ages was not made known unto the sons of men, as it is now revealed unto his holy apostles and prophets by the Spirit; [6] That the Gentiles should be fellowheirs, and of the same body, and partakers of his promise in Christ by the gospel:

[7] Whereof I was made a minister, according to the gift of the grace of God given unto me by the effectual working of his power. [8] Unto me, who am less than the least of all saints, is this grace given, that I should preach among the Gentiles the unsearchable riches of Christ; [9] And to make all men see what is the fellowship of the mystery, which from the beginning of the world hath been hid in God, who created all things by Jesus Christ: [10] To the intent that now unto the principalities and powers in heavenly places might be known by the church the manifold wisdom of God, [11] According to the eternal purpose which he purposed in Christ Jesus our Lord:

Ephesians 4:13-16: Till we all come in the unity of the faith, and of the knowledge of the Son of God, unto a perfect man, unto the measure of the stature of the fulness of Christ: [14] That we henceforth be no more children, tossed to and fro, and carried about with every wind of doctrine, by the sleight of men, and cunning craftiness, whereby they lie in wait to deceive;

[15] But speaking the truth in love, may grow up into him in all things, which is the head, even Christ: [16] From whom the whole body fitly joined together and compacted by that which every joint supplieth, according to the effectual working in the measure of every part, maketh increase of the body unto the edifying of itself in love. (RSV: "until we all attain to the unity of the faith and of the knowledge of the Son of God, to mature manhood")

Colossians 1:9-10: For this cause we also, since the day we heard it, do not cease to pray for you, and to desire that ye might be filled with the knowledge of his will in all wisdom and spiritual understanding; [10] That ye might walk worthy of the Lord unto all pleasing, being fruitful in every good work, and increasing in the knowledge of God;

Colossians 1:25-28: Whereof I am made a minister, according to the dispensation of God which is given to me for you, to fulfil the word of God;

[26] Even the mystery which hath been hid from ages and from generations, but now is made manifest to his saints: [27] To whom God would make known what is the riches of the glory of this mystery among the Gentiles; which is Christ in you, the hope of glory: [28] Whom we preach, warning every man, and teaching every man in all wisdom; that we may present every man perfect in Christ Jesus: (RSV: "the divine office which was given to me for you, to make the word of God fully known, . . . that we may present every man mature in Christ")

Colossians 2:2-3: That their hearts might be comforted, being knit together in love, and unto all riches of the full assurance of understanding, to the acknowledgement of the mystery of God, and of the Father, and of Christ; [3] In whom are hid all the treasures of wisdom and knowledge.

Colossians 2:16-19: Let no man therefore judge you in meat, or in drink, or in respect of an holyday, or of the new moon, or of the sabbath days: [17] Which are a shadow of things to come; but the body is of Christ. [18] Let no man beguile you of your reward in a voluntary humility and worshipping of angels, intruding into those things which he hath not seen, vainly puffed up by his fleshly mind, [19] And not holding the Head, from which all the body by joints and bands having nourishment ministered, and knit together, increaseth with the increase of God. (RSV: "grows with a growth that is from God")

Hebrews 8:13: In that he saith, A new covenant, he hath made the first old. Now that which decayeth and waxeth old is ready to vanish away. (RSV: "In speaking of a new covenant he treats the first as obsolete"; cf. 9:15; 12:24; Luke 22:20; 1 Cor. 11:25)

2 Peter 3:18: But grow in grace, and in the knowledge of our Lord and Saviour Jesus Christ . . .

Christianity has developed out of Judaism

Matthew 5:17-18: Think not that I am come to destroy the law, or the prophets: I am not come to destroy, but to fulfil. [18] For verily I say unto you, Till heaven and earth pass, one jot or one tittle shall in no wise pass from the law, till all be fulfilled. (RSV: "until all is accomplished")

Matthew 23:1-3: Then spake Jesus to the multitude, and to his disciples, [2] Saying, The scribes and the Pharisees sit in Moses' seat: [3] All therefore whatsoever they bid you observe, that observe and do; but do not ye after their works: for they say, and do not.

Luke 16:17: And it is easier for heaven and earth to pass, than one tittle of the law to fail. (RSV: "than for one dot of the law to become void")

John 11:49-52: And one of them, named Caiaphas, being the high priest that same year, said unto them, Ye know nothing at all,
[50] Nor consider that it is expedient for us, that one man should die for the people, and that the whole nation perish not.
[51] And this spake he not of himself: but being high priest that year, he prophesied that Jesus should die for that nation;
[52] And not for that nation only, but that also he should gather together in one the children of God that were scattered abroad.

Acts 2:46: . . . continuing daily with one accord in the temple . . .

Acts 3:1: Now Peter and John went up together into the temple at the hour of prayer, being the ninth hour.

The ninth hour in Hebrew reckoning was 3 p.m.: an hour of sacrifice and prayer at the temple (see Exod. 29:39; Lev. 6:20).

Acts 13:14-16: But when they departed from Perga, they came to Antioch in Pisidia, and went into the synagogue on the sabbath day, and sat down. [15] And after the reading of the law and the prophets the rulers of the synagogue sent unto them, saying, Ye men and brethren, if ye have any word of exhortation for the people, say on. [16] Then Paul stood up, and beckoning with his hand said, Men of Israel, and ye that fear God, give audience.

Acts 21:6-7: And when we had taken our leave one of another, we took ship; and they returned home again. [7] And when we had finished our course from Tyre, we came to Ptolemais, and saluted the brethren, and abode with them one day.

Acts 22:17: And it came to pass, that, when I was come again to Jerusalem, even while I prayed in the temple, I was in a trance;

Acts 23:1-6: And Paul, earnestly beholding the council, said, Men and brethren, I have lived in all good conscience before God until this day. [2] And the high priest Ananias commanded them that stood by him to smite him on the mouth. [3] Then said Paul unto him, God shall smite thee, thou whited wall: for sittest thou to judge me after the law, and commandest me to be smitten contrary to the law? [4] And they that stood by said, Revilest thou God's high priest? [5] Then said Paul, I wist not, brethren, that he was the high priest: for it is written, Thou shalt not speak evil of the ruler of thy people. [6] But when Paul perceived that the one part were Sadducees, and the other Pharisees, he cried out in the council, Men and brethren, I am a Pharisee, the son of a Pharisee: of the hope and resurrection of the dead I am called in question.

Acts 24:11-12: Because that thou mayest understand, that there are yet but twelve days since I went up to Jerusalem for to worship. [12] And they neither found me in the temple disputing with any man, neither raising up the people, neither in the synagogues, nor in the city:

Acts 24:17-18: Now after many years' I came to bring alms to my nation, and offerings. [18] Whereupon certain Jews from Asia found me purified in the temple, neither with multitude, nor with tumult.

Acts 25:8: While he answered for himself, Neither against the law of the Jews, neither against the temple, nor yet against Caesar, have I offended any thing at all.

Acts 26:5: Which knew me from the beginning, if they would testify, that after the most straitest sect of our religion I lived a Pharisee.

Romans 7:12-14: Wherefore the law is holy, and the commandment holy, and just, and good. [13] Was then that which is good made death unto me? God forbid. But sin, that it might appear sin, working death in me by that which is good; that sin by the commandment might become exceeding sinful.

[14] For we know that the law is spiritual: but I am carnal, sold under sin.

Philippians 3:5: Circumcised the eighth day, of the stock of Israel, of the tribe of Benjamin, an Hebrew of the Hebrews; as touching the law, a Pharisee;

Chapter Two

The Authority of
the Catholic Church

Jesus deliberately established a visible, institutional, universal church

Matthew 5:13-15: Ye are the salt of the earth: but if the salt have lost his savour, wherewith shall it be salted? it is thenceforth good for nothing, but to be cast out, and to be trodden under foot of men. [14] Ye are the light of the world. A city that is set on an hill cannot be hid. [15] Neither do men light a candle, and put it under a bushel, but on a candlestick; and it giveth light unto all that are in the house.

Matthew 16:18-19: And I say also unto thee, That thou art Peter, and upon this rock I will build my church; and the gates of hell shall not prevail against it. [19] And I will give unto thee the keys of the kingdom of heaven: and whatsoever thou shalt bind on earth shall be bound in heaven: and whatsoever thou shalt loose on earth shall be loosed in heaven.

Matthew 18:15-17: Moreover if thy brother shall trespass against thee, go and tell him his fault between thee and him alone: if he shall hear thee, thou hast gained thy brother. [16] But if he will not hear thee, then take with thee one or two more, that in the mouth of two or three witnesses every word may be established. [17] And if he shall neglect to hear them, tell it unto the church: but if he neglect to hear the church, let him be unto thee as an heathen man and a publican.

Acts 8:3: As for Saul, he made havock of the church . . . (RSV: "ravaging the church")

Acts 9:3-6: And as he journeyed, he came near Damascus: and suddenly there shined round about him a light from heaven:

[4] And he fell to the earth, and heard a voice saying unto him, Saul, Saul, why persecutest thou me? [5] And he said, Who art thou, Lord? And the Lord said, I am Jesus whom thou persecutest: it is hard for thee to kick against the pricks. (RSV: "rise and enter the city, and you will be told what you are to do")

This appears to refer to the Church as the "Body of Christ."

Even the Apostle Paul was under the authority of the Church. Compare Galatians 1:18 (RSV): "Then after three years I went up to Jerusalem to visit Cephas, and remained with him fifteen days." And Galatians 2:9 (RSV): "and when they perceived the grace that was given to me, James and Cephas [Peter] and John, who were reputed to be pillars, gave to me and Barnabas the right hand of fellowship, that we should go to the Gentiles and they to the circumcised." Paul was also sent out by the church at Antioch (Acts 13:1-4), which was in contact with the church at Jerusalem (Acts 11:19-27). Later on, Paul reported back to Antioch (Acts 14:26-28).

Acts 20:28: Take heed therefore unto yourselves, and to all the flock, over the which the Holy Ghost hath made you overseers, to feed the church of God, which he hath purchased with his own blood.

Romans 7:4: Wherefore, my brethren, ye also are become dead to the law by the body of Christ; that ye should be married to another, even to him who is raised from the dead, that we should bring forth fruit unto God.

1 Corinthians 5:12: For what have I to do to judge them also that are without? do not ye judge them that are within? (RSV: "Is it not those inside the church whom you are to judge?")

1 Corinthians 10:17: For we being many are one bread, and one body: for we are all partakers of that one bread.

1 Corinthians 10:32: Give none offence, neither to the Jews, nor to the Gentiles, nor to the church of God:

1 Corinthians 11:22: . . . despise ye the church of God . . .

1 Corinthians 12:12-13: For as the body is one, and hath many members, and all the members of that one body, being many, are one body: so also is Christ. [13] For by one Spirit are we all baptized into one body, whether we be Jews or Gentiles, whether we be bond or free; and have been all made to drink into one Spirit. (cf. 12:14-27)

1 Corinthians 12:28: And God hath set some in the church, first apostles, secondarily prophets, thirdly teachers, after that miracles, then gifts of healings, helps, governments, diversities of tongues.

1 Corinthians 15:9: For I am the least of the apostles, that am not meet to be called an apostle, because I persecuted the church of God.

Galatians 1:13: For ye have heard of my conversation in time past in the Jews' religion, how that beyond measure I persecuted the church of God, and wasted it: (cf. Phil. 3:6)

Ephesians 1:22: And hath put all things under his feet, and gave him to be the head over all things to the church,

Ephesians 2:19-22: Now therefore ye are no more strangers and foreigners, but fellowcitizens with the saints, and of the household of God; [20] And are built upon the foundation of the apostles and prophets, Jesus Christ himself being the chief corner stone; [21] In whom all the building fitly framed together groweth unto an holy temple in the Lord: [22] In whom ye also are builded together for an habitation of God through the Spirit.

Ephesians 3:10: To the intent that now unto the principalities and powers in heavenly places might be known by the church the manifold wisdom of God,

Ephesians 3:21: Unto him be glory in the church by Christ Jesus throughout all ages, world without end. Amen.

Ephesians 4:1-5: I therefore, the prisoner of the Lord, beseech you that ye walk worthy of the vocation wherewith ye are called,

[2] With all lowliness and meekness, with longsuffering, forbearing one another in love; [3] Endeavouring to keep the unity of the Spirit in the bond of peace. [4] There is one body, and one Spirit, even as ye are called in one hope of your calling;

[5] One Lord, one faith, one baptism,

Ephesians 4:12: For the perfecting of the saints, for the work of the ministry, for the edifying of the body of Christ:

Ephesians 5:23-24: For the husband is the head of the wife, even as Christ is the head of the church: and he is the saviour of the body. [24] Therefore as the church is subject unto Christ, so let the wives be to their own husbands in every thing. (cf. 5:25, 27, 29)

Ephesians 5:32: This is a great mystery: but I speak concerning Christ and the church.

Colossians 1:18: And he is the head of the body, the church: who is the beginning, the firstborn from the dead; that in all things he might have the preeminence.

Colossians 1:24: Who now rejoice in my sufferings for you, and fill up that which is behind of the afflictions of Christ in my flesh for his body's sake, which is the church:

1 Timothy 3:15: . . . the house of God, which is the church of the living God, the pillar and ground of the truth. (RSV: "household of God . . . pillar and bulwark of the truth"; cf. 3:5)

Priests are called by Jesus or the Holy Spirit

Matthew 4:18-22: And Jesus, walking by the sea of Galilee, saw two brethren, Simon called Peter, and Andrew his brother, casting a net into the sea: for they were fishers. [19] And he saith unto them, Follow me, and I will make you fishers of men. [20] And they straightway left their nets, and followed him. [21] And going on from thence, he saw other two brethren, James the son of Zebedee, and John his brother, in a ship with Zebedee their father, mending their nets; and he called them. [22] And they immediately left the ship and their father, and followed him.

Matthew 9:9: And as Jesus passed forth from thence, he saw a man, named Matthew, sitting at the receipt of custom: and he saith unto him, Follow me. And he arose, and followed him.

Matthew 22:14: For many are called, but few are chosen.

Mark 1:20: And straightway he called them: and they left their father Zebedee in the ship with the hired servants, and went after him. (RSV: ". . . and followed him")

Mark 3:13-14: And he goeth up into a mountain, and calleth unto him whom he would: and they came unto him. [14] And he ordained twelve, that they should be with him, and that he might send them forth to preach,

Mark 6:7: And he called unto him the twelve, and began to send them forth by two and two; and gave them power over unclean spirits;

Luke 6:13: And when it was day, he called unto him his disciples: and of them he chose twelve, whom also he named apostles;

Luke 9:1: Then he called his twelve disciples together, and gave them power and authority over all devils, and to cure diseases.

John 13:18: I speak not of you all: I know whom I have chosen: but that the scripture may be fulfilled, He that eateth bread with me hath lifted up his heel against me.

John 15:16, 19: Ye have not chosen me, but I have chosen you, and ordained you, that ye should go and bring forth fruit, and that your fruit should remain: that whatsoever ye shall ask of the Father in my name, he may give it you. . . . [19] If ye were of the world, the world would love his own: but because ye are not of the world, but I have chosen you out of the world, therefore the world hateth you.

Acts 1:2: Until the day in which he was taken up, after that he through the Holy Ghost had given commandments unto the apostles whom he had chosen:

Acts 10:41: Not to all the people, but unto witnesses chosen before of God, even to us, who did eat and drink with him after he rose from the dead.

Acts 20:28: Take heed therefore unto yourselves, and to all the flock, over the which the Holy Ghost hath made you overseers, to feed the church of God, which he hath purchased with his own blood.

Acts 26:16: But rise, and stand upon thy feet: for I have appeared unto thee for this purpose, to make thee a minister and a witness both of these things which thou hast seen, and of those things in the which I will appear unto thee;

Romans 1:1: Paul, a servant of Jesus Christ, called to be an apostle, separated unto the gospel of God,

1 Corinthians 1:1: Paul, called to be an apostle of Jesus Christ through the will of God, and Sosthenes our brother,

1 Corinthians 7:17, 20, 24: But as God hath distributed to every man, as the Lord hath called every one, so let him walk. And so ordain I in all churches . . . [20] Let every man abide in the same calling wherein he was called . . . [24] Brethren, let every man, wherein he is called, therein abide with God.

1 Corinthians 9:16-17: For though I preach the gospel, I have nothing to glory of: for necessity is laid upon me; yea, woe is unto me, if I preach not the gospel! [17] For if I do this thing willingly, I have a reward: but if against my will, a dispensation of the gospel is committed unto me.

1 Corinthians 12:28-29: And God hath set some in the church, first apostles, secondarily prophets, thirdly teachers, after that miracles, then gifts of healings, helps, governments, diversities of tongues. [29] Are all apostles? are all prophets? are all teachers? are all workers of miracles?

2 Corinthians 1:1: Paul, an apostle of Jesus Christ by the will of God, and Timothy our brother, unto the church of God which is at Corinth, with all the saints which are in all Achaia . . .

Galatians 1:1: Paul, an apostle, (not of men, neither by man, but by Jesus Christ, and God the Father, who raised him from the dead;)

Ephesians 1:1: Paul, an apostle of Jesus Christ by the will of God, to the saints which are at Ephesus, and to the faithful in Christ Jesus:

Ephesians 4:11: And he gave some, apostles; and some, prophets; and some, evangelists; and some, pastors and teachers;

Colossians 1:1: Paul, an apostle of Jesus Christ by the will of God, and Timotheus our brother,. . .

Colossians 1:25: Whereof I am made a minister, according to the dispensation of God which is given to me for you, to fulfil the word of God;

1 Timothy 1:1, 12: Paul, an apostle of Jesus Christ by the commandment of God our Saviour, and Lord Jesus Christ, which is our hope . . . [12] And I thank Christ Jesus our Lord, who hath enabled me, for that he counted me faithful, putting me into the ministry; (RSV: "he judged me faithful by appointing me to his service,")

1 Timothy 2:7: Whereunto I am ordained a preacher, and an apostle, (I speak the truth in Christ, and lie not;) a teacher of the Gentiles in faith and verity. (RSV: "For this I was appointed a preacher . . .")

2 Timothy 1:1, 11: Paul, an apostle of Jesus Christ by the will of God, according to the promise of life which is in Christ Jesus, . . . [11] Whereunto I am appointed a preacher, and an apostle, and a teacher of the Gentiles.

Priests are given authority
by Jesus or the Holy Spirit

Matthew 10:1: And when he had called unto him his twelve disciples, he gave them power against unclean spirits, to cast them out, and to heal all manner of sickness and all manner of disease.

Matthew 10:5: These twelve Jesus sent forth, and commanded them, saying, Go not into the way of the Gentiles, and into any city of the Samaritans enter ye not:

Matthew 10:16: Behold, I send you forth as sheep in the midst of wolves: be ye therefore wise as serpents, and harmless as doves.

Mark 3:14-15: And he ordained twelve, that they should be with him, and that he might send them forth to preach, [15] And to have power to heal sicknesses, and to cast out devils:

Mark 6:7: And he called unto him the twelve, and began to send them forth by two and two; and gave them power over unclean spirits;

Luke 9:1-2: Then he called his twelve disciples together, and gave them power and authority over all devils, and to cure diseases. [2] And he sent them to preach the kingdom of God, and to heal the sick.

Luke 10:1-3: After these things the Lord appointed other seventy also, and sent them two and two before his face into every city and place, whither he himself would come. [2] Therefore said he unto them, The harvest truly is great, but the labourers are few: pray ye therefore the Lord of the harvest, that he would send forth labourers into his harvest. [3] Go your ways: behold, I send you forth as lambs among wolves.

Luke 10:19: Behold, I give unto you power to tread on serpents and scorpions, and over all the power of the enemy: and nothing shall by any means hurt you.

Luke 11:49: Therefore also said the wisdom of God, I will send them prophets and apostles, and some of them they shall slay and persecute:

Luke 22:35: And he said unto them, When I sent you without purse, and scrip, and shoes, lacked ye any thing? And they said, Nothing.

John 4:38: I sent you to reap that whereon ye bestowed no labour: other men laboured, and ye are entered into their labours.

John 17:18: As thou hast sent me into the world, even so have I also sent them into the world.

John 20:21: Then said Jesus to them again, Peace be unto you: as my Father hath sent me, even so send I you.

Acts 1:8: But ye shall receive power, after that the Holy Ghost is come upon you: and ye shall be witnesses unto me both in Jerusalem, and in all Judaea, and in Samaria, and unto the uttermost part of the earth.

Acts 9:15: But the Lord said unto him, Go thy way: for he is a chosen vessel unto me, to bear my name before the Gentiles, and kings, and the children of Israel:

Acts 13:2-4: As they ministered to the Lord, and fasted, the Holy Ghost said, Separate me Barnabas and Saul for the work whereunto I have called them. [3] And when they had fasted and prayed, and laid their hands on them, they sent them away.

[4] So they, being sent forth by the Holy Ghost, departed unto Seleucia; and from thence they sailed to Cyprus.

Priests are given authority by Jesus or the Holy Spirit

Acts 16:10: And after he had seen the vision, immediately we endeavored to go into Macedonia, assuredly gathering that the Lord had called us for to preach the gospel unto them.

Acts 22:21: And he said unto me, Depart: for I will send thee far hence unto the Gentiles.

Acts 26:17: Delivering thee from the people, and from the Gentiles, unto whom now I send thee,

1 Corinthians 1:17: For Christ sent me not to baptize, but to preach the gospel: not with wisdom of words, lest the cross of Christ should be made of none effect.

2 Corinthians 10:8: For though I should boast somewhat more of our authority, which the Lord hath given us for edification, and not for your destruction, I should not be ashamed:

2 Corinthians 13:10: Therefore I write these things being absent, lest being present I should use sharpness, according to the power which the Lord hath given me to edification, and not to destruction.

The Church calls and commissions
men for the work of ministry

Acts 9:22-30: But Saul increased the more in strength, and confounded the Jews which dwelt at Damascus, proving that this is very Christ. [23] And after that many days were fulfilled, the Jews took counsel to kill him: [24] But their laying await was known of Saul. And they watched the gates day and night to kill him. [25] Then the disciples took him by night, and let him down by the wall in a basket. [26] And when Saul was come to Jerusalem, he assayed to join himself to the disciples: but they were all afraid of him, and believed not that he was a disciple.

[27] But Barnabas took him, and brought him to the apostles, and declared unto them how he had seen the Lord in the way, and that he had spoken to him, and how he had preached boldly at Damascus in the name of Jesus. [28] And he was with them coming in and going out at Jerusalem. [29] And he spake boldly in the name of the Lord Jesus, and disputed against the Grecians: but they went about to slay him. [30] Which when the brethren knew, they brought him down to Caesarea, and sent him forth to Tarsus.

Acts 11:22: Then tidings of these things came unto the ears of the church which was in Jerusalem: and they sent forth Barnabas, that he should go as far as Antioch.

Acts 14:23: And when they had ordained them elders in every church, and had prayed with fasting, they commended them to the Lord, on whom they believed.

The Church calls and commissions men for ministry

Acts 15:1-4: And certain men which came down from Judaea taught the brethren, and said, Except ye be circumcised after the manner of Moses, ye cannot be saved. [2] When therefore Paul and Barnabas had no small dissension and disputation with them, they determined that Paul and Barnabas, and certain other of them, should go up to Jerusalem unto the apostles and elders about this question. [3] And being brought on their way by the church, they passed through Phenice and Samaria, declaring the conversion of the Gentiles: and they caused great joy unto all the brethren. [4] And when they were come to Jerusalem, they were received of the church, and of the apostles and elders, and they declared all things that God had done with them.

Acts 15:22, 25: Then pleased it the apostles and elders, with the whole church, to send chosen men of their own company to Antioch with Paul and Barnabas; namely, Judas surnamed Barsabas, and Silas, chief men among the brethren . . . [25] It seemed good unto us, being assembled with one accord, to send chosen men unto you with our beloved Barnabas and Paul,

Acts 15:27, 30, 33: We have sent therefore Judas and Silas, who shall also tell you the same things by mouth . . . [30] So when they were dismissed, they came to Antioch: and when they had gathered the multitude together, they delivered the epistle . . . [33] And after they had tarried there a space, they were let go in peace from the brethren unto the apostles. (RSV: "they were sent off in peace by the brethren to those who had sent them")

Acts 17:10, 14: And the brethren immediately sent away Paul and Silas by night unto Berea: who coming thither went into the synagogue of the Jews . . . [14] And then immediately the brethren sent away Paul to go as it were to the sea: but Silas and Timotheus abode there still.

Romans 10:15: And how shall they preach, except they be sent? as it is written, How beautiful are the feet of them that preach the gospel of peace, and bring glad tidings of good things!

1 Corinthians 4:17: For this cause have I sent unto you Timotheus, who is my beloved son, and faithful in the Lord, who shall bring you into remembrance of my ways which be in Christ, as I teach every where in every church.

2 Corinthians 8:16-23: But thanks be to God, which put the same earnest care into the heart of Titus for you. [17] For indeed he accepted the exhortation; but being more forward, of his own accord he went unto you. [18] And we have sent with him the brother, whose praise is in the gospel throughout all the churches;

[19] And not that only, but who was also chosen of the churches to travel with us with this grace, which is administered by us to the glory of the same Lord, and declaration of your ready mind:

[20] Avoiding this, that no man should blame us in this abundance which is administered by us: [21] Providing for honest things, not only in the sight of the Lord, but also in the sight of men. [22] And we have sent with them our brother, whom we have oftentimes proved diligent in many things, but now much more diligent, upon the great confidence which I have in you.

[23] Whether any do inquire of Titus, he is my partner and fellowhelper concerning you: or our brethren be inquired of, they are the messengers of the churches, and the glory of Christ.

Galatians 1:18; 2:9: Then after three years I went up to Jerusalem to see Peter, and abode with him fifteen days . . . And when James, Cephas, and John, who seemed to be pillars, perceived the grace that was given unto me, they gave to me and Barnabas the right hands of fellowship; that we should go unto the heathen, and they unto the circumcision.

Ephesians 6:21-22: But that ye also may know my affairs, and how I do, Tychicus, a beloved brother and faithful minister in the Lord, shall make known to you all things: [22] Whom I have sent unto you for the same purpose, that ye might know our affairs, and that he might comfort your hearts.

Philippians 2:25: Yet I supposed it necessary to send to you Epaphroditus, my brother, and companion in labour, and fellowsoldier, but your messenger, and he that ministered to my wants. (cf. 2:19, 23, 28)

Colossians 4:7-10: All my state shall Tychicus declare unto you, who is a beloved brother, and a faithful minister and fellowservant in the Lord: [8] Whom I have sent unto you for the same purpose, that he might know your estate, and comfort your hearts; [9] With Onesimus, a faithful and beloved brother, who is one of you. They shall make known unto you all things which are done here. [10] Aristarchus my fellowprisoner saluteth you, and Marcus, sister's son to Barnabas, (touching whom ye received commandments: if he come unto you, receive him;)

1 Thessalonians 3:2: And sent Timotheus, our brother, and minister of God, and our fellowlabourer in the gospel of Christ, to establish you, and to comfort you concerning your faith:

Titus 1:5: For this cause left I thee in Crete, that thou shouldest set in order the things that are wanting, and ordain elders in every city, as I had appointed thee: (cf. 1 Tim. 3:1-13)

Men are ordained through the laying on of hands

Acts 6:1-6: And in those days, when the number of the disciples was multiplied, there arose a murmuring of the Grecians against the Hebrews, because their widows were neglected in the daily ministration. [2] Then the twelve called the multitude of the disciples unto them, and said, It is not reason that we should leave the word of God, and serve tables. [3] Wherefore, brethren, look ye out among you seven men of honest report, full of the Holy Ghost and wisdom, whom we may appoint over this business. [4] But we will give ourselves continually to prayer, and to the ministry of the word. [5] And the saying pleased the whole multitude: and they chose Stephen, a man full of faith and of the Holy Ghost, and Philip, and Prochorus, and Nicanor, and Timon, and Parmenas, and Nicolas a proselyte of Antioch:

[6] Whom they set before the apostles: and when they had prayed, they laid their hands on them.

Acts 9:17: And Ananias went his way, and entered into the house; and putting his hands on him said, Brother Saul, the Lord, even Jesus, that appeared unto thee in the way as thou camest, hath sent me, that thou mightest receive thy sight, and be filled with the Holy Ghost.

Acts 13:1-4: Now there were in the church that was at Antioch certain prophets and teachers; as Barnabas, and Simeon that was called Niger, and Lucius of Cyrene, and Manaen, which had been brought up with

Herod the tetrarch, and Saul. [2] As they ministered to the Lord, and fasted, the Holy Ghost said, Separate me Barnabas and Saul for the work whereunto I have called them. [3] And when they had fasted and prayed, and laid their hands on them, they sent them away. [4] So they, being sent forth by the Holy Ghost, departed unto Seleucia; and from thence they sailed to Cyprus.

1 Timothy 4:11-16: These things command and teach.

[12] Let no man despise thy youth; but be thou an example of the believers, in word, in conversation, in charity, in spirit, in faith, in purity. [13] Till I come, give attendance to reading, to exhortation, to doctrine. [14] Neglect not the gift that is in thee, which was given thee by prophecy, with the laying on of the hands of the presbytery. [15] Meditate upon these things; give thyself wholly to them; that thy profiting may appear to all.

[16] Take heed unto thyself, and unto the doctrine; continue in them: for in doing this thou shalt both save thyself, and them that hear thee. (cf. 1 Tim. 5:22; Heb. 6:2)

2 Timothy 1:6: Wherefore I put thee in remembrance that thou stir up the gift of God, which is in thee by the putting on of my hands.

Priests are direct representatives of Jesus

Matthew 10:40: He that receiveth you receiveth me, and he that receiveth me receiveth him that sent me.

Luke 10:16: He that heareth you heareth me; and he that despiseth you despiseth me; and he that despiseth me despiseth him that sent me.

John 13:20: Verily, verily, I say unto you, He that receiveth whomsoever I send receiveth me; and he that receiveth me receiveth him that sent me.

2 Corinthians 5:20: Now then we are ambassadors for Christ, as though God did beseech you by us: we pray you in Christ's stead, be ye reconciled to God.

Priests are God's fellowworkers for the Kingdom

Mark 16:20: And they went forth, and preached everywhere, the Lord working with them, and confirming the word with signs following. Amen.

John 15:13-15: Greater love hath no man than this, that a man lay down his life for his friends. [14] Ye are my friends, if ye do whatsoever I command you. [15] Henceforth I call you not servants; for the servant knoweth not what his lord doeth: but I have called you friends; for all things that I have heard of my Father I have made known unto you.

1 Corinthians 3:9: For we are labourers together with God: ye are God's husbandry, ye are God's building. (RSV: "For we are God's fellow workers; you are God's field, God's building")

1 Corinthians 9:22: To the weak became I as weak, that I might gain the weak: I am made all things to all men, that I might by all means save some. (RSV: "I have become all things to all men")

2 Corinthians 4:15: For all things [i.e., his many sufferings: 4:8-12, 17] are for your sakes, that the abundant grace might through the thanksgiving of many redound to the glory of God.

2 Corinthians 6:1: We then, as workers together with him, beseech you also that ye receive not the grace of God in vain. (RSV: "Working together with him")

Ephesians 3:1-2: For this cause I, Paul, the prisoner of Jesus Christ for you Gentiles, [2] If ye have heard of the dispensation of the grace of God which is given me to youward: (RSV: "the stewardship of God's grace that was given to me for you")

1 Timothy 4:16: Take heed unto thyself, and unto the doctrine; continue in them: for in doing this thou shalt both save thyself, and them that hear thee. (RSV: "Take heed to yourself and to your teaching; hold to that, for by so doing you will save both yourself and your hearers")

Jesus' followers are God's servants

Matthew 6:24: No man can serve two masters: for either he will hate the one, and love the other; or else he will hold to the one, and despise the other. Ye cannot serve God and mammon. (cf. Luke 16:13)

Mark 9:35: And he sat down, and called the twelve, and saith unto them, If any man desire to be first, the same shall be last of all, and servant of all. (cf. 10:43; Matt. 10:24; 20:26; 23:11; Luke 16:13)

Luke 22:26: But ye shall not be so: but he that is greatest among you, let him be as the younger; and he that is chief, as he that doth serve.

John 12:26: If any man serve me, let him follow me; and where I am, there shall also my servant be: if any man serve me, him will my Father honour. (cf. John 13:16; 15:20)

1 Corinthians 3:5-10: Who then is Paul, and who is Apollos, but ministers by whom ye believed, even as the Lord gave to every man? [6] I have planted, Apollos watered; but God gave the increase. [7] So then neither is he that planteth any thing, neither he that watereth; but God that giveth the increase. [8] Now he that planteth and he that watereth are one: and every man shall receive his own reward according to his own labour. [9] For we are labourers together with God: ye are God's husbandry, ye are God's building. [10] According to the grace of God which is given unto me, as a wise masterbuilder, I have laid the foundation, and another buildeth thereon. But let every man take heed how he buildeth thereupon.

1 Corinthians 4:1: Let a man so account of us, as of the ministers of Christ, and stewards of the mysteries of God. (RSV: "servants of Christ")

2 Corinthians 4:5: For we preach not ourselves, but Christ Jesus the Lord; and ourselves your servants for Jesus' sake.

2 Corinthians 6:4: But in all things approving ourselves as the ministers of God, in much patience, in afflictions, in necessities, in distresses,

Galatians 1:10: For do I now persuade men, or God? or do I seek to please men? for if I yet pleased men, I should not be the servant of Christ.

Philippians 1:1: Paul and Timotheus, the servants of Jesus Christ . . .

Colossians 1:7: As ye also learned of Epaphras our dear fellowservant, who is for you a faithful minister of Christ;

Colossians 4:7: All my state shall Tychicus declare unto you, who is a beloved brother, and a faithful minister and fellowservant in the Lord: (cf. 1 Thess. 3:2)

Titus 1:1: Paul, a servant of God, and an apostle of Jesus Christ . . .

James 1:1: James, a servant of God and of the Lord Jesus Christ . . .

1 Peter 5:1-5: The elders which are among you I exhort, who am also an elder, and a witness of the sufferings of Christ, and also a partaker of the glory that shall be revealed: [2] Feed the flock of God which is among you, taking the oversight thereof, not by constraint, but willingly; not for filthy lucre, but of a ready mind; [3] Neither as being lords over God's heritage, but being ensamples to the flock. [4] And when the chief Shepherd shall appear, ye shall receive a crown of glory that fadeth not away.

[5] Likewise, ye younger, submit yourselves unto the elder. Yea, all of you be subject one to another, and be clothed with humility: for God resisteth the proud, and giveth grace to the humble.

2 Peter 1:1: Simon Peter, a servant and an apostle of Jesus Christ . . .

Revelation 1:1: The Revelation of Jesus Christ, which God gave unto him, to shew unto his servants things which must shortly come to pass; and he sent and signified it by his angel unto his servant John:

Priests preside over the Eucharist and the Mass

Isaiah 66:18, 21: For I know their works and their thoughts: it shall come, that I will gather all nations and tongues; and they shall come, and see my glory . . . [21] And I will also take of them for priests and for Levites, saith the LORD.

Malachi 1:11: For from the rising of the sun even unto the going down of the same my name shall be great among the Gentiles; and in every place incense shall be offered unto my name, and a pure offering: for my name shall be great among the heathen, saith the LORD of hosts.

Luke 22:19-20: And he took bread, and gave thanks, and brake it, and gave unto them, saying, This is my body which is given for you: this do in remembrance of me. [20] Likewise also the cup after supper, saying, This cup is the new testament in my blood, which is shed for you.

Acts 2:42,46: And they continued stedfastly in the apostles' doctrine and fellowship, and in breaking of bread, and in prayers . . . [46] And they, continuing daily with one accord in the temple, and breaking bread from house to house, did eat their meat with gladness and singleness of heart, (cf. Acts 20:7)

1 Corinthians 10:16: The cup of blessing which we bless, is it not the communion of the blood of Christ? The bread which we break, is it not the communion of the body of Christ? (RSV: "is it not a participation in the blood of Christ? . . . participation in the body of Christ?")

Hebrews 5:1: For every high priest taken from among men is ordained for men in things pertaining to God, that he may offer both gifts and sacrifices for sins:

Hebrews 8:3: For every high priest is ordained to offer gifts and sacrifices: wherefore it is of necessity that this man have somewhat also to offer.

Priests' authority to forgive sins, grant indulgences, and impose penances

Leviticus 5:5-6: And it shall be, when he shall be guilty in one of these things, that he shall confess that he hath sinned in that thing: [6] And he shall bring his trespass offering unto the LORD for his sin which he hath sinned, a female from the flock, a lamb or a kid of the goats, for a sin offering; and the priest shall make an atonement for him concerning his sin.

Leviticus 19:21-22: And he shall bring his trespass offering unto the LORD, unto the door of the tabernacle of the congregation, even a ram for a trespass offering. [22] And the priest shall make an atonement for him with the ram of the trespass offering before the LORD for his sin which he hath done: and the sin which he hath done shall be forgiven him.

Numbers 5:6-7: Speak unto the children of Israel, When a man or woman shall commit any sin that men commit, to do a trespass against the LORD, and that person be guilty; [7] Then they shall confess their sin which they have done: and he shall recompense his trespass with the principal thereof, and add unto it the fifth part thereof, and give it unto him against whom he hath trespassed.

2 Samuel 12:12-13: For thou didst it secretly: but I will do this thing before all Israel, and before the sun. [13] And David said unto Nathan, I have sinned against the LORD. And Nathan said unto David, The LORD also hath put away thy sin; thou shalt not die.

Psalm 32:5: I acknowledged my sin unto thee, and mine iniquity have I not hid. I said, I will confess my transgressions unto the LORD; and thou forgavest the iniquity of my sin. Selah.

Psalm 38:18: For I will declare mine iniquity; I will be sorry for my sin.

Proverbs 28:13: He that covereth his sins shall not prosper: but whoso confesseth and forsaketh them shall have mercy.

Isaiah 43:25: I, even I, am he that blotteth out thy transgressions for mine own sake, and will not remember thy sins.

Matthew 3:6: And were baptized of him in Jordan, confessing their sins.

Matthew 18:18: Verily I say unto you, Whatsoever ye shall bind on earth shall be bound in heaven: and whatsoever ye shall loose on earth shall be loosed in heaven. (cf. Matt. 16:19: to Peter alone)

Mark 1:4-5: John did baptize in the wilderness, and preach the baptism of repentance for the remission of sins. And there went out unto him all the land of Judaea, and they of Jerusalem, and were all baptized of him in the river of Jordan, confessing their sins.

Luke 24:47: And that repentance and remission of sins should be preached in his name among all nations, beginning at Jerusalem.

John 20:22-23: And when he had said this, he breathed on them, and saith unto them, Receive ye the Holy Ghost: [23] Whose soever sins ye remit, they are remitted unto them; and whose soever sins ye retain, they are retained. (RSV: "If you forgive the sins of any, they are forgiven; if you retain the sins of any, they are retained")

Acts 19:18: And many that believed came, and confessed, and shewed their deeds. (RSV: "Many also of those who were now believers came, confessing and divulging their practices")

1 Corinthians 5:3-5: For I verily, as absent in body, but present in spirit, have judged already, as though I were present, concerning him that hath so done this deed, [4] In the name of our Lord Jesus Christ, when ye are gathered together, and my spirit, with the power of our Lord Jesus Christ, [5] To deliver such an one unto Satan for the destruction of the flesh, that the spirit may be saved in the day of the Lord Jesus.

2 Corinthians 2:6-11: Sufficient to such a man is this punishment, which was inflicted of many. [7] So that contrariwise ye ought rather to forgive him, and comfort him, lest perhaps such a one should be swallowed up with overmuch sorrow. [8] Wherefore I beseech you that ye would confirm your love toward him. [9] For to this end also did I write, that I might know the proof of you, whether ye be obedient in all things. [10] To whom ye forgive any thing, I forgive also: for if I forgave any thing, to whom I forgave it, for your sakes forgave I it in the person of Christ; [11] Lest Satan should get an advantage of us: for we are not ignorant of his devices. (RSV: "What I have forgiven, if I have forgiven anything, has been for your sake in the presence of Christ"

The above two passages offer explicit biblical proof of the doctrine of indulgences. St. Paul binds in 1 Corinthians 5:3-5 and looses in 2 Corinthians 2:6-7, 10. He forgives, and exhorts the Corinthians to forgive also, even though the offense was not committed against them personally. Both parties act as God's representatives in the matter of penance, the forgiveness of sins and the remission of sin's temporal penalties. This latter type of remission is exactly what Catholics mean by an "indulgence."

2 Corinthians 5:18-20: And all things are of God, who hath reconciled us to himself by Jesus Christ, and hath given to us the ministry of reconciliation; [19] To wit, that God was in Christ, reconciling the world unto himself, not imputing their trespasses unto them; and hath committed unto us the word of reconciliation. [20] Now then we are ambassadors for Christ, as though God did beseech you by us: we pray you in Christ's stead, be ye reconciled to God.

1 Timothy 1:18-20: This charge I commit unto thee, son Timothy, according to the prophecies which went before on thee, that thou by them mightest war a good warfare; [19] Holding faith, and a good conscience; which some having put away concerning faith have made shipwreck: [20] Of whom is Hymenaeus and Alexander; whom I have delivered unto Satan, that they may learn not to blaspheme.

James 5:14-15: Is any sick among you? let him call for the elders of the church; and let them pray over him, anointing him with oil in the name of the Lord: [15] And the prayer of faith shall save the sick, and the Lord shall raise him up; and if he have committed sins, they shall be forgiven him.

1 John 1:8-9: If we say that we have no sin, we deceive ourselves, and the truth is not in us. [9] If we confess our sins, he is faithful and just to forgive us our sins, and to cleanse us from all unrighteousness.

Priests administer the sacraments

Matthew 28:19: Go ye therefore, and teach all nations, baptizing them in the name of the Father, and of the Son, and of the Holy Ghost:

John 4:1-3: When therefore the Lord knew how the Pharisees had heard that Jesus made and baptized more disciples than John,
[2] (Though Jesus himself baptized not, but his disciples,)
[3] He left Judaea, and departed again into Galilee.

Acts 2:38, 41: Then Peter said unto them, Repent, and be baptized every one of you in the name of Jesus Christ for the remission of sins, and ye shall receive the gift of the Holy Ghost . . . [41] Then they that gladly received his word were baptized: and the same day there were added unto them about three thousand souls.

Acts 8:12: But when they believed Philip preaching the things concerning the kingdom of God, and the name of Jesus Christ, they were baptized, both men and women.

Acts 10:48: And he commanded them to be baptized in the name of the Lord . . .

Acts 18:8: And Crispus, the chief ruler of the synagogue, believed on the Lord with all his house; and many of the Corinthians hearing believed, and were baptized.

Acts 22:16: And now why tarriest thou? arise, and be baptized, and wash away thy sins, calling on the name of the Lord.

1 Corinthians 4:1-2: Let a man so account of us, as of the ministers of Christ, and stewards of the mysteries of God. [2] Moreover it is required in stewards, that a man be found faithful.

Latin sacramentum *means "mystery."*

James 5:14: Is any sick among you? let him call for the elders of the church; and let them pray over him, anointing him with oil in the name of the Lord:

Ministry calls for sacrifice

Matthew 4:22: And they immediately left the ship and their father, and followed him.

Matthew 5:10-12: Blessed are they which are persecuted for righteousness' sake: for theirs is the kingdom of heaven.

[11] Blessed are ye, when men shall revile you, and persecute you, and shall say all manner of evil against you falsely, for my sake. [12] Rejoice, and be exceeding glad: for great is your reward in heaven: for so persecuted they the prophets which were before you.

Matthew 10:22: And ye shall be hated of all men for my name's sake: but he that endureth to the end shall be saved.

Matthew 10:38: And he that taketh not his cross, and followeth after me, is not worthy of me.

Matthew 16:24: Then said Jesus unto his disciples, If any man will come after me, let him deny himself, and take up his cross, and follow me.

Matthew 19:27-29: Then answered Peter and said unto him, Behold, we have forsaken all, and followed thee; what shall we have therefore? [28] And Jesus said unto them, Verily I say unto you, That ye which have followed me, in the regeneration when the Son of man shall sit in the throne of his glory, ye also shall sit upon twelve thrones, judging the twelve tribes of Israel. [29] And every one that hath forsaken houses, or brethren, or sisters, or father, or mother, or wife, or children, or lands, for my name's sake, shall receive an hundredfold, and shall inherit everlasting life.

Matthew 23:34: Wherefore, behold, I send unto you prophets, and wise men, and scribes: and some of them ye shall kill and crucify; and some of them shall ye scourge in your synagogues, and persecute them from city to city: (cf. Luke 11:49)

Matthew 24:9: Then shall they deliver you up to be afflicted, and shall kill you: and ye shall be hated of all nations for my name's sake.

Mark 6:8: And commanded them that they should take nothing for their journey, save a staff only; no scrip, no bread, no money in their purse:

Mark 8:34: And when he had called the people unto him with his disciples also, he said unto them, Whosoever will come after me, let him deny himself, and take up his cross, and follow me.

Mark 10:28-31: Then Peter began to say unto him, Lo, we have left all, and have followed thee. [29] And Jesus answered and said, Verily I say unto you, There is no man that hath left house, or brethren, or sisters, or father, or mother, or wife, or children, or lands, for my sake, and the gospel's, [30] But he shall receive an hundredfold now in this time, houses, and brethren, and sisters, and mothers, and children, and lands, with persecutions; and in the world to come eternal life. [31] But many that are first shall be last; and the last first.

Mark 13:13: And ye shall be hated of all men for my name's sake: but he that shall endure unto the end, the same shall be saved.

Luke 6:22, 26: Blessed are ye, when men shall hate you, and when they shall separate you from their company, and shall reproach you, and cast out your name as evil, for the Son of man's sake . . . [26] Woe unto you, when all men shall speak well of you! for so did their fathers to the false prophets.

Luke 9:3: And he said unto them, Take nothing for your journey, neither staves, nor scrip, neither bread, neither money; neither have two coats apiece.

Luke 9:23: And he said to them all, If any man will come after me, let him deny himself, and take up his cross daily, and follow me.

Luke 9:57-62: And it came to pass, that, as they went in the way, a certain man said unto him, Lord, I will follow thee whithersoever thou goest. [58] And Jesus said unto him, Foxes have holes, and birds of the air have nests; but the Son of man hath not where to lay his head. [59] And he said unto another, Follow me. But he said, Lord, suffer me first to go and bury my father. [60] Jesus said unto him, Let the dead bury their dead: but go thou and preach the kingdom of God. [61] And another also said, Lord, I will follow thee; but let me first go bid them farewell, which are at home at my house. [62] And Jesus said unto him, No man, having put his hand to the plough, and looking back, is fit for the kingdom of God. (cf. Matt. 8:19-20)

Luke 10:16: He that heareth you heareth me; and he that despiseth you despiseth me; and he that despiseth me despiseth him that sent me. (RSV: "he who rejects you rejects me")

Luke 14:26-27: If any man come to me, and hate not his father, and mother, and wife, and children, and brethren, and sisters, yea, and his own life also, he cannot be my disciple. [27] And whosoever doth not bear his cross, and come after me, cannot be my disciple.

Luke 16:13: No servant can serve two masters: for either he will hate the one, and love the other; or else he will hold to the one, and despise the other. Ye cannot serve God and mammon.

Luke 21:12, 17: . . . they shall lay their hands on you, and persecute you, delivering you up to the synagogues, and into prisons, being brought before kings and rulers for my name's sake . . . [17] And ye shall be hated of all men for my name's sake.

John 12:25: He that loveth his life shall lose it; and he that hateth his life in this world shall keep it unto life eternal.

John 15:18-20: If the world hate you, ye know that it hated me before it hated you. [19] If ye were of the world, the world would love his own: but because ye are not of the world, but I have chosen you out of the world, therefore the world hateth you.

[20] Remember the word that I said unto you, The servant is not greater than his lord. If they have persecuted me, they will also persecute you . . .

John 17:14: I have given them thy word; and the world hath hated them, because they are not of the world, even as I am not of the world.

1 Corinthians 4:9-15: For I think that God hath set forth us the apostles last, as it were appointed to death: for we are made a spectacle unto the world, and to angels, and to men.

[10] We are fools for Christ's sake, but ye are wise in Christ; we are weak, but ye are strong; ye are honourable, but we are despised. [11] Even unto this present hour we both hunger, and thirst, and are naked, and are buffeted, and have no certain dwellingplace; [12] And labour, working with our own hands: being reviled, we bless; being persecuted, we suffer it:

[13] Being defamed, we intreat: we are made as the filth of the world, and are the offscouring of all things unto this day.

[14] I write not these things to shame you, but as my beloved sons I warn you. [15] For though ye have ten thousand instructors in Christ, yet have ye not many fathers: for in Christ Jesus I have begotten you through the gospel.

1 Corinthians 9:12, 18-19: If others be partakers of this power over you, are not we rather? Nevertheless we have not used this power; but suffer all things, lest we should hinder the gospel of Christ . . . [18] What is my reward then? Verily that, when I preach the gospel, I may make the gospel of Christ without charge, that I abuse not my power in the gospel.

[19] For though I be free from all men, yet have I made myself servant unto all, that I might gain the more.

2 Corinthians 4:7-17: But we have this treasure in earthen vessels, that the excellency of the power may be of God, and not of us. [8] We are troubled on every side, yet not distressed; we are perplexed, but not in despair; [9] Persecuted, but not forsaken; cast down, but not destroyed; [10] Always bearing about in the body the dying of the Lord Jesus, that the life also of Jesus might be made manifest in our body. [11] For we which live are alway delivered unto death for Jesus' sake, that the life also of Jesus might be made manifest in our mortal flesh. [12] So then death worketh in us, but life in you. [13] We having the same spirit of faith, according as it is written, I believed, and therefore have I spoken; we also believe, and therefore speak; [14] Knowing that he which raised up the Lord Jesus shall raise up us also by Jesus, and shall present us with you. [15] For all things are for your sakes, that the abundant grace might through the thanksgiving of many redound to the glory of God. [16] For which cause we faint not; but though our outward man perish, yet the inward man is renewed day by day. [17] For our light affliction, which is but for a moment, worketh for us a far more exceeding and eternal weight of glory;

2 Corinthians 6:4-5: But in all things approving ourselves as the ministers of God, in much patience, in afflictions, in necessities, in distresses, [5] In stripes, in imprisonments, in tumults, in labours, in watchings, in fastings;

2 Corinthians 11:23-28: Are they ministers of Christ? (I speak as a fool) I am more; in labours more abundant, in stripes above measure, in prisons more frequent, in deaths oft. [24] Of the Jews five times received I forty stripes save one. [25] Thrice was I beaten with rods, once was I stoned, thrice I suffered shipwreck, a night and a day I have been in the deep; [26] In journeyings often, in perils of waters, in perils of robbers, in perils by mine own countrymen, in perils by the heathen, in perils in the city, in perils in the wilderness, in perils in the sea, in perils among false brethren; [27] In weariness and painfulness, in watchings often, in hunger and thirst, in fastings often, in cold and nakedness. [28] Beside those things that are without, that which cometh upon me daily, the care of all the churches.

2 Timothy 3:12: Yea, and all that will live godly in Christ Jesus shall suffer persecution.

1 John 3:13: Marvel not, my brethren, if the world hate you.

Celibacy fosters undistracted
devotion to the Lord

Jeremiah 16:1-2: The word of the LORD came also unto me, saying, [2] Thou shalt not take thee a wife, neither shalt thou have sons or daughters in this place.

Matthew 19:12: For there are some eunuchs, which were so born from their mother's womb: and there are some eunuchs, which were made eunuchs of men: and there be eunuchs, which have made themselves eunuchs for the kingdom of heaven's sake. He that is able to receive it, let him receive it.

Luke 18:29-30: And he said unto them, Verily I say unto you, There is no man that hath left house, or parents, or brethren, or wife, or children, for the kingdom of God's sake, [30] Who shall not receive manifold more in this present time, and in the world to come life everlasting. (cf. Matt. 19:29-30; Mark 10:29-31)

1 Corinthians 7:7-9, 17, 32-35, 38: For I would that all men were even as I myself. But every man hath his proper gift of God, one after this manner, and another after that. [8] I say therefore to the unmarried and widows, It is good for them if they abide even as I. [9] But if they cannot contain, let them marry: for it is better to marry than to burn . . . [17] But as God hath distributed to every man, as the Lord hath called every one, so let him walk. And so ordain I in all churches . . . [32] But I would have you without carefulness. He that is unmarried careth for the things that belong to the Lord, how he may please the Lord: [33] But he that is married careth for the things that are of the world, how he may please his wife. [34] There is difference also between a wife and a virgin. The unmarried woman careth for the things of the Lord, that she may be holy both in body and in spirit: but she that is married careth for the things of the world, how she may please her husband. [35] And this I speak for your own profit; not that I may cast a snare upon you, but for that which is comely, and that ye may attend upon the Lord without distraction . . . [38] So then he that giveth her in marriage doeth well; but he that giveth her not in marriage doeth better.

God's ministers are entitled to pay

Luke 10:7: And in the same house remain, eating and drinking such things as they give: for the labourer is worthy of his hire. Go not from house to house.

1 Corinthians 9:3-14: Mine answer to them that do examine me is this, [4] Have we not power to eat and to drink?

[5] Have we not power to lead about a sister, a wife, as well as other apostles, and as the brethren of the Lord, and Cephas?

[6] Or I only and Barnabas, have not we power to forbear working? [7] Who goeth a warfare any time at his own charges? who planteth a vineyard, and eateth not of the fruit thereof? or who feedeth a flock, and eateth not of the milk of the flock?

[8] Say I these things as a man? or saith not the law the same also? [9] For it is written in the law of Moses, Thou shalt not muzzle the mouth of the ox that treadeth out the corn. Doth God take care for oxen? [10] Or saith he it altogether for our sakes? For our sakes, no doubt, this is written: that he that ploweth should plow in hope; and that he that thresheth in hope should be partaker of his hope. [11] If we have sown unto you spiritual things, is it a great thing if we shall reap your carnal things?

[12] If others be partakers of this power over you, are not we rather? Nevertheless we have not used this power; but suffer all things, lest we should hinder the gospel of Christ.

[13] Do ye not know that they which minister about holy things live of the things of the temple? and they which wait at the alter are partakers with the alter? [14] Even so hath the Lord ordained that they which preach the gospel should live of the gospel.

1 Timothy 5:17-18: Let the elders that rule well be counted worthy of double honour, especially they who labour in the word and doctrine. [18] For the scripture saith, Thou shalt not muzzle the ox that treadeth out the corn. And, The labourer is worthy of his reward.

Priests are appropriately called "Father"

Acts 7:2: And he said, Men, brethren, and fathers, hearken; The God of glory appeared unto our father Abraham, when he was in Mesopotamia, before he dwelt in Charran,

Romans 4:12: And the father of circumcision to them who are not of the circumcision only, but who also walk in the steps of that faith of our father Abraham, which he had being yet uncircumcised.

Romans 4:16-17: Therefore it is of faith, that it might be by grace; to the end the promise might be sure to all the seed; not to that only which is of the law, but to that also which is of the faith of Abraham; who is the father of us all, [17] (As it is written, I have made thee a father of many nations,) before him whom he believed, even God, who quickeneth the dead, and calleth those things which be not as though they were.

Romans 9:10: And not only this; but when Rebecca also had conceived by one, even by our father Isaac;

1 Corinthians 4:15: For though ye have ten thousand instructors in Christ, yet have ye not many fathers: for in Christ Jesus I have begotten you through the gospel. (RSV: "For though you have countless guides in Christ, you do not have many fathers. For I became your father in Christ Jesus through the gospel")

Philippians 2:22: But ye know the proof of him, that, as a son with the father, he hath served with me in the gospel.

James 2:21: Was not Abraham our father justified by works, when he had offered Isaac his son upon the altar?

In other words, Jesus' statement, "call no man your father on earth, for you have one Father, who is in heaven" (Matt. 23:9: RSV) utilized the common Hebrew method of exaggeration or hyperbole (see Matt. 19:24; 23:24; Luke 6:42; 14:26) to teach that God the Father is the ultimate source of all authority. Interpreting this absolutely literally would prohibit all uses of the word father whatsoever; even biological fathers. But Jesus Himself uses the term father many times (Matt. 15:4-6; 19:5, 19, 29; 21:31; Luke 16:24, 27, 30; John 8:56, etc.), and we see other examples above. Thus, the objection to calling Catholic priests father must be discarded.

A related issue with some critics of Catholicism, is the address, "holy father" as applied to popes (it is claimed that only God could be called that). All that remains, then, is to find "holy men" referred to in the Bible. The writer of Hebrews calls the recipients of his epistle "holy brethren" (RSV). Peter refers to a "holy priesthood" (1 Pet. 2:5: RSV and KJV) and "holy women" such as Sarah (1 Pet. 3:5: RSV and KJV) and "holy prophets" (2 Pet. 3:2: RSV and KJV; cf. Acts 3:21 [also Peter]; Zechariah's prophecy in Luke 1:70). John the Baptist is referred to as a "righteous and holy man" (Mark 6:20: RSV). Jesus refers to a "righteous man" in Matthew 10:41 (RSV and KJV). Therefore, men can be called "holy" in Scripture, and by extension, since "father" as an address for priests is perfectly biblical as well, the two could be put together for "holy father."

Priests are successors to the Apostles

1 Chronicles 27:33-34: And Ahithophel was the king's counseller: and Hushai the Archite was the king's companion:

[34] And after Ahithophel was Jehoiada the son of Benaiah, and Abiathar: and the general of the king's army was Joab.

This is an example of succession of office in the Old Testament.

Acts 1:20-26: For it is written in the book of Psalms, Let his habitation be desolate, and let no man dwell therein: and his bishoprick let another take. [21] Wherefore of these men which have companied with us all the time that the Lord Jesus went in and out among us, [22] Beginning from the baptism of John, unto that same day that he was taken up from us, must one be ordained to be a witness with us of his resurrection. [23] And they appointed two, Joseph called Barsabas, who was surnamed Justus, and Matthias. [24] And they prayed, and said, Thou, Lord, which knowest the hearts of all men, shew whether of these two thou hast chosen, [25] That he may take part of this ministry and apostleship, from which Judas by transgression fell, that he might go to his own place. [26] And they gave forth their lots; and the lot fell upon Matthias; and he was numbered with the eleven apostles.

Ephesians 2:19-20: Now therefore ye are no more strangers and foreigners, but fellowcitizens with the saints, and of the household of God; [20] And are built upon the foundation of the apostles and prophets, Jesus Christ himself being the chief corner stone;

1 Timothy 6:20: O Timothy, keep that which is committed to thy trust . . .

2 Timothy 1:6: Wherefore I put thee in remembrance that thou stir up the gift of God, which is in thee by the putting on of my hands.

2 Timothy 1:13-14: Hold fast the form of sound words, which thou hast heard of me, in faith and love which is in Christ Jesus.
[14] That good thing which was committed unto thee keep by the Holy Ghost which dwelleth in us.

2 Timothy 2:1-2: Thou therefore, my son, be strong in the grace that is in Christ Jesus. [2] And the things that thou hast heard of me among many witnesses, the same commit thou to faithful men, who shall be able to teach others also. (RSV: "what you have heard from me before many witnesses entrust to faithful men who will be able to teach others also")

2 Timothy 4:1-6: I charge thee therefore before God, and the Lord Jesus Christ, who shall judge the quick and the dead at his appearing and his kingdom; [2] Preach the word; be instant in season, out of season; reprove, rebuke, exhort with all longsuffering and doctrine. [3] For the time will come when they will not endure sound doctrine; but after their own lusts shall they heap to themselves teachers, having itching ears; [4] And they shall turn away their ears from the truth, and shall be turned unto fables. [5] But watch thou in all things, endure afflictions, do the work of an evangelist, make full proof of thy ministry. [6] For I am now ready to be offered, and the time of my departure is at hand.

Hebrews 7:5: And verily they that are of the sons of Levi, who receive the office of the priesthood, have a commandment to take tithes of the people according to the law, that is, of their brethren, though they come out of the loins of Abraham:

Bishops have special authority

Numbers 4:16: And to the office of Eleazar the son of Aaron the priest pertaineth the oil for the light, and the sweet incense, and the daily meat offering, and the anointing oil, and the oversight of all the tabernacle, and of all that therein is, in the sanctuary, and in the vessels thereof.

2 Kings 11:18: . . . And the priest appointed officers over the house of the LORD.

2 Chronicles 34:12, 17: And the men did the work faithfully: and the overseers of them were Jahath and Obadiah, the Levites, of the sons of Merari; and Zechariah and Meshullam, of the sons of the Kohathites, to set it forward; and other of the Levites, all that could skill of instruments of musick . . . [17] And they have gathered together the money that was found in the house of the LORD, and have delivered it into the hand of the overseers, and to the hand of the workmen.

Nehemiah 11:9: And Joel the son of Zichri was their overseer: and Judah the son of Senuah was second over the city.

Isaiah 60:17: I will also make thy officers peace, and thine exactors righteousness. (RSV: "I will make your overseers peace and your taskmasters righteousness")

In all of the above passages in the Old Testament, the ancient Greek Septuagint translation of the Bible used the word episkopos.

Acts 1:20: For it is written in the book of Psalms, Let his habitation be desolate, and let no man dwell therein: and his bishoprick let another take. (RSV: "'His office let another take'")

Acts 20:28: Take heed therefore unto yourselves, and to all the flock, over the which the Holy Ghost hath made you overseers, to feed the church of God, which he hath purchased with his own blood. (RSV: "to care for the church of God which he obtained with the blood of his own Son")

Philippians 1:1: Paul and Timotheus, the servants of Jesus Christ, to all the saints in Christ Jesus which are at Philippi, with the bishops and deacons:

1 Thessalonians 5:12-13: And we beseech you, brethren, to know them which labour among you, and are over you in the Lord, and admonish you; [13] And to esteem them very highly in love for their work's sake. And be at peace among yourselves.

1 Timothy 3:1-5: This is a true saying, If a man desire the office of a bishop, he desireth a good work. [2] A bishop then must be blameless, the husband of one wife, vigilant, sober, of good behaviour, given to hospitality, apt to teach; [3] Not given to wine, no striker, not greedy of filthy lucre; but patient, not a brawler, not covetous; [4] One that ruleth well his own house, having his children in subjection with all gravity; [5] (For if a man know not how to rule his own house, how shall he take care of the church of God?) (RSV: "He must manage his own household well, keeping his children submissive and respectful in every way; for if a man does not know how to manage his own household, how can he care for God's church?")

1 Timothy 4:11: These things command and teach.

Titus 1:5-9: For this cause left I thee in Crete, that thou shouldest set in order the things that are wanting, and ordain elders in every city, as I had appointed thee: [6] If any be blameless, the husband of one wife, having faithful children not accused of riot or unruly.

[7] For a bishop must be blameless, as the steward of God; not selfwilled, not soon angry, not given to wine, no striker, not given to filthy lucre; [8] But a lover of hospitality, a lover of good men, sober, just, holy, temperate; [9] Holding fast the faithful word as he hath been taught, that he may be able by sound doctrine both to exhort and to convince the gainsayers.

Titus 1:13: This witness is true. Wherefore rebuke them sharply, that they may be sound in the faith;

Titus 2:15: These things speak, and exhort, and rebuke with all authority. Let no man despise thee.

Titus 3:8: This is a faithful saying, and these things I will that thou affirm constantly, that they which have believed in God might be careful to maintain good works. These things are good and profitable unto men. (RSV: "I desire you to insist on these things . . .")

Hebrews 13:7: Remember them which have the rule over you, who have spoken unto you the word of God: whose faith follow, considering the end of their conversation. (RSV: "Remember your leaders")

Hebrews 13:17: Obey them that have the rule over you, and submit yourselves: for they watch for your souls, as they that must give account, that they may do it with joy, and not with grief: for that is unprofitable for you. (RSV: "Obey your leaders . . .")

The New Testament refers basically to three types of permanent offices in the Church (apostles and prophets were to cease): bishops (episkopos), elders (presbuteros, from which are derived Presbyterian and priest), and deacons (diakonos). The usual Greek word in Holy Scripture translated as elder in English translations, is presbuteros and its cognates (Acts 15:2-6; 21:18; 1 Tim. 5:1-2, 17, 19; Titus 1:5; Heb. 11:2; James 5:14; 1 Pet. 5:1, 5; at least eighteen times in the book of Acts in KJV). Protestants view these leaders as analogous to current-day pastors, while Catholics regard them as priests. KJV (according to Young's Concordance) translates presbuteros *as* elder *sixty-two times, and never as* bishop. *But* episkopos *and related words are never translated as* elder.

Deacons (often, minister *in English translations) are mentioned in the same fashion as Christian elders, with similar frequency (e.g., 1 Cor. 3:5, Phil. 1:1; 1 Thess. 3:2; 1 Tim. 3:8-13). Some argue that bishops, elders, and deacons are all synonymous biblical terms for the same office: roughly that of today's conception of a pastor, and that bishops are no higher in rank than these other offices. But in Titus 1:5 the bishop is charged to "ordain" (RSV: "appoint") elders "in every city." This suggests both hierarchy and regional administration or jurisdiction.*

Bishops and deacons are both mentioned in Philippians 1:1, which would be odd if they were synonymous. 1 Timothy 3:1-7 also discusses bishops, then goes on to treat deacons separately in 3:8-10. We would fully expect some overlapping or variability in function of ministers in the early Church, at the beginning of the development of ecclesiology. Even St. Paul called himself a "minister" or deacon (Greek: diakonos*) more than once (1 Cor. 3:5; 4:1; 2 Cor. 3:6; 6:4; 11:23; Eph. 3:7; Col. 1:23-25), but no one thinks that is all he was. Likewise, St. Peter calls himself a fellow "elder" (1 Pet. 5:1).*

1 Peter 2:25: For ye were as sheep going astray; but are now returned unto the Shepherd and Bishop of your souls. (RSV: "Shepherd and Guardian of your souls")

Jesus himself is referred to as episkopos, *thus demonstrating the analogy of authority and oversight in the Church. God is over all, and human beings also oversee the Church.*

The authority of the Church
and its councils is infallible

Matthew 10:20: For it is not ye that speak, but the Spirit of your Father which speaketh in you.

Luke 10:16: He that heareth you heareth me; and he that despiseth you despiseth me; and he that despiseth me despiseth him that sent me.

Luke 12:12: For the Holy Ghost shall teach you in the same hour what ye ought to say.

John 14:16-17: And I will pray the Father, and he shall give you another Comforter, that he may abide with you for ever;
[17] Even the Spirit of truth; whom the world cannot receive, because it seeth him not, neither knoweth him: but ye know him; for he dwelleth with you, and shall be in you.

John 14:26: But the Comforter, which is the Holy Ghost, whom the Father will send in my name, he shall teach you all things, and bring all things to your remembrance, whatsoever I have said unto you.

John 15:26: But when the Comforter is come, whom I will send unto you from the Father, even the Spirit of truth, which proceedeth from the Father, he shall testify of me:

John 16:13: Howbeit when he, the Spirit of truth, is come, he will guide you into all truth: for he shall not speak of himself; but whatsoever he shall hear, that shall he speak: and he will shew you things to come.

Acts 15:1-32: And certain men which came down from Judaea taught the brethren, and said, Except ye be circumcised after the manner of Moses, ye cannot be saved. [2] When therefore Paul and Barnabas had no small dissension and disputation with them, they determined that Paul and Barnabas, and certain other of them, should go up to Jerusalem unto the apostles and elders about this question. [3] And being brought on their way by the church, they passed through Phenice and Samaria, declaring the conversion of the Gentiles: and they caused great joy unto all the brethren. [4] And when they were come to Jerusalem, they were received of the church, and of the apostles and elders, and they declared all things that God had done with them. [5] But there rose up certain of the sect of the Pharisees which believed, saying, That it was needful to circumcise them, and to command them to keep the law of Moses. [6] And the apostles and elders came together for to consider of this matter. [7] And when there had been much disputing, Peter rose up, and said unto them, Men and brethren, ye know how that a good while ago God made choice among us, that the Gentiles by my mouth should hear the word of the gospel, and believe. [8] And God, which knoweth the hearts, bare them witness, giving them the Holy Ghost, even as he did unto us; [9] And put no difference between us and them, purifying their hearts by faith. [10] Now therefore why tempt ye God, to put a yoke upon the neck of the disciples, which neither our fathers nor we were able to bear? [11] But we believe that through the grace of the Lord Jesus Christ we shall be saved, even as they. [12] Then all the multitude kept silence, and gave audience to Barnabas and Paul, declaring what miracles and wonders God had wrought among the Gentiles by them.

[13] And after they had held their peace, James answered, saying, Men and brethren, hearken unto me: [14] Simeon hath declared how God at

the first did visit the Gentiles, to take out of them a people for his name. [15] And to this agree the words of the prophets; as it is written, [16] After this I will return, and will build again the tabernacle of David, which is fallen down; and I will build again the ruins thereof, and I will set it up:

[17] That the residue of men might seek after the Lord, and all the Gentiles, upon whom my name is called, saith the Lord, who doeth all these things. [18] Known unto God are all his works from the beginning of the world. [19] Wherefore my sentence is, that we trouble not them, which from among the Gentiles are turned to God: [20] But that we write unto them, that they abstain from pollutions of idols, and from fornication, and from things strangled, and from blood. [21] For Moses of old time hath in every city them that preach him, being read in the synagogues every sabbath day. [22] Then pleased it the apostles and elders, with the whole church, to send chosen men of their own company to Antioch with Paul and Barnabas; namely, Judas surnamed Barsabas, and Silas, chief men among the brethren: [23] And they wrote letters by them after this manner; The apostles and elders and brethren send greeting unto the brethren which are of the Gentiles in Antioch and Syria and Cilicia: [24] Forasmuch as we have heard, that certain which went out from us have troubled you with words, subverting your souls, saying, Ye must be circumcised, and keep the law: to whom we gave no such commandment: [25] It seemed good unto us, being assembled with one accord, to send chosen men unto you with our beloved Barnabas and Paul, [26] Men that have hazarded their lives for the name of our Lord Jesus Christ. [27] We have sent therefore Judas and Silas, who shall also tell you the same things by mouth.

[28] For it seemed good to the Holy Ghost, and to us, to lay upon you no greater burden than these necessary things; [29] That ye abstain from meats offered to idols, and from blood, and from things strangled, and from fornication: from which if ye keep yourselves, ye shall do well. Fare ye well. [30] So when they were dismissed, they came to Antioch: and when they had gathered the multitude together, they delivered the epistle:

[31] Which when they had read, they rejoiced for the consolation.

[32] And Judas and Silas, being prophets also themselves, exhorted the brethren with many words, and confirmed them.

Acts 16:4-5: And as they went through the cities, they delivered them the decrees for to keep, that were ordained of the apostles and elders which were at Jerusalem. [5] And so were the churches established in the faith, and increased in number daily. (RSV: "they delivered to them for observance the decisions which had been reached by the apostles and elders")

Ephesians 3:10: To the intent that now unto the principalities and powers in heavenly places might be known by the church the manifold wisdom of God,

The Church has authority to excommunicate and to pronounce anathemas

Matthew 16:19: . . . whatsoever thou shalt bind on earth shall be bound in heaven . . .

Matthew 18:15-17: Moreover if thy brother shall trespass against thee, go and tell him his fault between thee and him alone: if he shall hear thee, thou hast gained thy brother. [16] But if he will not hear thee, then take with thee one or two more, that in the mouth of two or three witnesses every word may be established.

[17] And if he shall neglect to hear them, tell it unto the church: but if he neglect to hear the church, let him be unto thee as an heathen man and a publican.

Matthew 18:18: . . . Whatsoever ye shall bind on earth shall be bound in heaven . . .

John 20:23: . . . whose soever sins ye retain, they are retained (RSV: "if you retain the sins of any, they are retained")

Romans 16:17: Now I beseech you, brethren, mark them which cause divisions and offences contrary to the doctrine which ye have learned; and avoid them.

1 Corinthians 5:1-5: It is reported commonly that there is fornication among you, and such fornication as is not so much as named among the Gentiles, that one should have his father's wife.

[2] And ye are puffed up, and have not rather mourned, that he that hath done this deed might be taken away from among you.

[3] For I verily, as absent in body, but present in spirit, have judged already, as though I were present, concerning him that hath so done this deed, [4] In the name of our Lord Jesus Christ, when ye are gathered together, and my spirit, with the power of our Lord Jesus Christ, [5] To deliver such an one unto Satan for the destruction of the flesh, that the spirit may be saved in the day of the Lord Jesus.

1 Corinthians 16:22: If any man love not the Lord Jesus Christ, let him be Anathema Maranatha.

2 Corinthians 2:5-11: But if any have caused grief, he hath not grieved me, but in part: that I may not overcharge you all.

[6] Sufficient to such a man is this punishment, which was inflicted of many. [7] So that contrariwise ye ought rather to forgive him, and comfort him, lest perhaps such a one should be swallowed up with overmuch sorrow. [8] Wherefore I beseech you that ye would confirm your love toward him.

[9] For to this end also did I write, that I might know the proof of you, whether ye be obedient in all things. [10] To whom ye forgive any thing, I forgive also: for if I forgave any thing, to whom I forgave it, for your sakes forgave I it in the person of Christ; [11] Lest Satan should get an advantage of us: for we are not ignorant of his devices.

Galatians 1:8-9: But though we, or an angel from heaven, preach any other gospel unto you than that which we have preached unto you, let him be accursed. [9] As we said before, so say I now again, If any man preach any other gospel unto you than that ye have received, let him be accursed.

2 Thessalonians 3:6: Now we command you, brethren, in the name of our Lord Jesus Christ, that ye withdraw yourselves from every brother that walketh disorderly, and not after the tradition which he received of us.

1 Timothy 1:19-20: Holding faith, and a good conscience; which some having put away concerning faith have made shipwreck:

[20] Of whom is Hymenaeus and Alexander; whom I have delivered unto Satan, that they may learn not to blaspheme.

1 Timothy 5:20: Them that sin rebuke before all, that others also may fear.

2 Timothy 2:16-18: But shun profane and vain babblings: for they will increase unto more ungodliness. [17] And their word will eat as doth a canker: of whom is Hymenaeus and Philetus; [18] Who concerning the truth have erred, saying that the resurrection is past already; and overthrow the faith of some.

2 Timothy 4:14-15: Alexander the coppersmith did me much evil: the Lord reward him according to his works: [15] Of whom be thou ware also; for he hath greatly withstood our words.

Titus 1:10-11: For there are many unruly and vain talkers and deceivers, specially they of the circumcision: [11] Whose mouths must be stopped, who subvert whole houses, teaching things which they ought not, for filthy lucre's sake.

Titus 3:10: A man that is an heretick after the first and second admonition reject; (RSV: "As for a man who is factious, after admonishing him once or twice, have nothing more to do with him")

Priests have authority to cast out demons (exorcism)

Matthew 10:8: Heal the sick, cleanse the lepers, raise the dead, cast out devils: freely ye have received, freely give. (RSV: "demons")

Mark 3:14-15: And he ordained twelve, that they should be with him, and that he might send them forth to preach, [15] And to have power to heal sicknesses, and to cast out devils: (RSV: "demons")

Mark 6:13: And they cast out many devils, and anointed with oil many that were sick, and healed them. (RSV: "demons")

Mark 9:38-40: And John answered him, saying, Master, we saw one casting out devils in thy name, and he followeth not us: and we forbad him, because he followeth not us. [39] But Jesus said, Forbid him not: for there is no man which shall do a miracle in my name, that can lightly speak evil of me. [40] For he that is not against us is on our part. (RSV: "demons")

Mark 16:17: And these signs shall follow them that believe; In my name shall they cast out devils; they shall speak with new tongues; (RSV: "demons")

Luke 9:1: Then he called his twelve disciples together, and gave them power and authority over all devils, and to cure diseases. (RSV: "demons")

Luke 10:17: And the seventy returned again with joy, saying, Lord, even the devils are subject unto us through thy name. (RSV: "demons")

Acts 19:12: So that from his body were brought unto the sick handkerchiefs or aprons, and the diseases departed from them, and the evil spirits went out of them.

Unity is vital to the Church / denominationalism and divisiveness

Matthew 12:25: And Jesus knew their thoughts, and said unto them, Every kingdom divided against itself is brought to desolation; and every city or house divided against itself shall not stand:

John 10:16: . . . and there shall be one fold, and one shepherd.

John 17:20-23: Neither pray I for these alone, but for them also which shall believe on me through their word; [21] That they all may be one; as thou, Father, art in me, and I in thee, that they also may be one in us: that the world may believe that thou hast sent me. [22] And the glory which thou gavest me I have given them; that they may be one, even as we are one: [23] I in them, and thou in me, that they may be made perfect in one; and that the world may know that thou hast sent me, and hast loved them, as thou hast loved me.

Acts 4:32: And the multitude of them that believed were of one heart and of one soul: neither said any of them that ought of the things which he possessed was his own; but they had all things common.

Romans 2:8: But unto them that are contentious, and do not obey the truth, but obey unrighteousness, indignation and wrath,

Romans 16:17: Now I beseech you, brethren, mark them which cause divisions and offences contrary to the doctrine which ye have learned; and avoid them. (cf. 13:13)

1 Corinthians 1:10-13: Now I beseech you, brethren, by the name of our Lord Jesus Christ, that ye all speak the same thing, and that there be no divisions among you; but that ye be perfectly joined together in the same mind and in the same judgment.

[11] For it hath been declared unto me of you, my brethren, by them which are of the house of Chloe, that there are contentions among you. [12] Now this I say, that every one of you saith, I am of Paul; and I of Apollos; and I of Cephas; and I of Christ. [13] Is Christ divided? was Paul crucified for you? or were ye baptized in the name of Paul?

1 Corinthians 3:3-4: For ye are yet carnal: for whereas there is among you envying, and strife, and divisions, are ye not carnal, and walk as men? [4] For while one saith, I am of Paul; and another, I am of Apollos; are ye not carnal?

1 Corinthians 10:17: For we being many are one bread, and one body: for we are all partakers of that one bread.

1 Corinthians 11:16-19: But if any man seem to be contentious, we have no such custom, neither the churches of God.

[17] Now in this that I declare unto you I praise you not, that ye come together not for the better, but for the worse.

[18] For first of all, when ye come together in the church, I hear that there be divisions among you; and I partly believe it. [19] For there must be also heresies among you, that they which are approved may be made manifest among you.

1 Corinthians 12:20-21: But now are they many members, yet but one body. [21] And the eye cannot say unto the hand, I have no need of thee: nor again the head to the feet, I have no need of you.

1 Corinthians 12:25: That there should be no schism in the body; but that the members should have the same care one for another.

2 Corinthians 12:20: For I fear, lest, when I come, I shall not find you such as I would, and that I shall be found unto you such as ye would not:

lest there be debates, envyings, wraths, strifes, backbitings, whisperings, swellings, tumults:

Galatians 5:19-20: Now the works of the flesh are manifest, which are these; Adultery, fornication, uncleanness, lasciviousness, [20] Idolatry, witchcraft, hatred, variance, emulations, wrath, strife, seditions, heresies,

Ephesians 4:1-5: I therefore, the prisoner of the Lord, beseech you that ye walk worthy of the vocation wherewith ye are called,
[2] With all lowliness and meekness, with longsuffering, forbearing one another in love; [3] Endeavouring to keep the unity of the Spirit in the bond of peace. [4] There is one body, and one Spirit, even as ye are called in one hope of your calling;
[5] One Lord, one faith, one baptism,

Philippians 1:27: Only let your conversation be as it becometh the gospel of Christ: that whether I come and see you, or else be absent, I may hear of your affairs, that ye stand fast in one spirit, with one mind striving together for the faith of the gospel;

Philippians 2:2: Fulfil ye my joy, that ye be likeminded, having the same love, being of one accord, of one mind.

1 Timothy 6:3-5: If any man teach otherwise, and consent not to wholesome words, even the words of our Lord Jesus Christ, and to the doctrine which is according to godliness; [4] He is proud, knowing nothing, but doting about questions and strifes of words, whereof cometh envy, strife, railings, evil surmisings, [5] Perverse disputings of men of corrupt minds, and destitute of the truth, supposing that gain is godliness: from such withdraw thyself.

2 Timothy 2:23: But foolish and unlearned questions avoid, knowing that they do gender strifes.

Titus 3:9-11: But avoid foolish questions, and genealogies, and contentions, and strivings about the law; for they are unprofitable and vain. [10] A man that is an heretick after the first and second admonition reject; [11] Knowing that he that is such is subverted, and sinneth, being condemned of himself.

James 3:16: For where envying and strife is, there is confusion and every evil work.

2 Peter 2:1-2: But there were false prophets also among the people, even as there shall be false teachers among you, who privily shall bring in damnable heresies, even denying the Lord that bought them, and bring upon themselves swift destruction.

[2] And many shall follow their pernicious ways; by reason of whom the way of truth shall be evil spoken of.

Sinners are part of the Church in an imperfect fashion

Matthew 13:24-30: Another parable put he forth unto them, saying, The kingdom of heaven is likened unto a man which sowed good seed in his field: [25] But while men slept, his enemy came and sowed tares among the wheat, and went his way. [26] But when the blade was sprung up, and brought forth fruit, then appeared the tares also. [27] So the servants of the householder came and said unto him, Sir, didst not thou sow good seed in thy field? from whence then hath it tares?

[28] He said unto them, An enemy hath done this. The servants said unto him, Wilt thou then that we go and gather them up?

[29] But he said, Nay; lest while ye gather up the tares, ye root up also the wheat with them. [30] Let both grow together until the harvest: and in the time of harvest I will say to the reapers, Gather ye together first the tares, and bind them in bundles to burn them: but gather the wheat into my barn. (cf. 3:12)

Matthew 13:47-50: Again, the kingdom of heaven is like unto a net, that was cast into the sea, and gathered of every kind: [48] Which, when it was full, they drew to shore, and sat down, and gathered the good into vessels, but cast the bad away. [49] So shall it be at the end of the world: the angels shall come forth, and sever the wicked from among the just, [50] And shall cast them into the furnace of fire: there shall be wailing and gnashing of teeth. (cf. 25:1-30)

Jesus chose Judas as His disciple, even though He knew the future, and he was truly an apostle (Matt. 10:1, 4; Mark 3:14; John 6:70-71; Acts 1:17).

Matthew 22:2, 10: The kingdom of heaven is like unto a certain king, which made a marriage for his son, . . . [10] So those servants went out into the highways, and gathered together all as many as they found, both bad and good: and the wedding was furnished with guests.

Matthew 23:2-3: Saying, The scribes and the Pharisees sit in Moses' seat: [3] All therefore whatsoever they bid you observe, that observe and do; but do not ye after their works: for they say, and do not.

Luke 22:31-34: And the Lord said, Simon, Simon, behold, Satan hath desired to have you, that he may sift you as wheat: [32] But I have prayed for thee, that thy faith fail not: and when thou art converted, strengthen thy brethren. [33] And he said unto him, Lord, I am ready to go with thee, both into prison, and to death.

[34] And he said, I tell thee, Peter, the cock shall not crow this day, before that thou shalt thrice deny that thou knowest me.

Acts 20:29-30: For I know this, that after my departing shall grievous wolves enter in among you, not sparing the flock.

[30] Also of your own selves shall men arise, speaking perverse things, to draw away disciples after them.

1 Corinthians 3:3: For ye are yet carnal: for whereas there is among you envying, and strife, and divisions, are ye not carnal, and walk as men?

1 Corinthians 5:1: It is reported commonly that there is fornication among you, and such fornication as is not so much as named among the Gentiles, that one should have his father's wife. (RSV: "It is actually reported that there is immorality among you, and of a kind that is not found even among pagans; for a man is living with his father's wife")

1 Corinthians 6:8: Nay, ye do wrong, and defraud, and that your brethren.

1 Corinthians 11:17-18: Now in this that I declare unto you I praise you not, that ye come together not for the better, but for the worse. [18] For first of all, when ye come together in the church, I hear that there be divisions among you; and I partly believe it.

2 Corinthians 11:4: For if he that cometh preacheth another Jesus, whom we have not preached, or if ye receive another spirit, which ye have not received, or another gospel, which ye have not accepted, ye might well bear with him.

2 Corinthians 12:20-21: For I fear, lest, when I come, I shall not find you such as I would, and that I shall be found unto you such as ye would not: lest there be debates, envyings, wraths, strifes, backbitings, whisperings, swellings, tumults: [21] And lest, when I come again, my God will humble me among you, and that I shall bewail many which have sinned already, and have not repented of the uncleanness and fornication and lasciviousness which they have committed.

Despite all this sin in the Corinthian assemblies, St. Paul called it the "church of God" (1 Cor. 1:2; 2 Cor. 1:1; cf. 2 Cor. 11:2). We observe the same dynamic with regard to the seven "churches" of Revelation (Rev. 2:1, 7, 12, 18; 3:13-14), even though sternly rebuked for a multitude of serious sins, such as: abandoning their initial love for God (Rev. 2:4); idolatry and "immorality" (2:14, 20-21: RSV); lukewarmness (3:16); and being "wretched, pitiable, poor, blind, and naked" (3:17: RSV).

Galatians 3:1-3: O foolish Galatians, who hath bewitched you, that ye should not obey the truth, before whose eyes Jesus Christ hath been evidently set forth, crucified among you? [2] This only would I learn of you, Received ye the Spirit by the works of the law, or by the hearing of faith? [3] Are ye so foolish? having begun in the Spirit, are ye now made perfect by the flesh?

Galatians 4:9-11: But now, after that ye have known God, or rather are known of God, how turn ye again to the weak and beggarly elements, whereunto ye desire again to be in bondage?

[10] Ye observe days, and months, and times, and years. [11] I am afraid of you, lest I have bestowed upon you labour in vain.

Galatians 5:7: Ye did run well; who did hinder you that ye should not obey the truth?

Yet St. Paul calls these congregations the "churches of Galatia" (Gal. 1:2).

1 Timothy 1:15: This is a faithful saying, and worthy of all acceptation, that Christ Jesus came into the world to save sinners; of whom I am chief.

2 Timothy 2:20: But in a great house there are not only vessels of gold and of silver, but also of wood and of earth; and some to honour, and some to dishonour.

1 John 1:8-10: If we say that we have no sin, we deceive ourselves, and the truth is not in us. [9] If we confess our sins, he is faithful and just to forgive us our sins, and to cleanse us from all unrighteousness. [10] If we say that we have not sinned, we make him a liar, and his word is not in us.

1 John 2:1-2: My little children, these things write I unto you, that ye sin not. And if any man sin, we have an advocate with the Father, Jesus Christ the righteous: [2] And he is the propitiation for our sins: and not for ours only, but also for the sins of the whole world.

Sacred buildings of worship are worthy of extravagant beauty

2 Samuel 7:2: That the king said unto Nathan the prophet, See now, I dwell in an house of cedar, but the ark of God dwelleth within curtains.

1 Kings 7:50: And the bowls, and the snuffers, and the basons, and the spoons, and the censers of pure gold; and the hinges of gold, both for the doors of the inner house, the most holy place, and for the doors of the house, to wit, of the temple.

2 Kings 18:16: At that time did Hezekiah cut off the gold from the doors of the temple of the LORD, and from the pillars which Hezekiah king of Judah had overlaid, and gave it to the king of Assyria.

1 Chronicles 22:5: And David said, Solomon my son is young and tender, and the house that is to be builded for the LORD must be exceeding magnifical, of fame and of glory throughout all countries: I will therefore now make preparation for it. So David prepared abundantly before his death.

1 Chronicles 28:11-19: Then David gave to Solomon his son the pattern of the porch, and of the houses thereof, and of the treasuries thereof, and of the upper chambers thereof, and of the inner parlours thereof, and of the place of the mercy seat,

[12] And the pattern of all that he had by the spirit, of the courts of the house of the LORD, and of all the chambers round about, of the treasuries

of the house of God, and of the treasuries of the dedicated things: [13] Also for the courses of the priests and the Levites, and for all the work of the service of the house of the LORD, and for all the vessels of service in the house of the LORD. [14] He gave of gold by weight for things of gold, for all instruments of all manner of service; silver also for all instruments of silver by weight, for all instruments of every kind of service: [15] Even the weight for the candlesticks of gold, and for their lamps of gold, by weight for every candlestick, and for the lamps thereof: and for the candlesticks of silver by weight, both for the candlestick, and also for the lamps thereof, according to the use of every candlestick. [16] And by weight he gave gold for the tables of shewbread, for every table; and likewise silver for the tables of silver: [17] Also pure gold for the fleshhooks, and the bowls, and the cups: and for the golden basons he gave gold by weight for every bason; and likewise silver by weight for every bason of silver: [18] And for the altar of incense refined gold by weight; and gold for the pattern of the chariot of the cherubims, that spread out their wings, and covered the ark of the covenant of the LORD. [19] All this, said David, the LORD made me understand in writing by his hand upon me, even all the works of this pattern.

1 Chronicles 29:1-9, 16: Furthermore David the king said unto all the congregation, Solomon my son, whom alone God hath chosen, is yet young and tender, and the work is great: for the palace is not for man, but for the LORD God. [2] Now I have prepared with all my might for the house of my God the gold for things to be made of gold, and the silver for things of silver, and the brass for things of brass, the iron for things of iron, and wood for things of wood; onyx stones, and stones to be set, glistering stones, and of divers colours, and all manner of precious stones, and marble stones in abundance. [3] Moreover, because I have set my affection to the house of my God, I have of mine own proper good, of gold and silver, which I have given to the house of my God, over and above all that I have prepared for the holy house,

[4] Even three thousand talents of gold, of the gold of Ophir, and seven thousand talents of refined silver, to overlay the walls of the houses withal: [5] The gold for things of gold, and the silver for things of silver, and for all manner of work to be made by the hands of artificers. And who then is willing to consecrate his service this day unto the LORD? [6] Then the chief of the fathers and princes of the tribes of Israel, and the captains of thousands and of hundreds, with the rulers of the king's work, offered willingly, [7] And gave for the service of the house of God of gold five thousand talents and ten thousand drams, and of silver ten thousand talents, and of brass eighteen thousand talents, and one hundred thousand talents of iron. [8] And they with whom precious stones were found gave them to the treasure of the house of the LORD, by the hand of Jehiel the Gershonite. [9] Then the people rejoiced, for that they offered willingly, because with perfect heart they offered willingly to the LORD: and David the king also rejoiced with great joy . . . [16] O LORD our God, all this store that we have prepared to build thee an house for thine holy name cometh of thine hand, and is all thine own.

2 Chronicles 2:1, 5: And Solomon determined to build an house for the name of the LORD, and an house for his kingdom . . . [5] And the house which I build is great: for great is our God above all gods.

2 Chronicles 3:4-10: And the porch that was in the front of the house, the length of it was according to the breadth of the house, twenty cubits, and the height was an hundred and twenty: and he overlaid it within with pure gold. [5] And the greater house he cieled with fir tree, which he overlaid with fine gold, and set thereon palm trees and chains. [6] And he garnished the house with precious stones for beauty: and the gold was gold of Parvaim. [7] He overlaid also the house, the beams, the posts, and the walls thereof, and the doors thereof, with gold; and graved cherubims on the walls. [8] And he made the most holy house, the length whereof was according to the breadth of the house, twenty cubits, and the breadth thereof twenty cubits: and he overlaid it with fine gold, amounting to six hundred talents.

[9] And the weight of the nails was fifty shekels of gold. And he overlaid the upper chambers with gold. [10] And in the most holy house he made two cherubims of image work, and overlaid them with gold.

2 Chronicles 4:7-8: And he made ten candlesticks of gold according to their form, and set them in the temple, five on the right hand, and five on the left. [8] He made also ten tables, and placed them in the temple, five on the right side, and five on the left. And he made an hundred basons of gold.

2 Chronicles 4:18-22: Thus Solomon made all these vessels in great abundance: for the weight of the brass could not be found out. [19] And Solomon made all the vessels that were for the house of God, the golden altar also, and the tables whereon the shewbread was set; [20] Moreover the candlesticks with their lamps, that they should burn after the manner before the oracle, of pure gold; [21] And the flowers, and the lamps, and the tongs, made he of gold, and that perfect gold; [22] And the snuffers, and the basons, and the spoons, and the censers, of pure gold: and the entry of the house, the inner doors thereof for the most holy place, and the doors of the house of the temple, were of gold.

Isaiah 64:11: Our holy and our beautiful house, where our fathers praised thee, is burned up with fire: and all our pleasant things are laid waste.

Jeremiah 52:18: The caldrons also, and the shovels, and the snuffers, and the bowls, and the spoons, and all the vessels of brass wherewith they ministered, took they away.

Daniel 5:3: Then they brought the golden vessels that were taken out of the temple of the house of God which was at Jerusalem . . .

Hosea 8:14: For Israel hath forgotten his Maker, and buildeth temples; and Judah hath multiplied fenced cities: but I will send a fire upon his cities, and it shall devour the palaces thereof.

Mark 13:1-2: And as he went out of the temple, one of his disciples saith unto him, Master, see what manner of stones and what buildings are here! [2] And Jesus answering said unto him, Seest thou these great buildings? there shall not be left one stone upon another, that shall not be thrown down. (RSV: "one of his disciples said to him, 'Look, Teacher, what wonderful stones and what wonderful buildings!'")

Luke 21:5: . . . some spake of the temple, how it was adorned with goodly stones and gifts . . . (cf. Acts 3:2. 10)

Churches and sacred sites are "holy places"

Exodus 3:2-5: And the angel of the LORD appeared unto him in a flame of fire out of the midst of a bush: and he looked, and, behold, the bush burned with fire, and the bush was not consumed. [3] And Moses said, I will now turn aside, and see this great sight, why the bush is not burnt. [4] And when the LORD saw that he turned aside to see, God called unto him out of the midst of the bush, and said, Moses, Moses. And he said, Here am I. [5] And he said, Draw not nigh hither: put off thy shoes from off thy feet, for the place whereon thou standest is holy ground. (cf. Acts 7:33)

Exodus 26:33-34: And thou shalt hang up the vail under the taches, that thou mayest bring in thither within the vail the ark of the testimony: and the vail shall divide unto you between the holy place and the most holy. [34] And thou shalt put the mercy seat upon the ark of the testimony in the most holy place.

Exodus 28:35: And it shall be upon Aaron to minister: and his sound shall be heard when he goeth in unto the holy place before the LORD, and when he cometh out, that he die not. (cf. 28:29, 43; 29:30-31; 31:11; 35:19; 39:1, 41)

Exodus 40:9-10: And thou shalt take the anointing oil, and anoint the tabernacle, and all that is therein, and shalt hallow it, and all the vessels thereof: and it shall be holy. [10] And thou shalt anoint the altar of the burnt offering, and all his vessels, and sanctify the altar: and it shall be an altar most holy.

Leviticus 6:26: The priest that offereth it for sin shall eat it: in the holy place shall it be eaten, in the court of the tabernacle of the congregation. (cf. 6:16, 27, 30; 7:6; 10:13; 14:13)

Leviticus 16:2: And the LORD said unto Moses, Speak unto Aaron thy brother, that he come not at all times into the holy place within the vail before the mercy seat, which is upon the ark; that he die not: for I will appear in the cloud upon the mercy seat. (cf. 16:3)

Leviticus 16:16: And he shall make an atonement for the holy place, because of the uncleanness of the children of Israel, and because of their transgressions in all their sins: and so shall he do for the tabernacle of the congregation, that remaineth among them in the midst of their uncleanness. (cf. 16:17, 20, 23-24, 27; 24:9; Num 18:10; 28:7)

Leviticus 26:2: Ye shall keep my sabbaths, and reverence my sanctuary: I am the LORD. (cf. 19:30)

1 Kings 6:16: And he built twenty cubits on the sides of the house, both the floor and the walls with boards of cedar: he even built them for it within, even for the oracle, even for the most holy place. (cf. 7:50)

1 Kings 8:6: And the priests brought in the ark of the covenant of the LORD unto his place, into the oracle of the house, to the most holy place, even under the wings of the cherubims. (cf. 8:8, 10)

Nehemiah 11:1: . . . Jerusalem the holy city . . . (cf. 11:18)

Psalm 5:7: But as for me, I will come into thy house in the multitude of thy mercy: and in thy fear will I worship toward thy holy temple. (cf. 65:4; 79:1)

Psalm 28:2: Hear the voice of my supplications, when I cry unto thee, when I lift up my hands toward thy holy oracle. (RSV: "holy sanctuary").

Psalm 43:3: . . . thy holy hill . . . (cf. Jer. 31:23)

Psalm 78:54: And he brought them to the border of his sanctuary, even to this mountain, which his right hand had purchased. (RSV: "his holy land")

Psalm 79:1: . . . thy holy temple . . .

Psalm 138:2: I will worship toward thy holy temple, and praise thy name for thy lovingkindness and for thy truth: for thou hast magnified thy word above all thy name. (cf. Jon. 2:4,7; Mic. 1:2; Hab. 2:20)

Isaiah 48:2: . . . the holy city . . . (cf. 52:1; 64:10)

Jeremiah 31:40: And the whole valley of the dead bodies, and of the ashes, and all the fields unto the brook of Kidron, unto the corner of the horse gate toward the east, shall be holy unto the LORD; it shall not be plucked up, nor thrown down any more for ever.

Jeremiah 51:51: . . . strangers are come into the sanctuaries of the LORD's house.

Ezekiel 20:40: For in mine holy mountain, in the mountain of the height of Israel, saith the Lord GOD, there shall all the house of Israel, all of them in the land, serve me: there will I accept them, and there will I require your offerings, and the firstfruits of your oblations, with all your holy things.

Ezekiel 44:27: And in the day that he goeth into the sanctuary, unto the inner court, to minister in the sanctuary, he shall offer his sin offering, saith the Lord GOD. (RSV: "the holy place")

Ezekiel 48:12: And this oblation of the land that is offered shall be unto them a thing most holy by the border of the Levites. (RSV: "the holy portion of the land, a most holy place"; cf. 45:1, 3-4, 6-7)

Daniel 9:24: Seventy weeks are determined upon thy people and upon thy holy city, to finish the transgression, and to make an end of sins, and to make reconciliation for iniquity, and to bring in everlasting righteousness, and to seal up the vision and prophecy, and to anoint the most Holy. (RSV: "to anoint a most holy place")

Zechariah 2:12: And the LORD shall inherit Judah his portion in the holy land, and shall choose Jerusalem again.

Matthew 4:5: Then the devil taketh him up into the holy city, and setteth him on a pinnacle of the temple,

Matthew 23:16-19: Woe unto you, ye blind guides, which say, Whosoever shall swear by the temple, it is nothing; but whosoever shall swear by the gold of the temple, he is a debtor! [17] Ye fools and blind: for whether is greater, the gold, or the temple that sanctifieth the gold? [18] And, Whosoever shall swear by the altar, it is nothing; but whosoever sweareth by the gift that is upon it, he is guilty. [19] Ye fools and blind: for whether is greater, the gift, or the altar that sanctifieth the gift?

Matthew 24:15: When ye therefore shall see the abomination of desolation, spoken of by Daniel the prophet, stand in the holy place, (whoso readeth, let him understand:)

Matthew 27:53: And came out of the graves after his resurrection, and went into the holy city, and appeared unto many. (cf. Rev. 11:2)

Ephesians 2:19-22: Now therefore ye are no more strangers and foreigners, but fellowcitizens with the saints, and of the household of God; [20] And are built upon the foundation of the apostles and prophets, Jesus Christ himself being the chief corner stone; [21] In whom all the building fitly framed together groweth unto an holy temple in the Lord: [22] In whom ye also are builded together for an habitation of God through the Spirit.

Further analogy of Christians as a holy "temple" due to being indwelt by the Holy Spirit occurs in 1 Corinthians 3:16-17 (cf. 6:19; 2 Cor. 6:16).

Hebrews 9:2-3: For there was a tabernacle made; the first, wherein was the candlestick, and the table, and the shewbread; which is called the sanctuary. [3] And after the second veil, the tabernacle which is called the Holiest of all;

Hebrews 9:12: Neither by the blood of goats and calves, but by his own blood he entered in once into the holy place, having obtained eternal redemption for us.

2 Peter 1:18: And this voice which came from heaven we heard, when we were with him in the holy mount.

Further instances of "holy place" occur in RSV in 1 Chronicles 6:49, 2 Chronicles (nine), Ezra 9:8, Psalms (four), Ezekiel (seven more). See also: "holy mountain" (RSV): Ps. 48:1; 87:1; 99:9; 110:3; Isa. 11:9; 27:13; 56:7; 57:13; 65:11, 25; 66:20; Ezek. 20:40; 28:14; Dan. 11:25; Joel 2:1; 3:17; Obad. 1:16; Zeph. 3:11; Zech. 8:3.

Sacred items are part of worship

Exodus 28:2: And thou shalt make holy garments for Aaron thy brother for glory and for beauty. (cf. 28:4; 29:29; 31:10; 35:19, 21; 39:1, 41; 40:13; Lev. 16:4, 32)

Exodus 28:38: And it shall be upon Aaron's forehead, that Aaron may bear the iniquity of the holy things, which the children of Israel shall hallow in all their holy gifts; and it shall be always upon his forehead, that they may be accepted before the LORD.

Exodus 29:6: And thou shalt put the mitre upon his head, and put the holy crown upon the mitre. (cf. 39:30; Lev. 8:9)

Exodus 29:37: Seven days thou shalt make an atonement for the altar, and sanctify it; and it shall be an altar most holy: whatsoever toucheth the altar shall be holy.

Exodus 30:25: And thou shalt make it an oil of holy ointment, an ointment compound after the art of the apothecary: it shall be an holy anointing oil. (cf. 30:31-32; 37:29; Num. 35:25)

Exodus 40:9-10: And thou shalt take the anointing oil, and anoint the tabernacle, and all that is therein, and shalt hallow it, and all the vessels thereof: and it shall be holy. [10] And thou shalt anoint the altar of the burnt offering, and all his vessels, and sanctify the altar: and it shall be an altar most holy.

Leviticus 5:15: . . . holy things of the LORD . . . (cf. Lev. 22:2-7; 14-16)

Leviticus 16:2: And the LORD said unto Moses, Speak unto Aaron thy brother, that he come not at all times into the holy place within the vail before the mercy seat, which is upon the ark; that he die not: for I will appear in the cloud upon the mercy seat. (cf. 16:3)

Numbers 4:19-20: But thus do unto them, that they may live, and not die, when they approach unto the most holy things: Aaron and his sons shall go in, and appoint them every one to his service and to his burden: [20] But they shall not go in to see when the holy things are covered, lest they die. (cf. 4:4,15)

Joshua 6:19: But all the silver, and gold, and vessels of brass and iron, are consecrated unto the LORD: they shall come into the treasury of the LORD. (RSV: "sacred to the LORD")

1 Samuel 21:6: So the priest gave him hallowed bread . . .

1 Kings 8:4: And they brought up the ark of the LORD, and the tabernacle of the congregation, and all the holy vessels that were in the tabernacle, even those did the priests and the Levites bring up. (cf. 1 Chron. 9:29; 22:19)

2 Chronicles 35:3: And said unto the Levites that taught all Israel, which were holy unto the LORD, Put the holy ark in the house which Solomon the son of David king of Israel did build; it shall not be a burden upon your shoulders: serve now the LORD your God, and his people Israel,

Ezekiel 44:13: And they shall not come near unto me, to do the office of a priest unto me, nor to come near to any of my holy things, in the most holy place: but they shall bear their shame, and their abominations which they have committed. (cf. Zeph. 3:4; Zech. 14:21; Jth. 4:3)

Matthew 7:6: Give not that which is holy unto the dogs, neither cast ye your pearls before swine, lest they trample them under their feet, and turn again and rend you.

Matthew 23:16-19: Woe unto you, ye blind guides, which say, Whosoever shall swear by the temple, it is nothing; but whosoever shall swear by the gold of the temple, he is a debtor!
[17] Ye fools and blind: for whether is greater, the gold, or the temple that sanctifieth the gold? [18] And, Whosoever shall swear by the altar, it is nothing; but whosoever sweareth by the gift that is upon it, he is guilty. [19] Ye fools and blind: for whether is greater, the gift, or the altar that sanctifieth the gift?

Romans 11:16: For if the firstfruit be holy, the lump is also holy: and if the root be holy, so are the branches.

Romans 12:1: I beseech you therefore, brethren, by the mercies of God, that ye present your bodies a living sacrifice, holy, acceptable unto God, which is your reasonable service.

Romans 16:16: Salute one another with an holy kiss . . . (cf. 1 Cor. 16:20; 2 Cor. 13:12; 1 Thess. 5:26)

Chapter Three

The Authority of Popes

Peter was the first pope

Genesis 41:39-41: And Pharaoh said unto Joseph, Forasmuch as God hath shewed thee all this, there is none so discreet and wise as thou art: [40] Thou shalt be over my house, and according unto thy word shall all my people be ruled: only in the throne will I be greater than thou. [41] And Pharaoh said unto Joseph, See, I have set thee over all the land of Egypt. (cf. 44:4)

Genesis 43:19: And they came near to the steward of Joseph's house, and they communed with him at the door of the house,

1 Kings 18:3: And Ahab called Obadiah, which was the governor of his house . . .

2 Kings 15:5: . . . And Jotham the king's son was over the house, judging the people of the land.

2 Kings 18:18: And when they had called to the king, there came out to them Eliakim the son of Hilkiah, which was over the household, and Shebna the scribe, and Joah the son of Asaph the recorder. (cf. 18:37; 19:2; Isa. 36:3, 22; 37:2)

Isaiah 22:15, 20-24: Thus saith the Lord GOD of hosts, Go, get thee unto this treasurer, even unto Shebna, which is over the house, and say . . . [20] And it shall come to pass in that day, that I will call my servant Eliakim the son of Hilkiah: [21] And I will clothe him with thy robe, and strengthen him with thy girdle, and I will commit thy government into his hand: and he shall be a father to the inhabitants of Jerusalem, and to the house of Judah. [22] And the key of the house of David will I lay upon his shoulder; so he shall open, and none shall shut; and he shall shut, and none shall open. [23] And I will fasten him as a nail in a sure place; and he shall be for a glorious throne to his father's house. [24] And they shall hang upon him all the glory of his father's house, the offspring and the issue, all vessels of small quantity, from the vessels of cups, even to all the vessels of flagons.

Matthew 16:15-17: He saith unto them, But whom say ye that I am? [16] And Simon Peter answered and said, Thou art the Christ, the Son of the living God. [17] And Jesus answered and said unto him, Blessed art thou, Simon Barjona: for flesh and blood hath not revealed it unto thee, but my Father which is in heaven.

Matthew 16:18-19: And I say also unto thee, That thou art Peter, and upon this rock I will build my church; and the gates of hell shall not prevail against it. [19] And I will give unto thee the keys of the kingdom of heaven: and whatsoever thou shalt bind on earth shall be bound in heaven: and whatsoever thou shalt loose on earth shall be loosed in heaven.

Luke 12:42: And the Lord said, Who then is that faithful and wise steward, whom his lord shall make ruler over his household, to give them their portion of meat in due season? (cf. Titus 1:7)

John 1:42: And he brought him to Jesus. And when Jesus beheld him, he said, Thou art Simon the son of Jona: thou shalt be called Cephas, which is by interpretation, A stone.

Revelation 3:7: And to the angel of the church in Philadelphia write; These things saith he that is holy, he that is true, he that hath the key of David, he that openeth, and no man shutteth; and shutteth, and no man openeth;

The "power of the keys" has to do with ecclesiastical discipline and administrative authority with regard to the requirements of the faith, including the use of censures, excommunication, absolution, baptismal discipline, the imposition of penances, and legislative powers. In the Old Testament a steward, or prime minister is a man who is "over a house" (see also 1 Kings 4:6; 16:9; 18:3; 2 Kings 10:5; 18:18).

"Binding" and "loosing" were technical rabbinical terms, which meant to "forbid" and "permit" with reference to the interpretation of the law, and secondarily to "condemn" or "acquit." Thus, St. Peter and the popes are given the authority to determine the rules for doctrine and life, by virtue of revelation and the Spirit's leading (John 16:13).

Only Peter, among the apostles, received a new name: Cephas, or Rock (cf. 1 Cor. 1:12; 3:22; 9:5; 15:5; Gal. 1:18; 2:9, 11, 14). He was the first to confess Christ's divinity (Matt. 16:16), and is told that he has received divine knowledge by a special revelation (Matt. 16:17).

Matthew 10:2: Now the names of the twelve apostles are these; The first, Simon, who is called Peter, and Andrew his brother; James the son of Zebedee, and John his brother;

Mark 3:14-17: And he ordained twelve, that they should be with him, and that he might send them forth to preach, [15] And to have power to heal sicknesses, and to cast out devils:

[16] And Simon he surnamed Peter; [17] And James the son of Zebedee, and John the brother of James; and he surnamed them Boanerges, which is, The sons of thunder:

Mark 16:5-7: And entering into the sepulchre, they saw a young man sitting on the right side, clothed in a long white garment; and they were affrighted. [6] And he saith unto them, Be not affrighted: Ye seek Jesus of Nazareth, which was crucified: he is risen; he is not here: behold the place where they laid him.

[7] But go your way, tell his disciples and Peter that he goeth before you into Galilee: there shall ye see him, as he said unto you.

Luke 6:13-14: And when it was day, he called unto him his disciples: and of them he chose twelve, whom also he named apostles; [14] Simon, (whom he also named Peter,) and Andrew his brother, James and John, Philip and Bartholomew,

Acts 1:13: And when they were come in, they went up into an upper room, where abode both Peter, and James, and John, and Andrew, Philip, and Thomas, Bartholomew, and Matthew, James the son of Alphaeus, and Simon Zelotes, and Judas the brother of James.

St. Peter's name occurs first in all lists of apostles. Judas Iscariot is always mentioned last. Peter is almost without exception named first whenever he appears with anyone else. His name is always the first listed of the "inner circle" of the disciples (Peter, James, and John: Matt. 17:1; 26:37, 40; Mark 5:37; 14:37). Peter's name is mentioned more often than all the other disciples put together: 191 times (162 as Peter or Simon Peter, twenty-three as Simon, and six as Cephas). John is next in frequency with only forty-eight appearances, and Peter is present half of the time we find St. John mentioned in the Bible.

2 Samuel 7:7: In all the places wherein I have walked with all the children of Israel spake I a word with any of the tribes of Israel, whom I commanded to feed my people Israel . . . (RSV: "the judges of Israel")

Psalm 78:70-72: He chose David also his servant, and took him from the sheepfolds: [71] From following the ewes great with young he brought him to feed Jacob his people, and Israel his inheritance. [72] So he fed them according to the integrity of his heart; and guided them by the skilfulness of his hands.

Isaiah 44:28: That saith of Cyrus, He is my shepherd, and shall perform all my pleasure: even saying to Jerusalem, Thou shalt be built; and to the temple, Thy foundation shall be laid.

Jeremiah 3:15: And I will give you pastors according to mine heart, which shall feed you with knowledge and understanding. (cf. 23:4)

Ezekiel 37:24: My servant David shall be king over them; and they shall all have one shepherd.

Luke 22:31-32: And the Lord said, Simon, Simon, behold, Satan hath desired to have you, that he may sift you as wheat: [32] But I have prayed for thee, that thy faith fail not: and when thou art converted, strengthen thy brethren.

John 21:15-17: So when they had dined, Jesus saith to Simon Peter, Simon, son of Jonas, lovest thou me more than these? He saith unto him, Yea, Lord; thou knowest that I love thee. He saith unto him, Feed my lambs. [16] He saith to him again the second time, Simon, son of Jonas, lovest thou me? He saith unto him, Yea, Lord; thou knowest that I love thee. He saith unto him, Feed my sheep. [17] He saith unto him the third time, Simon, son of Jonas, lovest thou me? Peter was grieved because he said unto him the third time, Lovest thou me? And he said unto him, Lord, thou knowest all things; thou knowest that I love thee. Jesus saith unto him, Feed my sheep.

The Good Shepherd, Jesus (John 10:11-16; cf. Ps. 23:1; 80:1; Isa. 40:11; Jer. 31:10; Matt. 26:31; Heb. 13:20; 1 Pet. 2:25; 5:4; Rev. 7:17), gives us other shepherds as well (John 21:15-17, above; Eph. 4:11). St. Peter is here regarded by Jesus as the Chief Shepherd after himself, singularly by name, and over the universal Church, even though others have a similar but subordinate role (Acts 20:28; 1 Pet. 5:2).

Luke 9:32: But Peter and they that were with him were heavy with sleep: and when they were awake, they saw his glory, and the two men that stood with him. (cf. Mark 1:36)

Acts 5:15: Insomuch that they brought forth the sick into the streets, and laid them on beds and couches, that at the least the shadow of Peter passing by might overshadow some of them.

Acts 5:29: Then Peter and the other apostles answered and said, We ought to obey God rather than men.

Acts 12:5: Peter therefore was kept in prison: but prayer was made without ceasing of the church unto God for him.

Acts 12:11: And when Peter was come to himself, he said, Now I know of a surety, that the Lord hath sent his angel, and hath delivered me out of the hand of Herod, and from all the expectation of the people of the Jews.

1 Corinthians 9:5: Have we not power to lead about a sister, a wife, as well as other apostles, and as the brethren of the Lord, and Cephas?

St. Peter is regarded by his fellow disciples and apostles, the Jewish leaders, and the common people alike as the leader and spokesman of Christianity, as indicated by his constantly being singled out or highlighted, or distinguished from others, in narratives (cf. Matt. 17:24; Acts 2:37-41; 4:1-13; 10:1-6). He is often the spokesman for the other apostles, especially at climactic moments (Mark 8:29; Matt. 18:21; Luke 9:5; 12:41; John 6:67 ff.), and usually the central figure relating to Jesus in dramatic gospel scenes such as Jesus' walking on the water (Matt. 14:28-32; Luke 5:1 ff.; Mark 10:28; Matt. 17:24 ff.).

He was the first person to speak (and the only speaker recorded) after Pentecost, so he was the first Christian to "preach the gospel" in the Church era (Acts 2:14-36), and the first to preach the necessity of baptism for entrance into Christianity and regeneration (Acts 2:38, 41).

Peter was the first traveling missionary, exercising what would now be called "visitation of the churches" (Acts 9:32-38, 43). Paul preached at Damascus immediately after his conversion (Acts 9:20), but hadn't traveled there for that purpose. His missionary journeys begin in Acts 13:2. Paul had gone to Jerusalem specifically to see Peter for fifteen days in the beginning of his ministry (Gal. 1:18), and was commissioned by Peter, James and John (Gal. 2:9) to preach to the Gentiles.

John 20:3-6: Peter therefore went forth, and that other disciple, and came to the sepulchre. [4] So they ran both together: and the other disciple did outrun Peter, and came first to the sepulchre.

[5] And he stooping down, and looking in, saw the linen clothes lying; yet went he not in. [6] Then cometh Simon Peter following him, and went into the sepulchre, and seeth the linen clothes lie,

Luke 24:33-34: And they rose up the same hour, and returned to Jerusalem, and found the eleven gathered together, and them that were with them, [34] Saying, The Lord is risen indeed, and hath appeared to Simon.

1 Corinthians 15:4-6: . . . he rose again the third day according to the scriptures: [5] And that he was seen of Cephas, then of the twelve: [6] After that, he was seen of above five hundred brethren at once; of whom the greater part remain unto this present, but some are fallen asleep.

St. Peter was the first apostle to enter the empty tomb and the first one to see the risen Jesus, and other disciples and apostles are aware of this.

Peter's letters are like papal encyclicals

Protestants believe that St. Peter wrote inspired Scripture; Catholics believe that he also could write infallible documents, too, as the first pope. Some Catholics have argued that 1 and 2 Peter are somewhat like a primitive papal encyclicals (just as 1 Clement was):

1 Peter 1:1: Peter, an apostle of Jesus Christ, to the strangers scattered throughout Pontus, Galatia, Cappadocia, Asia, and Bithynia,

1 Peter 5:1-4: The elders which are among you I exhort, who am also an elder, and a witness of the sufferings of Christ, and also a partaker of the glory that shall be revealed: [2] Feed the flock of God which is among you, taking the oversight thereof, not by constraint, but willingly; not for filthy lucre, but of a ready mind;

[3] Neither as being lords over God's heritage, but being ensamples to the flock. [4] And when the chief Shepherd shall appear, ye shall receive a crown of glory that fadeth not away.

The first letter of Peter is written to a wide variety of Christians, rather than to a specific church or individual, like St. Paul's epistles. He exhorts Church elders and urges others to be shepherds, just as Jesus urged him to do (John 21:15-17), because he is a "super-elder" and the shepherd of the whole flock, in an analogous sense to Jesus (5:4). The epistle is very "general" and broad and written much like the style of papal encyclicals today: wise, sage, almost proverbial: encouraging Christians to endure suffering (1:6-7; 3:13-14; 4:1, 12-17) and to be holy (1:14-23). He addresses the topic of husbands and wives (3:1-7).

2 Peter 1:1: Simon Peter, a servant and an apostle of Jesus Christ, to them that have obtained like precious faith with us through the righteousness of God and our Saviour Jesus Christ:

2 Peter 1:16-21: For we have not followed cunningly devised fables, when we made known unto you the power and coming of our Lord Jesus Christ, but were eyewitnesses of his majesty.

[17] For he received from God the Father honour and glory, when there came such a voice to him from the excellent glory, This is my beloved Son, in whom I am well pleased. [18] And this voice which came from heaven we heard, when we were with him in the holy mount. [19] We have also a more sure word of prophecy; whereunto ye do well that ye take heed, as unto a light that shineth in a dark place, until the day dawn, and the day star arise in your hearts: [20] Knowing this first, that no prophecy of the scripture is of any private interpretation. [21] For the prophecy came not in old time by the will of man: but holy men of God spake as they were moved by the Holy Ghost.

2 Peter 3:15-16: And account that the longsuffering of our Lord is salvation; even as our beloved brother Paul also according to the wisdom given unto him hath written unto you;

[16] As also in all his epistles, speaking in them of these things; in which are some things hard to be understood, which they that are unlearned and unstable wrest, as they do also the other scriptures, unto their own destruction.

St. Peter's second epistle is the same in these respects as his first. He is essentially writing to all Christians and authoritatively interprets prophecy: explaining that it is ultimately not private in nature (a "magisterial" sort of statement). He also refers to the difficult nature of some of St. Paul's writing (3:15-16). St. Paul writes directly to local flocks of Christians, but St. Peter is writing to the whole Church. Thus, he appears to be doing what popes do in their encyclicals, whereas Paul is functioning more as local bishops do.

St. Peter acted as a pope

Acts 2:33, 36-39: Therefore being by the right hand of God exalted, and having received of the Father the promise of the Holy Ghost, he hath shed forth this, which ye now see and hear.

. . . Therefore let all the house of Israel know assuredly, that God hath made that same Jesus, whom ye have crucified, both Lord and Christ. [37] Now when they heard this, they were pricked in their heart, and said unto Peter and to the rest of the apostles, Men and brethren, what shall we do? [38] Then Peter said unto them, Repent, and be baptized every one of you in the name of Jesus Christ for the remission of sins, and ye shall receive the gift of the Holy Ghost. [39] For the promise is unto you, and to your children, and to all that are afar off, even as many as the Lord our God shall call.

St. Peter's proclamation at Pentecost (Acts 2:14-41) contains a fully authoritative interpretation of Scripture, a doctrinal decision and a disciplinary decree concerning members of the "house of Israel" (2:36): an example of "binding and loosing."

Acts 5:1-10: But a certain man named Ananias, with Sapphira his wife, sold a possession, [2] And kept back part of the price, his wife also being privy to it, and brought a certain part, and laid it at the apostles' feet. [3] But Peter said, Ananias, why hath Satan filled thine heart to lie to the Holy Ghost, and to keep back part of the price of the land? [4] Whiles it remained, was it not thine own? and after it was sold, was it not in thine own power? why hast thou conceived this thing in thine heart? thou hast not lied unto men, but unto God. [5] And Ananias hearing these words fell down, and gave up the ghost: and great fear came on all them that heard these things. [6] And the young men arose, wound him up, and carried him out, and buried him. [7] And it was about the space of three hours after, when his wife, not knowing what was done, came in. [8] And Peter answered unto her, Tell me whether ye sold the land for so much? And she said, Yea, for so much.

[9] Then Peter said unto her, How is it that ye have agreed together to tempt the Spirit of the Lord? behold, the feet of them which have buried thy husband are at the door, and shall carry thee out. [10] Then fell she down straightway at his feet, and yielded up the ghost: and the young men came in, and found her dead, and, carrying her forth, buried her by her husband.

This is the first anathema (against Ananias and Sapphira): emphatically affirmed by God.

Acts 8:17-23: Then laid they their hands on them, and they received the Holy Ghost. [18] And when Simon saw that through laying on of the apostles' hands the Holy Ghost was given, he offered them money, [19] Saying, Give me also this power, that on whomsoever I lay hands, he may receive the Holy Ghost.

[20] But Peter said unto him, Thy money perish with thee, because thou hast thought that the gift of God may be purchased with money. [21] Thou hast neither part nor lot in this matter: for thy heart is not right in the sight of God.

[22] Repent therefore of this thy wickedness, and pray God, if perhaps the thought of thine heart may be forgiven thee.

[23] For I perceive that thou art in the gall of bitterness, and in the bond of iniquity.

St. Peter was the first to recognize and refute heresy (simony), and again issues an authoritative warning or anathema, so that Simon would repent.

Acts 3:2-8: And a certain man lame from his mother's womb was carried, whom they laid daily at the gate of the temple which is called Beautiful, to ask alms of them that entered into the temple;

[3] Who seeing Peter and John about to go into the temple asked an alms. [4] And Peter, fastening his eyes upon him with John, said, Look on us. [5] And he gave heed unto them, expecting to receive something of them. [6] Then Peter said, Silver and gold have I none; but such as I have give I thee: In the name of Jesus Christ of Nazareth rise up and walk. [7] And he took him by the right hand, and lifted him up: and immediately his feet and ankle bones received strength. [8] And he leaping up stood, and walked, and entered with them into the temple, walking, and leaping, and praising God.

Acts 9:36-41: Now there was at Joppa a certain disciple named Tabitha, which by interpretation is called Dorcas: this woman was full of good works and almsdeeds which she did. [37] And it came to pass in those days, that she was sick, and died: whom when they had washed, they laid her in an upper chamber. [38] And forasmuch as Lydda was nigh to Joppa, and the disciples had heard that Peter was there, they sent unto him two men, desiring him that he would not delay to come to them. [39] Then Peter arose and went with them. When he was come, they brought him into the upper chamber: and all the widows stood by him weeping, and shewing the coats and garments which Dorcas made, while she was with them. [40] But Peter put them all forth, and kneeled down, and prayed; and turning him to the body said, Tabitha, arise. And she opened her eyes: and when she saw Peter, she sat up. [41] And he gave her his hand, and lifted her up, and when he had called the saints and widows, presented her alive.

St. Peter performed the first miracle of the Church Age, healing a lame man (Acts 3:2-8). Even his shadow worked miracles (Acts 5:15). And he was the first person after Christ to raise the dead (Acts 9:40).

Acts 10:34-35: Then Peter opened his mouth, and said, Of a truth I perceive that God is no respecter of persons: [35] But in every nation he that feareth him, and worketh righteousness, is accepted with him.

Acts 10:44-48: While Peter yet spake these words, the Holy Ghost fell on all them which heard the word. [45] And they of the circumcision which believed were astonished, as many as came with Peter, because that on the Gentiles also was poured out the gift of the Holy Ghost. [46] For they heard them speak with tongues, and magnify God. Then answered Peter, [47] Can any man forbid water, that these should not be baptized, which have received the Holy Ghost as well as we? [48] And he commanded them to be baptized in the name of the Lord. Then prayed they him to tarry certain days.

St. Peter was the first apostle to receive the Gentiles, after a revelation from God (Acts 10:9-20), and to command them to be baptized.

Acts 15:7-15: And when there had been much disputing, Peter rose up, and said unto them, Men and brethren, ye know how that a good while ago God made choice among us, that the Gentiles by my mouth should hear the word of the gospel, and believe.

[8] And God, which knoweth the hearts, bare them witness, giving them the Holy Ghost, even as he did unto us;

[9] And put no difference between us and them, purifying their hearts by faith. [10] Now therefore why tempt ye God, to put a yoke upon the neck of the disciples, which neither our fathers nor we were able to bear? [11] But we believe that through the grace of the Lord Jesus Christ we shall be saved, even as they. [12] Then all the multitude kept silence, and gave audience to Barnabas and Paul, declaring what miracles and wonders God had wrought among the Gentiles by them. [13] And after they had held their peace, James answered, saying, Men and brethren, hearken unto me: [14] Simeon hath declared how God at the first did visit the Gentiles, to take out of them a people for his name.

[15] And to this agree the words of the prophets; as it is written,

St. Peter makes the authoritative doctrinal pronouncement at the Council of Jerusalem and seems to stop the debate cold in its tracks, as indicated by the assembly falling silent. St. Paul and St. Barnabas talk about signs and wonders, but no indication is given of any doctrinal proclamation from them. When St. James speaks, he refers back to Peter (even though Paul had spoken in the interim), and then basically confirmed what Peter had also said. All of this is harmonious with the notion of Peter functioning as a pope, the head of the Church, while working together with the apostles and bishops and elders.

Scripture offers examples
of the infallibility of individuals

Deuteronomy 5:5: (I stood between the LORD and you at that time, to shew you the work of the LORD: for ye were afraid by reason of the fire, and went not up into the mount;) . . . (RSV: "to declare to you the word of the LORD"; Moses; cf. 1 Chron 15:15; 2 Chron 35:6)

1 Samuel 15:10: Then came the word of the LORD unto Samuel, saying, (cf. 1 Chron. 11:3)

2 Samuel 7:4: And it came to pass that night, that the word of the LORD came unto Nathan, saying, (cf. 1 Chron 17:3)

2 Samuel 23:2: The Spirit of the LORD spake by me, and his word was in my tongue. (King David: cf. 1 Chron. 22:8)

2 Samuel 24:11: For when David was up in the morning, the word of the LORD came unto the prophet Gad, David's seer, saying,

1 Kings 6:11: And the word of the LORD came to Solomon, saying,

1 Kings 13:20-21: And it came to pass, as they sat at the table, that the word of the LORD came unto the prophet that brought him back: [21] And he cried unto the man of God that came from Judah, saying, Thus saith the LORD, Forasmuch as thou hast disobeyed the mouth of the LORD, and hast not kept the commandment which the LORD thy God commanded thee,

1 Kings 15:29: . . . according unto the saying of the LORD, which he spake by his servant Ahijah the Shilonite:

1 Kings 17:24: And the woman said to Elijah, Now by this I know that thou art a man of God, and that the word of the LORD in thy mouth is truth. (see also: 16:1, 7, 12 [Jehu]; 16:34 [Joshua]; 17:2, 8, 16 [Elijah]; 18:1 [Elijah])

2 Kings 1:17: So he died according to the word of the LORD which Elijah had spoken . . .

2 Kings 7:1: Then Elisha said, Hear ye the word of the LORD; Thus saith the LORD . . .

2 Kings 9:36: Wherefore they came again, and told him. And he said, This is the word of the LORD, which he spake by his servant Elijah the Tishbite . . . (cf. 10:17)

2 Kings 14:25: . . . according to the word of the LORD God of Israel, which he spake by the hand of his servant Jonah, the son of Amittai, the prophet . . .

2 Kings 20:4: And it came to pass, afore Isaiah was gone out into the middle court, that the word of the LORD came to him, saying, (cf. 20:16, 19; 23:16)

2 Kings 24:2: . . . according to the word of the LORD, which he spake by his servants the prophets.

2 Chronicles 11:2: But the word of the LORD came to Shemaiah the man of God, saying, (cf. 12:7)

2 Chronicles 24:19-20: Yet he sent prophets to them, to bring them again unto the LORD; and they testified against them: but they would not give ear. [20] And the Spirit of God came upon Zechariah the son of Jehoiada the priest, which stood above the people, and said unto them,

Thus saith God, Why transgress ye the commandments of the LORD, that ye cannot prosper? because ye have forsaken the LORD, he hath also forsaken you.

2 Chronicles 30:12: Also in Judah the hand of God was to give them one heart to do the commandment of the king and of the princes, by the word of the LORD.

2 Chronicles 36:21: To fulfil the word of the LORD by the mouth of Jeremiah . . . (cf. 36:22; Ezra 1:1; Jer. 1:2, 4; 2:4; 7:2; 13:3, 8; 14:1; 16:1; 18:5; 19:3; 21:11; 22:2, 29; 24:4; 28:12; 29:30; several more times in Jeremiah; Dan. 9:2)

Nehemiah 9:30: Yet many years didst thou forbear them, and testifiedst against them by thy spirit in thy prophets: . . . (RSV: "Many years thou didst bear with them, and didst warn them by thy Spirit through thy prophets")

Isaiah 38:4: Then came the word of the LORD to Isaiah, saying, (cf. 39:5, 8; 66:5)

Jeremiah 25:3: From the thirteenth year of Josiah the son of Amon king of Judah, even unto this day, that is the three and twentieth year, the word of the LORD hath come unto me, and I have spoken unto you, rising early and speaking; but ye have not hearkened.

Jeremiah 26:15: But know ye for certain, that if ye put me to death, ye shall surely bring innocent blood upon yourselves, and upon this city, and upon the inhabitants thereof: for of a truth the LORD hath sent me unto you to speak all these words in your ears.

Ezekiel 33:1: Again the word of the LORD came unto me, saying,
"Word of the LORD" appears sixty times in the book of Ezekiel, usually in reference to the prophet Ezekiel.

Hosea 1:1: The word of the LORD that came unto Hosea . . . (cf. 4:1)

Joel 1:1: The word of the LORD that came to Joel the son of Pethuel.

Amos 7:16: Now therefore hear thou the word of the LORD . . .

Jonah 1:1: Now the word of the LORD came unto Jonah the son of Amittai, saying, (cf. 3:1, 3)

Micah 1:1: The word of the LORD that came to Micah . . .

Zephaniah 1:1: The word of the LORD which came unto Zephaniah . . .

Haggai 1:13: Then spake Haggai the LORD's messenger in the LORD's message unto the people, saying, I am with you, saith the LORD. (cf. 1:1, 3; 2:1, 10, 20)

Zechariah 1:1: . . . the word of the LORD unto Zechariah . . . (cf. 1:7; 6:9; 7:1, 4, 8; 8:1, 18)

Zechariah 7:12: Yea, they made their hearts as an adamant stone, lest they should hear the law, and the words which the LORD of hosts hath sent in his spirit by the former prophets: therefore came a great wrath from the LORD of hosts.

Malachi 1:1: The burden of the word of the LORD to Israel by Malachi.

Malachi 2:6-8: The law of truth was in his mouth, and iniquity was not found in his lips: he walked with me in peace and equity, and did turn many away from iniquity. [7] For the priest's lips should keep knowledge, and they should seek the law at his mouth: for he is the messenger of the LORD of hosts. [8] But ye are departed out of the way; ye have caused many to stumble at the law; ye have corrupted the covenant of Levi, saith the LORD of hosts.

This passage is referring to Levites, who were teachers in Israel.

The prophets received their inspiration by the Holy Spirit (Num. 11:29; 2 Chron. 24:20; Neh. 9:30; Ezek. 3:24; 11:5; Zech. 7:12; Acts 28:25; 2 Pet. 1:21). The Holy Spirit (as a result of the New Covenant) is now given to all

Christians (John 15:26; 1 Cor. 3:16), so it is perfectly possible and plausible that an even greater measure of the Holy Spirit would be given to leaders of the Church who have the responsibility to teach, since James wrote: "Let not many of you become teachers, my brethren, for you know that we who teach shall be judged with greater strictness" (James 3:1). The disciples were reassured by Jesus: "When the Spirit of truth comes, he will guide you into all the truth" (John 16:13; cf. 8:32, RSV), so surely it makes sense that shepherds of the Christian flock would be given an extra measure of protection in order to better fulfill their duties.

Jesus called John the Baptist "more than a prophet" (Luke 7:26, RSV) and stated, "among those born of women none is greater than John; yet he who is least in the kingdom of God is greater than he" (Luke 7:28, RSV). Therefore, it is not in the least implausible that one man: the pope, could be infallible, which is a far lesser gift than the inspiration and direct revelation from God exhibited by the prophets.

Briefly put, then, the argument is: "If prophets spoke with inspiration, then popes can plausibly speak infallibly, since the latter is a far less extraordinary gift than the former." Or, from a different angle: "If those with lesser gifts can do the great thing (inspired utterance), then those with greater gifts can certainly do the lesser thing (infallible utterance)."

Matthew 1:22: Now all this was done, that it might be fulfilled which was spoken of the Lord by the prophet, saying, (cf. 2:15)

Luke 1:70: As he spake by the mouth of his holy prophets, which have been since the world began:

Acts 28:25: And when they agreed not among themselves, they departed, after that Paul had spoken one word, Well spake the Holy Ghost by Esaias the prophet unto our fathers,

2 Peter 1:21: For the prophecy came not in old time by the will of man: but holy men of God spake as they were moved by the Holy Ghost.

See further New Testament references to prophets and prophesying: Acts 2:16-18; 11:27-28; 13:1; 15:32; 19:6; 21:9-10; Rom. 12:6; 1 Cor. 11:4-5; 12:10, 28-29; 14:1, 3-6, 22, 24, 29, 31-32, 37, 39; Eph. 3:5; 4:11; 1 Thess. 5:20; 1 Tim. 1:18; 4:14).

Any non-Catholic Christian who believes in the inspiration of Holy Scripture, and who accepts the received canon of Scripture (either sixty-six or seventy-three books) — itself deriving from authoritative conciliar and papal pronouncements of an infallible Catholic Church — accepts the fact that St. Peter, the undisputed leader of the twelve disciples, and (we believe) the first pope, has written two inspired epistles (or proto-encyclicals). Inspiration means "God-breathed": a positive characteristic that includes being entirely free from error (as all God-inspired words of revelation are truth).

Infallibility is a limited, far less profound "negative" protection against error. Everyone who holds to the inspiration of Scripture already believes that St. Peter wrote inspired words from God in the Bible. Where, then, is the inherent difficulty in believing that he and his successors could be protected by the Holy Spirit to write infallible documents (see, e.g., John 14:26; 15:26; 16:13; Acts 15:28)? The more difficult thing to believe, the thing that requires far more faith, since it is a greater gift, is already accepted, so what insuperable prima facie difficulty remains in the notion of infallible (as opposed to inspired) popes (and an infallible Church)?

Chapter Four

The Theology of Salvation

We are saved through grace

Acts 15:11: But we believe that through the grace of the Lord Jesus Christ we shall be saved, even as they.

Acts 18:27: . . . to receive him: who, when he was come, helped them much which had believed through grace:

Acts 20:24, 32: . . . the ministry, which I have received of the Lord Jesus, to testify the gospel of the grace of God . . . And now, brethren, I commend you to God, and to the word of his grace, which is able to build you up, and to give you an inheritance among all them which are sanctified.

Romans 3:24: Being justified freely by his grace through the redemption that is in Christ Jesus:

Romans 4:16: Therefore it is of faith, that it might be by grace; to the end the promise might be sure to all the seed; not to that only which is of the law, but to that also which is of the faith of Abraham; who is the father of us all,

Romans 5:2: By whom also we have access by faith into this grace wherein we stand, and rejoice in hope of the glory of God.

Romans 5:15-17: But not as the offence, so also is the free gift. For if through the offence of one many be dead, much more the grace of God, and the gift by grace, which is by one man, Jesus Christ, hath abounded unto many. [16] And not as it was by one that sinned, so is the gift: for the judgment was by one to condemnation, but the free gift is of many offences unto justification. [17] For if by one man's offence death reigned by one; much more they which receive abundance of grace and of the gift of righteousness shall reign in life by one, Jesus Christ.)

Romans 5:20-21: Moreover the law entered, that the offence might abound. But where sin abounded, grace did much more abound: [21] That as sin hath reigned unto death, even so might grace reign through righteousness unto eternal life by Jesus Christ our Lord.

Romans 6:14: For sin shall not have dominion over you: for ye are not under the law, but under grace.

Romans 11:5-6: Even so then at this present time also there is a remnant according to the election of grace. [6] And if by grace, then is it no more of works: otherwise grace is no more grace. But if it be of works, then is it no more grace: otherwise work is no more work.

1 Corinthians 15:10: But by the grace of God I am what I am: and his grace which was bestowed upon me was not in vain; but I laboured more abundantly than they all: yet not I, but the grace of God which was with me.

Galatians 1:15: But when it pleased God, who separated me from my mother's womb, and called me by his grace,

Galatians 2:21: I do not frustrate the grace of God: for if righteousness come by the law, then Christ is dead in vain.

Ephesians 1:7: In whom we have redemption through his blood, the forgiveness of sins, according to the riches of his grace;

Ephesians 2:4-10: But God, who is rich in mercy, for his great love wherewith he loved us, [5] Even when we were dead in sins, hath quickened us together with Christ, (by grace ye are saved;)

[6] And hath raised us up together, and made us sit together in heavenly places in Christ Jesus: [7] That in the ages to come he might shew the exceeding riches of his grace in his kindness toward us through Christ Jesus.

[8] For by grace are ye saved through faith; and that not of yourselves: it is the gift of God:

[9] Not of works, lest any man should boast. [10] For we are his workmanship, created in Christ Jesus unto good works, which God hath before ordained that we should walk in them.

2 Thessalonians 2:16: Now our Lord Jesus Christ himself, and God, even our Father, which hath loved us, and hath given us everlasting consolation and good hope through grace,

2 Timothy 1:9: Who hath saved us, and called us with an holy calling, not according to our works, but according to his own purpose and grace, which was given us in Christ Jesus before the world began,

Titus 2:11: For the grace of God that bringeth salvation hath appeared to all men,

Titus 3:7: That being justified by his grace, we should be made heirs according to the hope of eternal life. (RSV: "so that we might be justified by his grace and become heirs in hope of eternal life")

1 Peter 1:10: Of which salvation the prophets have inquired and searched diligently, who prophesied of the grace that should come unto you:

Holy Scripture teaches that grace is primary in that it enables both faith and works that are organically tied to it in the process of sanctification and eventual eschatological salvation (i.e., when we actually get to heaven, or purgatory: which means we are saved, too, and inevitably on the way to heaven).

There is a biblical sense in which we are saved by grace alone, and this is asserted unambiguously without immediate qualification (as we see to the contrary in the cases of faith alone and works alone: see the next two sections). That highlights the nature of the difference compared with faith and works. "Grace alone," is, therefore, an entirely biblical, orthodox, Catholic statement, as long as it is understood exactly in its proper sense (i.e., not utterly excluding works and faith in the overall mix).

Salvation is not by faith alone

Ezekiel 33:12-19: Therefore, thou son of man, say unto the children of thy people, The righteousness of the righteous shall not deliver him in the day of his transgression: as for the wickedness of the wicked, he shall not fall thereby in the day that he turneth from his wickedness; neither shall the righteous be able to live for his righteousness in the day that he sinneth.

[13] When I shall say to the righteous, that he shall surely live; if he trust to his own righteousness, and commit iniquity, all his righteousnesses shall not be remembered; but for his iniquity that he hath committed, he shall die for it. [14] Again, when I say unto the wicked, Thou shalt surely die; if he turn from his sin, and do that which is lawful and right; [15] If the wicked restore the pledge, give again that he had robbed, walk in the statutes of life, without committing iniquity; he shall surely live, he shall not die. [16] None of his sins that he hath committed shall be mentioned unto him: he hath done that which is lawful and right; he shall surely live. [17] Yet the children of thy people say, The way of the Lord is not equal: but as for them, their way is not equal. [18] When the righteous turneth from his righteousness, and committeth iniquity, he shall even die thereby. [19] But if the wicked turn from his wickedness, and do that which is lawful and right, he shall live thereby.

James 2:14: What doth it profit, my brethren, though a man say he hath faith, and have not works? can faith save him?

James 2:17-18: Even so faith, if it hath not works, is dead, being alone. [18] Yea, a man may say, Thou hast faith, and I have works: shew me thy faith without thy works, and I will shew thee my faith by my works.

James 2:20: But wilt thou know, O vain man, that faith without works is dead?

James 2:22: Seest thou how faith wrought with his works, and by works was faith made perfect? (RSV: "You see that faith was active along with his works, and faith was completed by works,")

James 2:24: Ye see then how that by works a man is justified, and not by faith only. (RSV: "You see that a man is justified by works and not by faith alone")

James 2:26: For as the body without the spirit is dead, so faith without works is dead also.

We see above, directly in 2:24 and indirectly in all the others, that works also play a part in the sanctification and salvation process, but they are not by themselves. They are entirely enabled by God's free grace and accompanied by faith.

Salvation is not by works alone

James 2:21: Was not Abraham our father justified by works, when he had offered Isaac his son upon the altar?

James 2:25: Likewise also was not Rahab the harlot justified by works, when she had received the messengers, and had sent them out another way?

This "justification by works" is not by itself, any more than faith is operative by itself. James writes of Abraham being "justified by works" (2:21), but this can't be ripped from context, so as to distort his meaning, since in the verse immediately before, he ties faith organically in with works, and he does the same in the verse immediately after, as he does in the larger context of 2:14, 17-18 and 2:26. They simply can't be separated.

Likewise, when justification by works is asserted again in 2:24, it is qualified in 2:26, by connecting faith with it, and in the larger context before the statement, also in 2:14, 17-18, 20, 22. The works can't possibly be interpreted as on their own, then, without doing massive violence to the contextual meaning and teaching.

The same applies to 2:25 and the statement about Rahab the harlot being "justified by works" — it is qualified in the same way in context, by the consideration of 2:14, 17-18, 20, 22, 26. Moreover, salvation by works alone is flatly and explicitly denied by St. Paul in Ephesians 2:8-9 and 2 Timothy 1:9, and the same is strongly implied in Romans 11:5-6 (see the earlier section "We are saved through grace").

For the Catholic, justification is not the same thing as salvation or the attainment of eternal life. It can be lost or rejected by means of human free will and disobedience. So, to assert "justification by works," even in a qualified sense, is not at all the same as asserting salvation by works.

Therefore, it is scripturally improper to assert either salvation by works alone or salvation by faith alone. They are never taught in Holy Scripture, and are both denied more than once. Justification by faith or justification by works can be asserted in a limited sense, as Scripture does: always understood as hand-in-hand with the other two elements in the grace-faith-works triumvirate.

Grace, faith, works, action, and obedience lead to salvation

Romans 1:5: By whom we have received grace and apostleship, for obedience to the faith among all nations, for his name: (RSV: "through whom we have received grace and apostleship to bring about the obedience of faith "; cf. Acts 6:7)

Romans 1:17: For therein is the righteousness of God revealed from faith to faith: as it is written, The just shall live by faith. (RSV: "through faith for faith; as it is written, 'He who through faith is righteous shall live'")

Romans 2:6-7: Who will render to every man according to his deeds: [7] To them who by patient continuance in well doing seek for glory and honour and immortality, eternal life: (RSV: "For he will render to every man according to his works"; cf. 2:8; 2:10)

Romans 2:13: For not the hearers of the law are just before God, but the doers of the law shall be justified. (RSV: "righteous before God"; cf. James 1:22-23; 2:21-24)

Romans 3:22: Even the righteousness of God which is by faith of Jesus Christ unto all and upon all them that believe: for there is no difference: (RSV: "the righteousness of God through faith in Jesus Christ for all who believe")

Romans 3:31: Do we then make void the law through faith? God forbid: yea, we establish the law. (RSV: "Do we then overthrow the law by this faith? By no means! On the contrary, we uphold the law")

Romans 6:17: But God be thanked, that ye were the servants of sin, but ye have obeyed from the heart that form of doctrine which was delivered you.

Romans 8:13: For if ye live after the flesh, ye shall die: but if ye through the Spirit do mortify the deeds of the body, ye shall live. (cf. 2 Cor. 11:15)

Romans 8:28: And we know that all things work together for good to them that love God, to them who are the called according to his purpose.

Romans 10:16: But they have not all obeyed the gospel. For Esaias [Isaiah] saith, Lord, who hath believed our report?

Romans 14:23: And he that doubteth is damned if he eat, because he eateth not of faith: for whatsoever is not of faith is sin. (RSV: "whatever does not proceed from faith is sin")

Romans 15:17-18: I have therefore whereof I may glory through Jesus Christ in those things which pertain to God. [18] For I will not dare to speak of any of those things which Christ hath not wrought by me, to make the Gentiles obedient, by word and deed, (RSV: "In Christ Jesus, then, I have reason to be proud of my work for God. For I will not venture to speak of anything except what Christ has wrought through me to win obedience from the Gentiles, by word and deed,")

Romans 16:26: But now is made manifest, and by the scriptures of the prophets, according to the commandment of the everlasting God, made known to all nations for the obedience of faith: (RSV: "to bring about the obedience of faith"; cf. Heb. 11:8)

1 Corinthians 3:9: For we are labourers together with God: ye are God's husbandry, ye are God's building. (RSV: "For we are God's fellow workers; you are God's field"; cf. 3:8; Mark 16:20)

1 Corinthians 3:10: According to the grace of God which is given unto me, as a wise masterbuilder, I have laid the foundation, and another buildeth thereon. But let every man take heed how he buildeth thereupon.

1 Corinthians 9:27: But I keep under my body, and bring it into subjection: lest that by any means, when I have preached to others, I myself should be a castaway. (RSV: "but I pommel my body and subdue it, lest . . . I myself should be disqualified")

1 Corinthians 15:10: But by the grace of God I am what I am: and his grace which was bestowed upon me was not in vain; but I laboured more abundantly than they all: yet not I, but the grace of God which was with me.

1 Corinthians 15:58: Therefore, my beloved brethren, be ye stedfast, unmoveable, always abounding in the work of the Lord, forasmuch as ye know that your labour is not in vain in the Lord.

1 Corinthians 16:13: Watch ye, stand fast in the faith, quit you like men, be strong. (RSV: "Be watchful, stand firm in your faith, be courageous, be strong")

2 Corinthians 1:6: And whether we be afflicted, it is for your consolation and salvation, which is effectual in the enduring of the same sufferings which we also suffer: or whether we be comforted, it is for your consolation and salvation.

2 Corinthians 1:24: Not for that we have dominion over your faith, but are helpers of your joy: for by faith ye stand. (RSV: "Not that we lord it over your faith; we work with you for your joy, for you stand firm in your faith")

2 Corinthians 5:10: For we must all appear before the judgment seat of Christ; that every one may receive the things done in his body, according to that he hath done, whether it be good or bad.

2 Corinthians 6:1: We then, as workers together with him, beseech you also that ye receive not the grace of God in vain.

2 Corinthians 8:3-7: For to their power, I bear record, yea, and beyond their power they were willing of themselves;

[4] Praying us with much intreaty that we would receive the gift, and take upon us the fellowship of the ministering to the saints.

[5] And this they did, not as we hoped, but first gave their own selves to the Lord, and unto us by the will of God.

[6] Insomuch that we desired Titus, that as he had begun, so he would also finish in you the same grace also. [7] Therefore, as ye abound in every thing, in faith, and utterance, and knowledge, and in all diligence, and in your love to us, see that ye abound in this grace also. (RSV: "we have urged Titus that as he had already made a beginning, he should also complete among you this gracious work. Now as you excel in everything — in faith, in utterance . . . see that you excel in this gracious work also")

2 Corinthians 10:15: Not boasting of things without our measure, that is, of other men's labours; but having hope, when your faith is increased, that we shall be enlarged by you according to our rule abundantly,

2 Corinthians 11:23: Are they ministers of Christ? (I speak as a fool) I am more; in labours more abundant, in stripes above measure, in prisons more frequent, in deaths oft.

2 Corinthians 13:5: Examine yourselves, whether ye be in the faith; prove your own selves. Know ye not your own selves, how that Jesus Christ is in you, except ye be reprobates? (RSV: "whether you are holding to your faith. Test yourselves. Do you not realize that Jesus Christ is in you? — unless indeed you fail to meet the test!")

Galatians 2:20: I am crucified with Christ: nevertheless I live; yet not I, but Christ liveth in me: and the life which I now live in the flesh I live by the faith of the Son of God, who loved me, and gave himself for me.

Galatians 5:6-7: For in Jesus Christ neither circumcision availeth anything, nor uncircumcision; but faith which worketh by love.

[7] Ye did run well; who did hinder you that ye should not obey the truth?

Galatians 6:7-9: Be not deceived; God is not mocked: for whatsoever a man soweth, that shall he also reap. [8] For he that soweth to his flesh shall of the flesh reap corruption; but he that soweth to the Spirit shall of the Spirit reap life everlasting. [9] And let us not be weary in well doing: for in due season we shall reap, if we faint not.

Ephesians 2:10: For we are his workmanship, created in Christ Jesus unto good works, which God hath before ordained that we should walk in them.

Philippians 2:12-13: Wherefore, my beloved, as ye have always obeyed, not as in my presence only, but now much more in my absence, work out your own salvation with fear and trembling.

[13] For it is God which worketh in you both to will and to do of his good pleasure.

Philippians 2:14-16: Do all things without murmurings and disputings: [15] That ye may be blameless and harmless, the sons of God, without rebuke, in the midst of a crooked and perverse nation, among whom ye shine as lights in the world; [16] Holding forth the word of life; that I may rejoice in the day of Christ, that I have not run in vain, neither laboured in vain.

Philippians 3:9: And be found in him, not having mine own righteousness, which is of the law, but that which is through the faith of Christ, the righteousness which is of God by faith:

Philippians 4:3: And I intreat thee also, true yokefellow, help those women which laboured with me in the gospel, with Clement also, and with other my fellowlabourers, whose names are in the book of life.

Colossians 3:23-25: And whatsoever ye do, do it heartily, as to the Lord, and not unto men; [24] Knowing that of the Lord ye shall receive the reward of the inheritance: for ye serve the Lord Christ. [25] But he that doeth wrong shall receive for the wrong which he hath done: and there is no respect of persons.

1 Thessalonians 1:3: Remembering without ceasing your work of faith, and labour of love, and patience of hope in our Lord Jesus Christ, in the sight of God and our Father;

2 Thessalonians 1:8: In flaming fire taking vengeance on them that know not God, and that obey not the gospel of our Lord Jesus Christ:

2 Thessalonians 1:11: Wherefore also we pray always for you, that our God would count you worthy of this calling, and fulfil all the good pleasure of his goodness, and the work of faith with power:

1 Timothy 6:11: But thou, O man of God, flee these things; and follow after righteousness, godliness, faith, love, patience, meekness.

1 Timothy 6:18-19: That they do good, that they be rich in good works, ready to distribute, willing to communicate; [19] Laying up in store for themselves a good foundation against the time to come, that they may lay hold on eternal life.

2 Timothy 2:10: Therefore I endure all things for the elect's sakes, that they may also obtain the salvation which is in Christ Jesus with eternal glory.

2 Timothy 2:22: Flee also youthful lusts: but follow righteousness, faith, charity, peace, with them that call on the Lord out of a pure heart.

2 Timothy 4:7: I have fought a good fight, I have finished my course, I have kept the faith:

Titus 1:16: They profess that they know God; but in works they deny him, being abominable, and disobedient, and unto every good work reprobate.

Titus 3:8: This is a faithful saying, and these things I will that thou affirm constantly, that they which have believed in God might be careful to maintain good works. These things are good and profitable unto men.

Titus 3:14: And let ours also learn to maintain good works for necessary uses, that they be not unfruitful. (RSV: "apply themselves to good deeds, so as to help cases of urgent need, and not to be unfruitful")

Final judgment is always
associated with works

1 Samuel 28:15-19: And Samuel said to Saul, Why hast thou disquieted me, to bring me up? And Saul answered, I am sore distressed; for the Philistines make war against me, and God is departed from me, and answereth me no more, neither by prophets, nor by dreams: therefore I have called thee, that thou mayest make known unto me what I shall do. [16] Then said Samuel, Wherefore then dost thou ask of me, seeing the LORD is departed from thee, and is become thine enemy? [17] And the LORD hath done to him, as he spake by me: for the LORD hath rent the kingdom out of thine hand, and given it to thy neighbour, even to David: [18] Because thou obeyedst not the voice of the LORD, nor executedst his fierce wrath upon Amalek, therefore hath the LORD done this thing unto thee this day. [19] Moreover the LORD will also deliver Israel with thee into the hand of the Philistines: and to morrow shalt thou and thy sons be with me: the LORD also shall deliver the host of Israel into the hand of the Philistines.

2 Kings 22:13: Go ye, inquire of the LORD for me, and for the people, and for all Judah, concerning the words of this book that is found: for great is the wrath of the LORD that is kindled against us, because our fathers have not hearkened unto the words of this book, to do according unto all that which is written concerning us. (cf. 2 Chron. 34:21)

Psalm 7:8-10: The LORD shall judge the people: judge me, O LORD, according to my righteousness, and according to mine integrity that is in me. [9] Oh let the wickedness of the wicked come to an end; but establish the just: for the righteous God trieth the hearts and reins. [10] My defence is of God, which saveth the upright in heart.

Psalm 58:11: So that a man shall say, Verily there is a reward for the righteous: verily he is a God that judgeth in the earth.

Ecclesiastes 12:14: For God shall bring every work into judgment, with every secret thing, whether it be good, or whether it be evil.

Isaiah 59:18: According to their deeds, accordingly he will repay, fury to his adversaries, recompence to his enemies; to the islands he will repay recompence.

Jeremiah 4:4: Circumcise yourselves to the LORD, and take away the foreskins of your heart, ye men of Judah and inhabitants of Jerusalem: lest my fury come forth like fire, and burn that none can quench it, because of the evil of your doings. (cf. 21:12)

Ezekiel 7:3: Now is the end come upon thee, and I will send mine anger upon thee, and will judge thee according to thy ways, and will recompense upon thee all thine abominations. (cf. 7:8; 33:20)

Ezekiel 36:19: And I scattered them among the heathen, and they were dispersed through the countries: according to their way and according to their doings I judged them.

Micah 5:15: And I will execute vengeance in anger and fury upon the heathen, such as they have not heard.

Zephaniah 2:3: Seek ye the LORD, all ye meek of the earth, which have wrought his judgment; seek righteousness, seek meekness: it may be ye shall be hid in the day of the LORD's anger.

Matthew 5:22: But I say unto you, That whosoever is angry with his brother without a cause shall be in danger of the judgment: and whosoever shall say to his brother, Raca, shall be in danger of the council: but whosoever shall say, Thou fool, shall be in danger of hell fire.

Matthew 7:16-27: Ye shall know them by their fruits. Do men gather grapes of thorns, or figs of thistles? [17] Even so every good tree bringeth forth good fruit; but a corrupt tree bringeth forth evil fruit. [18] A good tree cannot bring forth evil fruit, neither can a corrupt tree bring forth good fruit.

[19] Every tree that bringeth not forth good fruit is hewn down, and cast into the fire. [20] Wherefore by their fruits ye shall know them. [21] Not every one that saith unto me, Lord, Lord, shall enter into the kingdom of heaven; but he that doeth the will of my Father which is in heaven. [22] Many will say to me in that day, Lord, Lord, have we not prophesied in thy name? and in thy name have cast out devils? and in thy name done many wonderful works? [23] And then will I profess unto them, I never knew you: depart from me, ye that work iniquity.

[24] Therefore whosoever heareth these sayings of mine, and doeth them, I will liken him unto a wise man, which built his house upon a rock: [25] And the rain descended, and the floods came, and the winds blew, and beat upon that house; and it fell not: for it was founded upon a rock. [26] And every one that heareth these sayings of mine, and doeth them not, shall be likened unto a foolish man, which built his house upon the sand:

[27] And the rain descended, and the floods came, and the winds blew, and beat upon that house; and it fell: and great was the fall of it.

Matthew 10:22: . . . he that endureth to the end shall be saved. (cf. Matt. 24:13; Mark 13:13)

Matthew 16:27: For the Son of man shall come in the glory of his Father with his angels; and then he shall reward every man according to his works.

Matthew 18:8-9: Wherefore if thy hand or thy foot offend thee, cut them off, and cast them from thee: it is better for thee to enter into life halt or maimed, rather than having two hands or two feet to be cast into ever-lasting fire. [9] And if thine eye offend thee, pluck it out, and cast it from thee: it is better for thee to enter into life with one eye, rather than having two eyes to be cast into hell fire. (cf. Mark 9:43, 47)

Matthew 25:14-30: For the kingdom of heaven is as a man travelling into a far country, who called his own servants, and delivered unto them his goods. [15] And unto one he gave five talents, to another two, and to another one; to every man according to his several ability; and straightway took his journey.

[16] Then he that had received the five talents went and traded with the same, and made them other five talents.

[17] And likewise he that had received two, he also gained other two. [18] But he that had received one went and digged in the earth, and hid his lord's money. [19] After a long time the lord of those servants cometh, and reckoneth with them. [20] And so he that had received five talents came and brought other five talents, saying, Lord, thou deliveredst unto me five talents: behold, I have gained beside them five talents more. [21] His lord said unto him, Well done, thou good and faithful servant: thou hast been faithful over a few things, I will make thee ruler over many things: enter thou into the joy of thy lord. [22] He also that had received two talents came and said, Lord, thou deliveredst unto me two talents: behold, I have gained two other talents beside them.

[23] His lord said unto him, Well done, good and faithful servant; thou hast been faithful over a few things, I will make thee ruler over many things: enter thou into the joy of thy lord.

[24] Then he which had received the one talent came and said, Lord, I knew thee that thou art an hard man, reaping where thou hast not sown, and gathering where thou hast not strawed:

[25] And I was afraid, and went and hid thy talent in the earth: lo, there thou hast that is thine. [26] His lord answered and said unto him, Thou wicked and slothful servant, thou knewest that I reap where I sowed not, and gather where I have not strawed:

[27] Thou oughtest therefore to have put my money to the exchangers, and then at my coming I should have received mine own with usury. [28] Take therefore the talent from him, and give it unto him which hath ten talents. [29] For unto every one that hath shall be given, and he shall have abundance: but from him that hath not shall be taken away even that which he hath.

[30] And cast ye the unprofitable servant into outer darkness: there shall be weeping and gnashing of teeth.

Matthew 25:31-46: When the Son of man shall come in his glory, and all the holy angels with him, then shall he sit upon the throne of his glory: [32] And before him shall be gathered all nations: and he shall separate them one from another, as a shepherd divideth his sheep from the goats: [33] And he shall set the sheep on his right hand, but the goats on the left. [34] Then shall the King say unto them on his right hand, Come, ye blessed of my Father, inherit the kingdom prepared for you from the foundation of the world: [35] For I was an hungred, and ye gave me meat: I was thirsty, and ye gave me drink: I was a stranger, and ye took me in: [36] Naked, and ye clothed me: I was sick, and ye visited me: I was in prison, and ye came unto me. [37] Then shall the righteous answer him, saying, Lord, when saw we thee an hungred, and fed thee? or thirsty, and gave thee drink? [38] When saw we thee a stranger, and took thee in? or naked, and clothed thee? [39] Or when saw we thee sick, or in prison, and came unto thee? [40] And the King shall answer and say unto them, Verily I say unto you, Inasmuch as ye have done it unto one of the least of these my brethren, ye have done it unto me. [41] Then shall he say also unto them on the left hand, Depart from me, ye cursed, into everlasting fire, prepared for the devil and his angels: [42] For I was an hungred, and ye gave me no meat: I was thirsty, and ye gave me no drink: [43] I was a stranger, and ye took me not in: naked, and ye clothed me not: sick, and in prison, and ye visited me not. [44] Then shall they also answer him, saying, Lord, when saw we thee an hungred, or athirst, or a stranger, or naked, or sick, or in prison, and did not minister unto thee? [45] Then shall he answer them, saying, Verily I say unto you, Inasmuch as ye did it not to one of the least of these, ye did it not to me. [46] And these shall go away into everlasting punishment: but the righteous into life eternal.

Luke 3:9: And now also the axe is laid unto the root of the trees: every tree therefore which bringeth not forth good fruit is hewn down, and cast into the fire. (cf. Matt. 3:10; 7:19)

Luke 14:13-14: But when thou makest a feast, call the poor, the maimed, the lame, the blind: [14] And thou shalt be blessed; for they cannot recompense thee: for thou shalt be recompensed at the resurrection of the just.

Luke 21:34-36: And take heed to yourselves, lest at any time your hearts be overcharged with surfeiting, and drunkenness, and cares of this life, and so that day come upon you unawares.

[35] For as a snare shall it come on all them that dwell on the face of the whole earth. [36] Watch ye therefore, and pray always, that ye may be accounted worthy to escape all these things that shall come to pass, and to stand before the Son of man.

John 5:26-29: For as the Father hath life in himself; so hath he given to the Son to have life in himself; [27] And hath given him authority to execute judgment also, because he is the Son of man.

[28] Marvel not at this: for the hour is coming, in the which all that are in the graves shall hear his voice, [29] And shall come forth; they that have done good, unto the resurrection of life; and they that have done evil, unto the resurrection of damnation.

Romans 1:18: For the wrath of God is revealed from heaven against all ungodliness and unrighteousness of men, who hold the truth in unrighteousness;

Romans 2:5-13: But after thy hardness and impenitent heart treasurest up unto thyself wrath against the day of wrath and revelation of the righteous judgment of God; [6] Who will render to every man according to his deeds: [7] To them who by patient continuance in well doing seek for glory and honour and immortality, eternal life: [8] But unto them that are contentious, and do not obey the truth, but obey unrighteousness, indignation and wrath, [9] Tribulation and anguish, upon every soul of man that doeth evil, of the Jew first, and also of the Gentile; [10] But glory, honour, and peace, to every man that worketh good, to the Jew first, and also to the Gentile: [11] For there is no respect of persons with God. [12] For as many as have sinned without law shall also perish without law: and as many as have sinned in the law shall be judged by the law; [13] (For not the hearers of the law are just before God, but the doers of the law shall be justified.

1 Corinthians 3:8-9: Now he that planteth and he that watereth are one: and every man shall receive his own reward according to his own labour. [9] For we are labourers together with God: ye are God's husbandry, ye are God's building.

2 Corinthians 5:10: For we must all appear before the judgment seat of Christ; that every one may receive the things done in his body, according to that he hath done, whether it be good or bad.

1 Thessalonians 3:12-13: And the Lord make you to increase and abound in love one toward another, and toward all men, even as we do toward you: [13] To the end he may stablish your hearts unblameable in holiness before God, even our Father, at the coming of our Lord Jesus Christ with all his saints.

1 Thessalonians 5:23: And the very God of peace sanctify you wholly; and I pray God your whole spirit and soul and body be preserved blameless unto the coming of our Lord Jesus Christ.

2 Thessalonians 1:7-12: And to you who are troubled rest with us, when the Lord Jesus shall be revealed from heaven with his mighty angels, [8] In flaming fire taking vengeance on them that know not God, and that obey not the gospel of our Lord Jesus Christ: [9] Who shall be punished with everlasting destruction from the presence of the Lord, and from the glory of his power;

[10] When he shall come to be glorified in his saints, and to be admired in all them that believe (because our testimony among you was believed) in that day. [11] Wherefore also we pray always for you, that our God would count you worthy of this calling, and fulfil all the good pleasure of his goodness, and the work of faith with power: [12] That the name of our Lord Jesus Christ may be glorified in you, and ye in him, according to the grace of our God and the Lord Jesus Christ.

Hebrews 6:7-8: For the earth which drinketh in the rain that cometh oft upon it, and bringeth forth herbs meet for them by whom it is dressed, receiveth blessing from God: [8] But that which beareth thorns and briers is rejected, and is nigh unto cursing; whose end is to be burned.

1 Peter 1:17: And if ye call on the Father, who without respect of persons judgeth according to every man's work, pass the time of your sojourning here in fear:

1 Peter 4:13: But rejoice, inasmuch as ye are partakers of Christ's sufferings; that, when his glory shall be revealed, ye may be glad also with exceeding joy. (cf. Rom. 8:17)

2 Peter 3:10-14: But the day of the Lord will come as a thief in the night; in the which the heavens shall pass away with a great noise, and the elements shall melt with fervent heat, the earth also and the works that are therein shall be burned up. [11] Seeing then that all these things shall be dissolved, what manner of persons ought ye to be in all holy conversation and godliness,

[12] Looking for and hasting unto the coming of the day of God, wherein the heavens being on fire shall be dissolved, and the elements shall melt with fervent heat? [13] Nevertheless we, according to his promise, look for new heavens and a new earth, wherein dwelleth righteousness.

[14] Wherefore, beloved, seeing that ye look for such things, be diligent that ye may be found of him in peace, without spot, and blameless.

Jude 6-16: And the angels which kept not their first estate, but left their own habitation, he hath reserved in everlasting chains under darkness unto the judgment of the great day. [7] Even as Sodom and Gomorrha, and the cities about them in like manner, giving themselves over to fornication, and going after strange flesh, are set forth for an example, suffering the vengeance of eternal fire. [8] Likewise also these filthy dreamers defile the flesh, despise dominion, and speak evil of dignities.

[9] Yet Michael the archangel, when contending with the devil he disputed about the body of Moses, durst not bring against him a railing accusation, but said, The Lord rebuke thee. [10] But these speak evil of those things which they know not: but what they know naturally, as brute beasts, in those things they corrupt themselves. [11] Woe unto them! for they have gone in the way of Cain, and ran greedily after the error of Balaam for reward, and perished in the gainsaying of Core. [12] These are spots in your feasts of charity, when they feast with you, feeding themselves without fear: clouds they are without water, carried about of winds; trees whose fruit withereth, without fruit, twice dead, plucked up by the roots; [13] Raging waves of the sea, foaming out their own shame; wandering stars, to whom is reserved the blackness of darkness for ever. [14] And Enoch also, the seventh from Adam, prophesied of these, saying, Behold, the Lord cometh with ten thousands of his saints, [15] To execute judgment upon all, and to convince all that are ungodly among them of all their ungodly deeds which they have ungodly committed, and of all their hard speeches which ungodly sinners have spoken against him. [16] These are murmurers, complainers, walking after their own lusts; and their mouth speaketh great swelling words, having men's persons in admiration because of advantage.

Jude 20-21: But ye, beloved, building up yourselves on your most holy faith, praying in the Holy Ghost, [21] Keep yourselves in the love of God, looking for the mercy of our Lord Jesus Christ unto eternal life.

Revelation 2:5: Remember therefore from whence thou art fallen, and repent, and do the first works; or else I will come unto thee quickly, and will remove thy candlestick out of his place, except thou repent.

Revelation 2:23: . . . I am he which searcheth the reins and hearts: and I will give unto every one of you according to your works.

Revelation 20:11-13: And I saw a great white throne, and him that sat on it, from whose face the earth and the heaven fled away; and there was found no place for them. [12] And I saw the dead, small and great, stand before God; and the books were opened: and another book was opened, which is the book of life: and the dead were judged out of those things which were written in the books, according to their works. [13] And the sea gave up the dead which were in it; and death and hell delivered up the dead which were in them: and they were judged every man according to their works.

Revelation 21:8: But the fearful, and unbelieving, and the abominable, and murderers, and whoremongers, and sorcerers, and idolaters, and all liars, shall have their part in the lake which burneth with fire and brimstone: which is the second death.

Revelation 22:12: And, behold, I come quickly; and my reward is with me, to give every man according as his work shall be.

Some sins are more serious than others

1 John 5:16-17: If any man see his brother sin a sin which is not unto death, he shall ask, and he shall give him life for them that sin not unto death. There is a sin unto death: I do not say that he shall pray for it. [17] All unrighteousness is sin: and there is a sin not unto death. (RSV: "If any one sees his brother committing what is not a mortal sin, he will ask, and God will give him life for those whose sin is not mortal. There is sin which is mortal; I do not say that one is to pray for that. All wrongdoing is sin, but there is a sin which is not mortal")

Some non-Catholic Christians think that all sins are exactly alike in the eyes of God: everything from a white lie or a child stealing a cookie to mass murder. This mistaken notion is decisively refuted by the above passage. Scripture provides several indications of this difference in seriousness of sin, and in subjective guiltiness for it:

Matthew 5:22: But I say unto you, That whosoever is angry with his brother without a cause shall be in danger of the judgment: and whosoever shall say to his brother, Raca, shall be in danger of the council: but whosoever shall say, Thou fool, shall be in danger of hell fire. (RSV: ". . . whoever insults his brother shall be liable to the council, and whoever says, 'You fool!' shall be liable to the hell of fire")

Luke 12:47-48: And that servant, which knew his lord's will, and prepared not himself, neither did according to his will, shall be beaten with many stripes. [48] But he that knew not, and did commit things worthy of stripes, shall be beaten with few stripes. For unto whomsoever much is given, of him shall be much required: and to whom men have committed much, of him they will ask the more.

Luke 23:34: Then said Jesus, Father, forgive them; for they know not what they do . . .

John 9:41: Jesus said unto them, If ye were blind, ye should have no sin: but now ye say, We see; therefore your sin remaineth. (RSV: "If you were blind, you would have no guilt; but now that you say, 'We see,' your guilt remains")

John 19:11: . . . he that delivered me unto thee hath the greater sin.

Acts 17:30: And the times of this ignorance God winked at; but now commandeth all men every where to repent: (RSV: "The times of ignorance God overlooked,")

Romans 3:25: Whom God hath set forth to be a propitiation through faith in his blood, to declare his righteousness for the remission of sins that are past, through the forbearance of God; (RSV: "to show God's righteousness, because in his divine forbearance he had passed over former sins;")

1 Timothy 1:13: Who was before a blasphemer, and a persecutor, and injurious: but I obtained mercy, because I did it ignorantly in unbelief.

Hebrews 10:26: For if we sin wilfully after that we have received the knowledge of the truth, there remaineth no more sacrifice for sins, (RSV: "if we sin deliberately . . .")

James 3:1: My brethren, be not many masters, knowing that we shall receive the greater condemnation. (RSV: "Let not many of you become teachers, my brethren, for you know that we who teach shall be judged with greater strictness")

The Bible also refers to (mortal) sins, which — if not repented of — will exclude one from heaven (e.g., 1 Cor. 6:9-10; Gal. 1:8; 5:19-21; Eph. 5:3-6;

Heb. 12:16; Rev. 21:8; 22:15). Objectors to these notions bring up James 2:10 (RSV): "For whoever keeps the whole law but fails in one point has become guilty of all of it." This doesn't prove that all sins are the same, equally destructive and worthy of judgment, because the passage is dealing with man's inability to keep the entire Law of God: a common theme in Scripture. James accepts differences in degrees of sin and righteousness elsewhere in the same letter, such as 3:1 (page 186). In James 1:12, the man who endures trial will receive a "crown of life." James also teaches that the "prayer of a righteous man has great power in its effects" (5:16, RSV), which implies that there are relatively more righteous people, whom God honors more, by making their prayers more effective (he used the prophet Elijah as an example). If there is a lesser and greater righteousness, then there are lesser and greater sins also, because to be less righteous is to be more sinful, and vice versa.

Quantifiable differences in grace

Acts 4:33: And with great power gave the apostles witness of the resurrection of the Lord Jesus: and great grace was upon them all.

Romans 5:20: Moreover the law entered, that the offence might abound. But where sin abounded, grace did much more abound:

Romans 6:1: What shall we say then? Shall we continue in sin, that grace may abound?

Romans 12:3: For I say, through the grace given unto me, to every man that is among you, not to think of himself more highly than he ought to think; but to think soberly, according as God hath dealt to every man the measure of faith.

2 Corinthians 8:7: Therefore, as ye abound in every thing, in faith, and utterance, and knowledge, and in all diligence, and in your love to us, see that ye abound in this grace also.

Ephesians 4:7: But unto every one of us is given grace according to the measure of the gift of Christ.

James 4:6: But he giveth more grace. Wherefore he saith, God resisteth the proud, but giveth grace unto the humble. (cf. 1 Pet. 5:5)

1 Peter 1:2: Elect according to the foreknowledge of God the Father, through sanctification of the Spirit, unto obedience and sprinkling of the blood of Jesus Christ: Grace unto you, and peace, be multiplied. (RSV: "May grace and peace be multiplied to you")

1 Peter 4:10: As every man hath received the gift, even so minister the same one to another, as good stewards of the manifold grace of God. (RSV: "good stewards of God's varied grace")

2 Peter 1:2: Grace and peace be multiplied unto you through the knowledge of God, and of Jesus our Lord,

2 Peter 3:18: But grow in grace, and in the knowledge of our Lord and Saviour Jesus Christ. . .

Our merit is based on our response to God's grace

Matthew 5:11-12: Blessed are ye, when men shall revile you, and persecute you, and shall say all manner of evil against you falsely, for my sake. [12] Rejoice, and be exceeding glad: for great is your reward in heaven: for so persecuted they the prophets which were before you.

Matthew 6:3-4: But when thou doest alms, let not thy left hand know what thy right hand doeth: [4] That thine alms may be in secret: and thy Father which seeth in secret himself shall reward thee openly. (cf. 6:5-6, 16-18)

Matthew 10:41-42: He that receiveth a prophet in the name of a prophet shall receive a prophet's reward; and he that receiveth a righteous man in the name of a righteous man shall receive a righteous man's reward. [42] And whosoever shall give to drink unto one of these little ones a cup of cold water only in the name of a disciple, verily I say unto you, he shall in no wise lose his reward.

Matthew 19:21: Jesus said unto him, If thou wilt be perfect, go and sell that thou hast, and give to the poor, and thou shalt have treasure in heaven: and come and follow me.

Matthew 19:29: And every one that hath forsaken houses, or brethren, or sisters, or father, or mother, or wife, or children, or lands, for my name's sake, shall receive an hundredfold, and shall inherit everlasting life.

Mark 9:41: For whosoever shall give you a cup of water to drink in my name, because ye belong to Christ, verily I say unto you, he shall not lose his reward.

Mark 10:29-30: And Jesus answered and said, Verily I say unto you, There is no man that hath left house, or brethren, or sisters, or father, or mother, or wife, or children, or lands, for my sake, and the gospel's, [30] But he shall receive an hundredfold now in this time, houses, and brethren, and sisters, and mothers, and children, and lands, with persecutions; and in the world to come eternal life.

Luke 6:35, 38: But love ye your enemies, and do good, and lend, hoping for nothing again; and your reward shall be great, and ye shall be the children of the Highest: for he is kind unto the unthankful and to the evil . . . Give, and it shall be given unto you; good measure, pressed down, and shaken together, and running over, shall men give into your bosom. For with the same measure that ye mete withal it shall be measured to you again.

Romans 15:17-18: I have therefore whereof I may glory through Jesus Christ in those things which pertain to God. [18] For I will not dare to speak of any of those things which Christ hath not wrought by me, to make the Gentiles obedient, by word and deed, (RSV: "In Christ Jesus, then, I have reason to be proud of my work for God. For I will not venture to speak of anything except what Christ has wrought through me to win obedience from the Gentiles, by word and deed,")

1 Corinthians 3:6-9: I have planted, Apollos watered; but God gave the increase. [7] So then neither is he that planteth any thing, neither he that watereth; but God that giveth the increase.

[8] Now he that planteth and he that watereth are one: and every man shall receive his own reward according to his own labour. [9] For we are labourers together with God: ye are God's husbandry, ye are God's building.

2 Corinthians 9:6: But this I say, He which soweth sparingly shall reap also sparingly; and he which soweth bountifully shall reap also bountifully.

Ephesians 6:8: knowing that whatever good any one does, he will receive the same again from the Lord, whether he is a slave or free. (cf. Matt. 16:27)

2 Timothy 2:15: Study to shew thyself approved unto God, a workman that needeth not to be ashamed, rightly dividing the word of truth.

2 Timothy 4:8: Henceforth there is laid up for me a crown of righteousness, which the Lord, the righteous judge, shall give me at that day: and not to me only, but unto all them also that love his appearing.

Hebrews 6:10: For God is not unrighteous to forget your work and labour of love, which ye have shewed toward his name, in that ye have ministered to the saints, and do minister.

Hebrews 10:35: Cast not away therefore your confidence, which hath great recompence of reward.

Hebrews 11:6: But without faith it is impossible to please him: for he that cometh to God must believe that he is, and that he is a rewarder of them that diligently seek him.

James 1:12: Blessed is the man that endureth temptation: for when he is tried, he shall receive the crown of life, which the Lord hath promised to them that love him.

2 John 1:8: Look to yourselves, that we lose not those things which we have wrought, but that we receive a full reward. (RSV: "may win a full reward")

Revelation 2:10: Fear none of those things which thou shalt suffer: behold, the devil shall cast some of you into prison, that ye may be tried; and ye shall have tribulation ten days: be thou faithful unto death, and I will give thee a crown of life.

Revelation 3:11-12: Behold, I come quickly: hold that fast which thou hast, that no man take thy crown. [12] Him that overcometh will I make a pillar in the temple of my God, and he shall go no more out: and I will write upon him the name of my God, and the name of the city of my God, which is new Jerusalem, which cometh down out of heaven from my God: and I will write upon him my new name.

We are God's coworkers

Mark 16:20: And they went forth, and preached everywhere, the Lord working with them, and confirming the word with signs following. Amen.

Romans 8:28: And we know that all things work together for good to them that love God, to them who are the called according to his purpose.

Romans 15:17-18: I have therefore whereof I may glory through Jesus Christ in those things which pertain to God. [18] For I will not dare to speak of any of those things which Christ hath not wrought by me, to make the Gentiles obedient, by word and deed, (RSV: "In Christ Jesus, then, I have reason to be proud of my work for God. For I will not venture to speak of anything except what Christ has wrought through me to win obedience from the Gentiles, by word and deed,")

1 Corinthians 3:9-10: For we are labourers together with God: ye are God's husbandry, ye are God's building. According to the grace of God which is given unto me, as a wise masterbuilder, I have laid the foundation, and another buildeth thereon. But let every man take heed how he buildeth thereupon. (RSV: "For we are God's fellow workers; you are God's field, God's building")

1 Corinthians 15:10: But by the grace of God I am what I am: and his grace which was bestowed upon me was not in vain; but I laboured more abundantly than they all: yet not I, but the grace of God which was with me.

1 Corinthians 15:58: Therefore, my beloved brethren, be ye stedfast, unmoveable, always abounding in the work of the Lord, forasmuch as ye know that your labour is not in vain in the Lord.

2 Corinthians 6:1: We then, as workers together with him, beseech you also that ye receive not the grace of God in vain. (RSV: "Working together with him . . .")

Ephesians 2:10: For we are his workmanship, created in Christ Jesus unto good works, which God hath before ordained that we should walk in them.

Philippians 2:12-13: Wherefore, my beloved, as ye have always obeyed, not as in my presence only, but now much more in my absence, work out your own salvation with fear and trembling.

[13] For it is God which worketh in you both to will and to do of his good pleasure.

2 Peter 1:10: Wherefore the rather, brethren, give diligence to make your calling and election sure: for if ye do these things, ye shall never fall:

We can participate in the distribution
of grace and in the salvation of others

Psalm 51:13: Then will I teach transgressors thy ways; and sinners shall be converted unto thee.

Acts 2:40-41: And with many other words did he testify and exhort, saying, Save yourselves from this untoward generation.

[41] Then they that gladly received his word were baptized: and the same day there were added unto them about three thousand souls.

Acts 11:14: Who shall tell thee words, whereby thou and all thy house shall be saved.

Acts 11:15: And as I began to speak, the Holy Ghost fell on them, as on us at the beginning.

Romans 11:13-14: For I speak to you Gentiles, inasmuch as I am the apostle of the Gentiles, I magnify mine office: [14] If by any means I may provoke to emulation them which are my flesh, and might save some of them.

Romans 15:17-18: I have therefore whereof I may glory through Jesus Christ in those things which pertain to God. [18] For I will not dare to speak of any of those things which Christ hath not wrought by me, to make the Gentiles obedient, by word and deed, (RSV: "In Christ Jesus, then, I have reason to be proud of my work for God. For I will not venture to speak of anything except what Christ has wrought through me to win obedience from the Gentiles, by word and deed,")

1 Corinthians 1:18, 21: For the preaching of the cross is to them that perish foolishness; but unto us which are saved it is the power of God . . . [21] For after that in the wisdom of God the world by wisdom knew not God, it pleased God by the foolishness of preaching to save them that believe.

1 Corinthians 7:16: For what knowest thou, O wife, whether thou shalt save thy husband? or how knowest thou, O man, whether thou shalt save thy wife?

1 Corinthians 9:22: To the weak became I as weak, that I might gain the weak: I am made all things to all men, that I might by all means save some.

2 Corinthians 1:6: And whether we be afflicted, it is for your consolation and salvation, which is effectual in the enduring of the same sufferings which we also suffer: or whether we be comforted, it is for your consolation and salvation.

2 Corinthians 2:10: To whom ye forgive any thing, I forgive also: for if I forgave any thing, to whom I forgave it, for your sakes forgave I it in the person of Christ; (RSV: "Any one whom you forgive, I also forgive. What I have forgiven, if I have forgiven anything, has been for your sake in the presence of Christ,")

2 Corinthians 4:8-15: We are troubled on every side, yet not distressed; we are perplexed, but not in despair; [9] Persecuted, but not forsaken; cast down, but not destroyed; [10] Always bearing about in the body the dying of the Lord Jesus, that the life also of Jesus might be made manifest in our body. [11] For we which live are alway delivered unto death for Jesus' sake, that the life also of Jesus might be made manifest in our mortal flesh. [12] So then death worketh in us, but life in you. [13] We having the same spirit of faith, according as it is written, I believed, and therefore have I spoken; we also believe, and therefore speak; [14] Knowing that he which raised up the Lord Jesus shall raise up us also by Jesus, and shall present us with you. [15] For all things are for your sakes, that the abundant grace might through the thanksgiving of many redound to the glory of God.

2 Corinthians 5:18-19: And all things are of God, who hath reconciled us to himself by Jesus Christ, and hath given to us the ministry of reconciliation; [19] To wit, that God was in Christ, reconciling the world unto himself, not imputing their trespasses unto them; and hath committed unto us the word of reconciliation.

Ephesians 3:2: If ye have heard of the dispensation of the grace of God which is given me to youward: (RSV: "assuming that you have heard of the stewardship of God's grace that was given to me for you")

Ephesians 4:29: Let no corrupt communication proceed out of your mouth, but that which is good to the use of edifying, that it may minister grace unto the hearers. (RSV: "impart grace . . .")

Philippians 1:7: Even as it is meet for me to think this of you all, because I have you in my heart; inasmuch as both in my bonds, and in the defence and confirmation of the gospel, ye all are partakers of my grace. (RSV: "you are all partakers with me of grace")

Philippians 1:19: For I know that this shall turn to my salvation through your prayer, and the supply of the Spirit of Jesus Christ, (RSV: "For I know that through your prayers and the help of the Spirit of Jesus Christ this will turn out for my deliverance,")

Philippians 2:12-13: Wherefore, my beloved, as ye have always obeyed, not as in my presence only, but now much more in my absence, work out your own salvation with fear and trembling.

[13] For it is God which worketh in you both to will and to do of his good pleasure.

1 Timothy 4:16: Take heed unto thyself, and unto the doctrine; continue in them: for in doing this thou shalt both save thyself, and them that hear thee. (RSV: "Take heed to yourself and to your teaching: hold to that, for by so doing you will save both yourself and your hearers")

2 Timothy 2:10: Therefore I endure all things for the elect's sakes, that they may also obtain the salvation which is in Christ Jesus with eternal glory.

Hebrews 10:24: And let us consider one another to provoke unto love and to good works:

James 5:15: And the prayer of faith shall save the sick, and the Lord shall raise him up; and if he have committed sins, they shall be forgiven him.

James 5:19-20: Brethren, if any of you do err from the truth, and one convert him; [20] Let him know, that he which converteth the sinner from the error of his way shall save a soul from death, and shall hide a multitude of sins. (RSV: "whoever brings back a sinner from the error of his way will save his soul from death and will cover a multitude of sins")

1 Peter 3:1: Likewise, ye wives, be in subjection to your own husbands; that, if any obey not the word, they also may without the word be won by the conversation of the wives;

1 Peter 4:8-10: And above all things have fervent charity among yourselves: for charity shall cover the multitude of sins.

[9] Use hospitality one to another without grudging.

[10] As every man hath received the gift, even so minister the same one to another, as good stewards of the manifold grace of God.

Moreover, when we pray for someone and God answers, they are blessed, and one might say that they are given more grace thereby, just as Paul often opens his epistles, "Grace to you and peace from God our Father and the Lord Jesus Christ" (2 Cor. 1:2, RSV). This common greeting of "grace to you" (cf. in RSV: Rom. 1:7; 1 Cor. 1:3; Gal. 1:3; Eph. 1:2; Phil. 1:2; Col. 1:2; 1 Thess. 1:1;

2 Thess. 1:2; Philem. 1:3; Rev. 1:4) is in the sense of "May God give you more grace." Thus, everyone who prays is potentially a "mini-distributor" of grace (and indirectly — in a limited sense — of salvation as well).

Revelation 1:4-5: John to the seven churches which are in Asia: Grace be unto you, and peace, from him which is, and which was, and which is to come; and from the seven Spirits which are before his throne; [5] And from Jesus Christ, who is the faithful witness . . .

The angels also participate in this spreading around of God's grace.

The psalms proclaim God's righteousness

Psalm 7:9: Oh let the wickedness of the wicked come to an end; but establish the just: for the righteous God trieth the hearts and reins.

Psalm 7:17: I will praise the LORD according to his righteousness: and will sing praise to the name of the LORD most high.

Psalm 11:7: For the righteous LORD loveth righteousness; his countenance doth behold the upright.

Psalm 22:3: But thou art holy, O thou that inhabitest the praises of Israel.

Psalm 33:5: He loveth righteousness and judgment: the earth is full of the goodness of the LORD.

Psalm 50:6: And the heavens shall declare his righteousness: for God is judge himself. Selah.

Psalm 71:16: I will go in the strength of the Lord GOD: I will make mention of thy righteousness, even of thine only.

Psalm 71:19: Thy righteousness also, O God, is very high, who hast done great things: O God, who is like unto thee!

Psalm 71:22: I will also praise thee with the psaltery, even thy truth, O my God: unto thee will I sing with the harp, O thou Holy One of Israel.

Psalm 77:13: Thy way, O God, is in the sanctuary: who is so great a God as our God?

Psalm 78:41: Yea, they turned back and tempted God, and limited the Holy One of Israel.

Psalm 89:14: Justice and judgment are the habitation of thy throne: mercy and truth shall go before thy face.

Psalm 89:18: For the LORD is our defence; and the Holy One of Israel is our king.

Psalm 92:15: To shew that the LORD is upright: he is my rock, and there is no unrighteousness in him.

Psalm 97:6: The heavens declare his righteousness, and all the people see his glory.

Psalm 99:5: Exalt ye the LORD our God, and worship at his footstool; for he is holy. (cf. 99:3, 9)

Psalm 111:3: His work is honourable and glorious: and his righteousness endureth for ever.

Psalm 116:5: Gracious is the LORD, and righteous; yea, our God is merciful.

Psalm 119:137: Righteous art thou, O LORD, and upright are thy judgments.

Psalm 119:142: Thy righteousness is an everlasting righteousness, and thy law is the truth.

God enables and establishes
human righteousness (Psalms)

Psalm 5:8: Lead me, O LORD, in thy righteousness because of mine enemies; make thy way straight before my face.

Psalm 7:9: Oh let the wickedness of the wicked come to an end; but establish the just: for the righteous God trieth the hearts and reins.

Psalm 7:10: My defence is of God, which saveth the upright in heart.

Psalm 10:17: LORD, thou hast heard the desire of the humble: thou wilt prepare their heart, thou wilt cause thine ear to hear:

Psalm 13:5: But I have trusted in thy mercy; my heart shall rejoice in thy salvation.

Psalm 14:5: There were they in great fear: for God is in the generation of the righteous.

Psalm 18:35: Thou hast also given me the shield of thy salvation: and thy right hand hath holden me up, and thy gentleness hath made me great.

Psalm 19:8: The statutes of the LORD are right, rejoicing the heart: the commandment of the LORD is pure, enlightening the eyes.

Psalm 21:2: Thou hast given him his heart's desire, and hast not withholden the request of his lips. Selah.

Psalm 23:3: He restoreth my soul: he leadeth me in the paths of righteousness for his name's sake.

Psalm 25:5: Lead me in thy truth, and teach me: for thou art the God of my salvation; on thee do I wait all the day.

Psalm 28:7: The LORD is my strength and my shield; my heart trusted in him, and I am helped: therefore my heart greatly rejoiceth; and with my song will I praise him.

Psalm 31:1: In thee, O LORD, do I put my trust; let me never be ashamed: deliver me in thy righteousness.

Psalm 31:3: For thou art my rock and my fortress; therefore for thy name's sake lead me, and guide me.

Psalm 31:23: O love the LORD, all ye his saints: for the LORD preserveth the faithful, and plentifully rewardeth the proud doer.

Psalm 33:21: For our heart shall rejoice in him, because we have trusted in his holy name.

Psalm 34:15: The eyes of the LORD are upon the righteous, and his ears are open unto their cry.

Psalm 34:19: Many are the afflictions of the righteous: but the LORD delivereth him out of them all.

Psalm 36:10: O continue thy lovingkindness unto them that know thee; and thy righteousness to the upright in heart.

Psalm 37:17: For the arms of the wicked shall be broken: but the LORD upholdeth the righteous.

Psalm 37:28: For the LORD loveth judgment, and forsaketh not his saints; they are preserved for ever: but the seed of the wicked shall be cut off.

Psalm 37:31: The law of his God is in his heart; none of his steps shall slide.

Psalm 37:39: But the salvation of the righteous is of the LORD: he is their strength in the time of trouble.

Psalm 40:8: I delight to do thy will, O my God: yea, thy law is within my heart.

Psalm 40:10: I have not hid thy righteousness within my heart; I have declared thy faithfulness and thy salvation: I have not concealed thy lovingkindness and thy truth from the great congregation.

Psalm 40:11: Withhold not thou thy tender mercies from me, O LORD: let thy lovingkindness and thy truth continually preserve me.

Psalm 45:7: Thou lovest righteousness, and hatest wickedness: therefore God, thy God, hath anointed thee with the oil of gladness above thy fellows.

Psalm 51:6-7: Behold, thou desirest truth in the inward parts: and in the hidden part thou shalt make me to know wisdom. [7] Purge me with hyssop, and I shall be clean: wash me, and I shall be whiter than snow.

Psalm 51:8: Make me to hear joy and gladness; that the bones which thou hast broken may rejoice.

Psalm 51:9: Hide thy face from my sins, and blot out all mine iniquities.

Psalm 51:10: Create in me a clean heart, O God; and renew a right spirit within me.

Psalm 51:11: Cast me not away from thy presence; and take not thy holy spirit from me.

Psalm 51:14: Deliver me from bloodguiltiness, O God, thou God of my salvation: and my tongue shall sing aloud of thy righteousness.

Psalm 55:22: Cast thy burden upon the LORD, and he shall sustain thee: he shall never suffer the righteous to be moved.

Psalm 71:2: Deliver me in thy righteousness, and cause me to escape: incline thine ear unto me, and save me.

Psalm 71:24: My tongue also shall talk of thy righteousness all the day long: for they are confounded, for they are brought unto shame, that seek my hurt.

Psalm 73:1: Truly God is good to Israel, even to such as are of a clean heart.

Psalm 78:72: So he fed them according to the integrity of his heart; and guided them by the skilfulness of his hands.

Psalm 79:9: Help us, O God of our salvation, for the glory of thy name: and deliver us, and purge away our sins, for thy name's sake.

Psalm 84:11: For the LORD God is a sun and shield: the LORD will give grace and glory: no good thing will he withhold from them that walk uprightly.

Psalm 85:8: I will hear what God the LORD will speak: for he will speak peace unto his people, and to his saints: but let them not turn again to folly.

Psalm 86:11: Teach me thy way, O LORD; I will walk in thy truth: unite my heart to fear thy name.

Psalm 104:15: And wine that maketh glad the heart of man, and oil to make his face to shine, and bread which strengtheneth man's heart.

Psalm 106:31: And that was counted unto him for righteousness unto all generations for evermore.

Psalm 118:14: The LORD is my strength and song, and is become my salvation.

Psalm 119:34: Give me understanding, and I shall keep thy law; yea, I shall observe it with my whole heart.

Psalm 119:40: Behold, I have longed after thy precepts: quicken me in thy righteousness.

Psalm 119:165: Great peace have those who love thy law; nothing can make them stumble.

Psalm 143:1: Hear my prayer, O LORD, give ear to my supplications: in thy faithfulness answer me, and in thy righteousness.

Psalm 143:11: Quicken me, O LORD, for thy name's sake: for thy righteousness' sake bring my soul out of trouble.

The psalms speak of human righteousness

Psalm 1:5: Therefore the ungodly shall not stand in the judgment, nor sinners in the congregation of the righteous.

Psalm 1:6: For the LORD knoweth the way of the righteous: but the way of the ungodly shall perish.

Psalm 7:8: The LORD shall judge the people: judge me, O LORD, according to my righteousness, and according to mine integrity that is in me.

Psalm 11:7: For the righteous LORD loveth righteousness; his countenance doth behold the upright.

Psalm 15:2: He that walketh uprightly, and worketh righteousness, and speaketh the truth in his heart.

Psalm 18:20: The LORD rewarded me according to my righteousness; according to the cleanness of my hands hath he recompensed me.

Psalm 18:24: Therefore hath the LORD recompensed me according to my righteousness, according to the cleanness of my hands in his eyesight.

Psalm 24:4: He that hath clean hands, and a pure heart; who hath not lifted up his soul unto vanity, nor sworn deceitfully.

Psalm 26:3: For thy lovingkindness is before mine eyes: and I have walked in thy truth.

Psalm 32:11: Be glad in the LORD, and rejoice, ye righteous: and shout for joy, all ye that are upright in heart.

Psalm 33:1: Rejoice in the LORD, O ye righteous: for praise is comely for the upright.

Psalm 37:3: Trust in the LORD, and do good; so shalt thou dwell in the land, and verily thou shalt be fed.

Psalm 37:18: The LORD knoweth the days of the upright: and their inheritance shall be for ever.

Psalm 37:27: Depart from evil, and do good; and dwell for evermore.

Psalm 37:37: Mark the perfect man, and behold the upright: for the end of that man is peace.

Psalm 44:18: Our heart is not turned back, neither have our steps declined from thy way;

Psalm 64:10: The righteous shall be glad in the LORD, and shall trust in him; and all the upright in heart shall glory.

Psalm 68:3: But let the righteous be glad; let them rejoice before God: yea, let them exceedingly rejoice.

Psalm 73:1: Truly God is good to Israel, even to such as are of a clean heart.

Psalm 89:5: And the heavens shall praise thy wonders, O LORD: thy faithfulness also in the congregation of the saints.

Psalm 92:12: The righteous shall flourish like the palm tree: he shall grow like a cedar in Lebanon.

Psalm 94:15: But judgment shall return unto righteousness: and all the upright in heart shall follow it.

Psalm 97:11: Light is sown for the righteous, and gladness for the upright in heart.

Psalm 97:12: Rejoice in the LORD, ye righteous; and give thanks at the remembrance of his holiness.

Psalm 106:3: Blessed are they that keep judgment, and he that doeth righteousness at all times.

Psalm 118:20: This gate of the LORD, into which the righteous shall enter.

Psalm 119:1: Blessed are the undefiled in the way, who walk in the law of the LORD.

Psalm 119:56: This I had, because I kept thy precepts.

Psalm 119:63: I am a companion of all them that fear thee, and of them that keep thy precepts.

Psalm 119:69: The proud have forged a lie against me: but I will keep thy precepts with my whole heart.

Psalm 119:87: They had almost consumed me upon earth; but I forsook not thy precepts.

Psalm 119:100: I understand more than the ancients, because I keep thy precepts.

Psalm 119:110: The wicked have laid a snare for me: yet I erred not from thy precepts.

Psalm 119:168: I have kept thy precepts and thy testimonies: for all my ways are before thee.

Psalm 125:4: Do good, O LORD, unto those that be good, and to them that are upright in their hearts.

Psalm 140:13: Surely the righteous shall give thanks unto thy name: the upright shall dwell in thy presence.

God's grace enables us to be righteous (prophets)

Isaiah 12:2: Behold, God is my salvation; I will trust, and not be afraid: for the LORD JEHOVAH is my strength and my song; he also is become my salvation.

Isaiah 26:7: The way of the just is uprightness: thou, most upright, dost weigh the path of the just.

Isaiah 26:9: With my soul have I desired thee in the night; yea, with my spirit within me will I seek thee early: for when thy judgments are in the earth, the inhabitants of the world will learn righteousness.

Isaiah 33:5: The LORD is exalted; for he dwelleth on high: he hath filled Zion with judgment and righteousness.

Isaiah 45:13: I have raised him up in righteousness, and I will direct all his ways: he shall build my city, and he shall let go my captives, not for price nor reward, saith the LORD of hosts.

Isaiah 45:22: Look unto me, and be ye saved, all the ends of the earth: for I am God, and there is none else.

Isaiah 45:24: Surely, shall one say, in the LORD have I righteousness and strength: even to him shall men come; and all that are incensed against him shall be ashamed.

Isaiah 48:18: O that thou hadst hearkened to my commandments! then had thy peace been as a river, and thy righteousness as the waves of the sea:

Isaiah 49:8: Thus saith the LORD, In an acceptable time have I heard thee, and in a day of salvation have I helped thee: and I will preserve thee, and give thee for a covenant of the people, to establish the earth, to cause to inherit the desolate heritages;

Isaiah 51:7: Hearken unto me, ye that know righteousness, the people in whose heart is my law; fear ye not the reproach of men, neither be ye afraid of their revilings.

Isaiah 54:14: In righteousness shalt thou be established: thou shalt be far from oppression; for thou shalt not fear: and from terror; for it shall not come near thee.

Isaiah 56:1: Thus saith the LORD, Keep ye judgment, and do justice: for my salvation is near to come, and my righteousness to be revealed.

Isaiah 57:15: For thus saith the high and lofty One that inhabiteth eternity, whose name is Holy; I dwell in the high and holy place, with him also that is of a contrite and humble spirit, to revive the spirit of the humble, and to revive the heart of the contrite ones.

Isaiah 61:10: I will greatly rejoice in the LORD, my soul shall be joyful in my God; for he hath clothed me with the garments of salvation, he hath covered me with the robe of righteousness, as a bridegroom decketh himself with ornaments, and as a bride adorneth herself with her jewels.

Isaiah 61:11: For as the earth bringeth forth her bud, and as the garden causeth the things that are sown in it to spring forth; so the Lord GOD will cause righteousness and praise to spring forth before all the nations.

Isaiah 62:12: And they shall call them, The holy people, The redeemed of the LORD: and thou shalt be called, Sought out, A city not forsaken.

Isaiah 64:5: Thou meetest him that rejoiceth and worketh righteousness, those that remember thee in thy ways: behold, thou art wroth; for we have sinned: in those is continuance, and we shall be saved.

Jeremiah 3:15: And I will give you pastors according to mine heart, which shall feed you with knowledge and understanding.

Jeremiah 15:20: And I will make thee unto this people a fenced brasen wall: and they shall fight against thee, but they shall not prevail against thee: for I am with thee to save thee and to deliver thee, saith the LORD.

Jeremiah 17:14: Heal me, O LORD, and I shall be healed; save me, and I shall be saved: for thou art my praise.

Jeremiah 30:11: For I am with thee, saith the LORD, to save thee: though I make a full end of all nations whither I have scattered thee, yet will I not make a full end of thee: but I will correct thee in measure, and will not leave thee altogether unpunished.

Jeremiah 31:33: But this shall be the covenant that I will make with the house of Israel; After those days, saith the LORD, I will put my law in their inward parts, and write it in their hearts; and will be their God, and they shall be my people.

Jeremiah 32:39: And I will give them one heart, and one way, that they may fear me for ever, for the good of them, and of their children after them:

Jeremiah 32:40: And I will make an everlasting covenant with them, that I will not turn away from them, to do them good; but I will put my fear in their hearts, that they shall not depart from me.

Jeremiah 32:41: Yea, I will rejoice over them to do them good, and I will plant them in this land assuredly with my whole heart and with my whole soul.

Jeremiah 39:18: For I will surely deliver thee, and thou shalt not fall by the sword, but thy life shall be for a prey unto thee: because thou hast put thy trust in me, saith the LORD.

Ezekiel 11:19: And I will give them one heart, and I will put a new spirit within you; and I will take the stony heart out of their flesh, and will give them an heart of flesh:

Ezekiel 18:31: Cast away from you all your transgressions, whereby ye have transgressed; and make you a new heart and a new spirit: for why will ye die, O house of Israel?

Ezekiel 36:26: A new heart also will I give you, and a new spirit will I put within you: and I will take away the stony heart out of your flesh, and I will give you an heart of flesh.

Daniel 9:18: O my God, incline thine ear, and hear; open thine eyes, and behold our desolations, and the city which is called by thy name: for we do not present our supplications before thee for our righteousnesses, but for thy great mercies.

Hosea 2:19: And I will betroth thee unto me for ever; yea, I will betroth thee unto me in righteousness, and in judgment, and in loving-kindness, and in mercies.

Hosea 10:12: Sow to yourselves in righteousness, reap in mercy; break up your fallow ground: for it is time to seek the LORD, till he come and rain righteousness upon you.

Hosea 14:4: I will heal their backsliding, I will love them freely: for mine anger is turned away from him.

Habakkuk 2:4: Behold, his soul which is lifted up is not upright in him: but the just shall live by his faith.

Sanctification is part of salvation

Psalm 51:2, 7-10: Wash me throughly from mine iniquity, and cleanse me from my sin . . . [7] Purge me with hyssop, and I shall be clean: wash me, and I shall be whiter than snow.

[8] Make me to hear joy and gladness; that the bones which thou hast broken may rejoice. [9] Hide thy face from my sins, and blot out all mine iniquities. [10] Create in me a clean heart, O God; and renew a right spirit within me.

Ezekiel 33:12-19: Therefore, thou son of man, say unto the children of thy people, The righteousness of the righteous shall not deliver him in the day of his transgression: as for the wickedness of the wicked, he shall not fall thereby in the day that he turneth from his wickedness; neither shall the righteous be able to live for his righteousness in the day that he sinneth.

[13] When I shall say to the righteous, that he shall surely live; if he trust to his own righteousness, and commit iniquity, all his righteousnesses shall not be remembered; but for his iniquity that he hath committed, he shall die for it. [14] Again, when I say unto the wicked, Thou shalt surely die; if he turn from his sin, and do that which is lawful and right; [15] If the wicked restore the pledge, give again that he had robbed, walk in the statutes of life, without committing iniquity; he shall surely live, he shall not die. [16] None of his sins that he hath committed shall be mentioned unto

him: he hath done that which is lawful and right; he shall surely live. [17] Yet the children of thy people say, The way of the Lord is not equal: but as for them, their way is not equal. [18] When the righteous turneth from his righteousness, and committeth iniquity, he shall even die thereby.

[19] But if the wicked turn from his wickedness, and do that which is lawful and right, he shall live thereby.

Ezekiel 37:23: Neither shall they defile themselves any more with their idols, nor with their detestable things, nor with any of their transgressions: but I will save them out of all their dwellingplaces, wherein they have sinned, and will cleanse them: so shall they be my people, and I will be their God.

Matthew 5:20: For I say unto you, That except your righteousness shall exceed the righteousness of the scribes and Pharisees, ye shall in no case enter into the kingdom of heaven.

John 17:17: Sanctify them through thy truth: thy word is truth.

Acts 3:19: Repent ye therefore, and be converted, that your sins may be blotted out, when the times of refreshing shall come from the presence of the Lord;

Acts 15:8-9: And God, which knoweth the hearts, bare them witness, giving them the Holy Ghost, even as he did unto us;

[9] And put no difference between us and them, purifying their hearts by faith. (RSV: "and he made no distinction between us and them, but cleansed their hearts by faith")

Acts 20:32: And now, brethren, I commend you to God, and to the word of his grace, which is able to build you up, and to give you an inheritance among all them which are sanctified.

Acts 26:18: To open their eyes, and to turn them from darkness to light, and from the power of Satan unto God, that they may receive forgiveness of sins, and inheritance among them which are sanctified by faith that is in me.

Romans 2:13: For not the hearers of the law are just before God, but the doers of the law shall be justified.

Romans 5:10: For if, when we were enemies, we were reconciled to God by the death of his Son, much more, being reconciled, we shall be saved by his life.

Romans 5:19: For as by one man's disobedience many were made sinners, so by the obedience of one shall many be made righteous.

Romans 6:13, 17: Neither yield ye your members as instruments of unrighteousness unto sin: but yield yourselves unto God, as those that are alive from the dead, and your members as instruments of righteousness unto God . . . [17] But God be thanked, that ye were the servants of sin, but ye have obeyed from the heart that form of doctrine which was delivered you.

Romans 6:19: I speak after the manner of men because of the infirmity of your flesh: for as ye have yielded your members servants to uncleanness and to iniquity unto iniquity; even so now yield your members servants to righteousness unto holiness. (RSV: "For just as you once yielded your members to impurity and to greater and greater iniquity, so now yield your members to righteousness for sanctification")

Romans 6:22: But now being made free from sin, and become servants to God, ye have your fruit unto holiness, and the end everlasting life. (RSV: "But now that you have been set free from sin and have become slaves of God, the return you get is sanctification and its end, eternal life")

Romans 8:10: And if Christ be in you, the body is dead because of sin; but the Spirit is life because of righteousness. (RSV: "But if Christ is in you, although your bodies are dead because of sin, your spirits are alive because of righteousness")

Romans 14:17: For the kingdom of God is not meat and drink; but righteousness, and peace, and joy in the Holy Ghost.

1 Corinthians 1:2: Unto the church of God which is at Corinth, to them that are sanctified in Christ Jesus, called to be saints, with all that in every place call upon the name of Jesus Christ our Lord, both theirs and ours:

1 Corinthians 6:11: And such were some of you: but ye are washed, but ye are sanctified, but ye are justified in the name of the Lord Jesus, and by the Spirit of our God. (RSV: "But you were washed, you were sanctified, you were justified")

2 Corinthians 7:1: Having therefore these promises, dearly beloved, let us cleanse ourselves from all filthiness of the flesh and spirit, perfecting holiness in the fear of God.

Ephesians 1:4: According as he hath chosen us in him before the foundation of the world, that we should be holy and without blame before him in love:

Ephesians 4:24: And that ye put on the new man, which after God is created in righteousness and true holiness. (RSV: "and put on the new nature, created after the likeness of God in true righteousness and holiness")

Ephesians 6:14: Stand therefore, having your loins girt about with truth, and having on the breastplate of righteousness;

Colossians 1:22: In the body of his flesh through death, to present you holy and unblameable and unreproveable in his sight:

Colossians 3:12: Put on therefore, as the elect of God, holy and beloved, bowels of mercies, kindness, humbleness of mind, meekness, longsuffering;

1 Thessalonians 3:13: To the end he may stablish your hearts unblameable in holiness before God, even our Father, at the coming of our Lord Jesus Christ with all his saints.

1 Thessalonians 4:3, 7: For this is the will of God, even your sanctification, that ye should abstain from fornication . . . [7] For God hath not called us unto uncleanness, but unto holiness.

1 Thessalonians 5:23: And the very God of peace sanctify you wholly; and I pray God your whole spirit and soul and body be preserved blameless unto the coming of our Lord Jesus Christ.

2 Thessalonians 2:13: But we are bound to give thanks alway to God for you, brethren beloved of the Lord, because God hath from the beginning chosen you to salvation through sanctification of the Spirit and belief of the truth:

1 Timothy 4:7: But refuse profane and old wives' fables, and exercise thyself rather unto godliness. (cf. 4:12; 6:3-6)

1 Timothy 6:11: But thou, O man of God, flee these things; and follow after righteousness, godliness, faith, love, patience, meekness.

2 Timothy 2:21-22: If a man therefore purge himself from these, he shall be a vessel unto honour, sanctified, and meet for the master's use, and prepared unto every good work. [22] Flee also youthful lusts: but follow righteousness, faith, charity, peace, with them that call on the Lord out of a pure heart.

2 Timothy 3:12: Yea, and all that will live godly in Christ Jesus shall suffer persecution.

Titus 2:12-14: Teaching us that, denying ungodliness and worldly lusts, we should live soberly, righteously, and godly, in this present world; [13] Looking for that blessed hope, and the glorious appearing of the great God and our Saviour Jesus Christ;
[14] Who gave himself for us, that he might redeem us from all iniquity, and purify unto himself a peculiar people, zealous of good works. (cf. 1:1)

Hebrews 9:12-14: Neither by the blood of goats and calves, but by his own blood he entered in once into the holy place, having obtained eternal redemption for us. [13] For if the blood of bulls and of goats, and the ashes of an heifer sprinkling the unclean, sanctifieth to the purifying of the flesh: [14] How much more shall the blood of Christ, who through the eternal Spirit offered himself without spot to God, purge your conscience from dead works to serve the living God?

Hebrews 10:10: By the which will we are sanctified through the offering of the body of Jesus Christ once for all.

Hebrews 10:14: For by one offering he hath perfected for ever them that are sanctified.

Hebrews 10:29: Of how much sorer punishment, suppose ye, shall he be thought worthy, who hath trodden under foot the Son of God, and hath counted the blood of the covenant, wherewith he was sanctified, an unholy thing, and hath done despite unto the Spirit of grace?

Hebrews 12:10, 14: For they verily for a few days chastened us after their own pleasure; but he for our profit, that we might be partakers of his holiness . . . [14] Follow peace with all men, and holiness, without which no man shall see the Lord:

Hebrews 13:12: Wherefore Jesus also, that he might sanctify the people with his own blood, suffered without the gate.

James 1:21, 26: Wherefore lay apart all filthiness and superfluity of naughtiness, and receive with meekness the engrafted word, which is able to save your souls . . . [26] If any man among you seem to be religious, and bridleth not his tongue, but deceiveth his own heart, this man's religion is vain.

James 4:8: Draw nigh to God, and he will draw nigh to you. Cleanse your hands, ye sinners; and purify your hearts, ye double minded.

1 Peter 1:2: Elect according to the foreknowledge of God the Father, through sanctification of the Spirit, unto obedience and sprinkling of the blood of Jesus Christ: Grace unto you, and peace, be multiplied.

1 Peter 1:14-15: As obedient children, not fashioning yourselves according to the former lusts in your ignorance: [15] But as he which hath called you is holy, so be ye holy in all manner of conversation;

1 Peter 1:22: Seeing ye have purified your souls in obeying the truth through the Spirit unto unfeigned love of the brethren, see that ye love one another with a pure heart fervently:

1 Peter 2:5, 9: Ye also, as lively stones, are built up a spiritual house, an holy priesthood, to offer up spiritual sacrifices, acceptable to God by Jesus Christ . . . [9] But ye are a chosen generation, a royal priesthood, an holy nation, a peculiar people; that ye should shew forth the praises of him who hath called you out of darkness into his marvellous light: (cf. 2:24)

2 Peter 1:9: But he that lacketh these things is blind, and cannot see afar off, and hath forgotten that he was purged from his old sins.

2 Peter 3:11: Seeing then that all these things shall be dissolved, what manner of persons ought ye to be in all holy conversation and godliness, (cf. 1:3, 6-7)

1 John 1:7-9: But if we walk in the light, as he is in the light, we have fellowship one with another, and the blood of Jesus Christ his Son cleanseth us from all sin. [8] If we say that we have no sin, we deceive ourselves, and the truth is not in us. [9] If we confess our sins, he is faithful and just to forgive us our sins, and to cleanse us from all unrighteousness.

1 John 3:3: And every man that hath this hope in him purifieth himself, even as he is pure. (cf. Jude 1:20-21)

Faith shows itself in obedience and in good works

John 3:36: He that believeth on the Son hath everlasting life: and he that believeth not the Son shall not see life; but the wrath of God abideth on him. (RSV: "he who does not obey the Son shall not see life,")

John 6:27-29: Labour not for the meat which perisheth, but for that meat which endureth unto everlasting life, which the Son of man shall give unto you: for him hath God the Father sealed.
[28] Then said they unto him, What shall we do, that we might work the works of God? [29] Jesus answered and said unto them, This is the work of God, that ye believe on him whom he hath sent.

Acts 5:32: And we are his witnesses of these things; and so is also the Holy Ghost, whom God hath given to them that obey him.

Romans 1:5: By whom we have received grace and apostleship, for obedience to the faith among all nations, for his name: (RSV: "the obedience of faith")

Romans 10:16: But they have not all obeyed the gospel . . .

Romans 16:26: But now is made manifest, and by the scriptures of the prophets, according to the commandment of the everlasting God, made known to all nations for the obedience of faith:

1 Corinthians 15:10: But by the grace of God I am what I am: and his grace which was bestowed upon me was not in vain; but I laboured more abundantly than they all: yet not I, but the grace of God which was with me. (cf. 15:58)

2 Corinthians 8:7: Therefore, as ye abound in every thing, in faith, and utterance, and knowledge, and in all diligence, and in your love to us, see that ye abound in this grace also.

2 Corinthians 9:13: Whiles by the experiment of this ministration they glorify God for your professed subjection unto the gospel of Christ, and for your liberal distribution unto them, and unto all men;

Galatians 5:6-7: For in Jesus Christ neither circumcision availeth anything, nor uncircumcision; but faith which worketh by love. [7] Ye did run well; who did hinder you that ye should not obey the truth?

1 Thessalonians 1:3: Remembering without ceasing your work of faith, and labour of love, and patience of hope in our Lord Jesus Christ, in the sight of God and our Father;

2 Thessalonians 1:8, 11: In flaming fire taking vengeance on them that know not God, and that obey not the gospel of our Lord Jesus Christ . . . [11] Wherefore also we pray always for you, that our God would count you worthy of this calling, and fulfil all the good pleasure of his goodness, and the work of faith with power:

Titus 1:16: They profess that they know God; but in works they deny him, being abominable, and disobedient, and unto every good work reprobate.

Hebrews 5:9: And being made perfect, he became the author of eternal salvation unto all them that obey him;

James 2:18: Yea, a man may say, Thou hast faith, and I have works: shew me thy faith without thy works, and I will shew thee my faith by my works.

James 2:22: Seest thou how faith wrought with his works, and by works was faith made perfect?

1 Peter 4:17: For the time is come that judgment must begin at the house of God: and if it first begin at us, what shall the end be of them that obey not the gospel of God?

1 John 5:2: By this we know that we love the children of God, when we love God, and keep his commandments.

Revelation 2:19: I know thy works, and charity, and service, and faith, and thy patience, and thy works; and the last to be more than the first.

Salvation is a process and
is not absolutely assured

1 Samuel 11:6; 18:12: And the Spirit of God came upon Saul when he heard those tidings, and his anger was kindled greatly . . . And Saul was afraid of David, because the LORD was with him, and was departed from Saul.

Ezekiel 18:24: But when the righteous turneth away from his righteousness, and committeth iniquity, and doeth according to all the abominations that the wicked man doeth, shall he live? All his righteousness that he hath done shall not be mentioned: in his trespass that he hath trespassed, and in his sin that he hath sinned, in them shall he die.

Ezekiel 33:12-19: Therefore, thou son of man, say unto the children of thy people, The righteousness of the righteous shall not deliver him in the day of his transgression: as for the wickedness of the wicked, he shall not fall thereby in the day that he turneth from his wickedness; neither shall the righteous be able to live for his righteousness in the day that he sinneth.

[13] When I shall say to the righteous, that he shall surely live; if he trust to his own righteousness, and commit iniquity, all his righteousnesses shall not be remembered; but for his iniquity that he hath committed, he shall die for it. [14] Again, when I say unto the wicked, Thou shalt surely die; if he turn from his sin, and do that which is lawful and right; [15] If the wicked restore the pledge, give again that he had robbed, walk in the

statutes of life, without committing iniquity; he shall surely live, he shall not die. [16] None of his sins that he hath committed shall be mentioned unto him: he hath done that which is lawful and right; he shall surely live. [17] Yet the children of thy people say, The way of the Lord is not equal: but as for them, their way is not equal. [18] When the righteous turneth from his righteousness, and committeth iniquity, he shall even die thereby.

[19] But if the wicked turn from his wickedness, and do that which is lawful and right, he shall live thereby.

Matthew 7:21: Not every one that saith unto me, Lord, Lord, shall enter into the kingdom of heaven; but he that doeth the will of my Father which is in heaven.

Matthew 13:19-21: When any one heareth the word of the kingdom, and understandeth it not, then cometh the wicked one, and catcheth away that which was sown in his heart. This is he which received seed by the way side. [20] But he that received the seed into stony places, the same is he that heareth the word, and anon with joy receiveth it; [21] Yet hath he not root in himself, but dureth for a while: for when tribulation or persecution ariseth because of the word, by and by he is offended.

Matthew 24:10-13: And then shall many be offended, and shall betray one another, and shall hate one another. [11] And many false prophets shall rise, and shall deceive many.

[12] And because iniquity shall abound, the love of many shall wax cold. [13] But he that shall endure unto the end, the same shall be saved. (cf. 10:22; Mark 13:13)

Mark 4:5-6,14-19: And some fell on stony ground, where it had not much earth; and immediately it sprang up, because it had no depth of earth: [6] But when the sun was up, it was scorched; and because it had no root, it withered away . . . [14] The sower soweth the word. [15] And these are they by the way side, where the word is sown; but when they have heard, Satan cometh immediately, and taketh away the word that was sown in their hearts. [16] And these are they likewise which are sown on stony ground; who, when they have heard the word, immediately receive it with gladness; [17] And have no root in themselves, and so endure but for a time: afterward, when affliction or persecution ariseth for the word's sake, immediately they are offended. [18] And these are they which are sown among thorns; such as hear the word, [19] And the cares of this world, and the deceitfulness of riches, and the lusts of other things entering in, choke the word, and it becometh unfruitful.

Luke 8:5-14: A sower went out to sow his seed: and as he sowed, some fell by the way side; and it was trodden down, and the fowls of the air devoured it. [6] And some fell upon a rock; and as soon as it was sprung up, it withered away, because it lacked moisture. [7] And some fell among thorns; and the thorns sprang up with it, and choked it. [8] And other fell on good ground, and sprang up, and bare fruit an hundredfold. And when he had said these things, he cried, He that hath ears to hear, let him hear.

[9] And his disciples asked him, saying, What might this parable be? [10] And he said, Unto you it is given to know the mysteries of the kingdom of God: but to others in parables; that seeing they might not see, and hearing they might not understand. [11] Now the parable is this: The seed is the word of God. [12] Those by the way side are they that hear; then cometh the devil, and taketh away the word out of their hearts, lest they should believe and be saved. [13] They on the rock are they, which, when they hear, receive the word with joy; and these have no root, which for a while believe, and in time of temptation fall away. [14] And that which fell among thorns are they, which, when they have heard, go forth, and are choked with cares and riches and pleasures of this life, and bring no fruit to perfection.

1 Corinthians 9:27: But I keep under my body, and bring it into subjection: lest that by any means, when I have preached to others, I myself should be a castaway. (RSV: "but I pommel my body and subdue it, lest after preaching to others I myself should be disqualified")

1 Corinthians 10:12: Wherefore let him that thinketh he standeth take heed lest he fall.

Galatians 4:8-9: Howbeit then, when ye knew not God, ye did service unto them which by nature are no gods. [9] But now, after that ye have known God, or rather are known of God, how turn ye again to the weak and beggarly elements, whereunto ye desire again to be in bondage?

Galatians 5:1, 4: Stand fast therefore in the liberty wherewith Christ hath made us free, and be not entangled again with the yoke of bondage . . . [4] Christ is become of no effect unto you, whosoever of you are justified by the law; ye are fallen from grace.

Philippians 3:11-14: If by any means I might attain unto the resurrection of the dead. [12] Not as though I had already attained, either were already perfect: but I follow after, if that I may apprehend that for which also I am apprehended of Christ Jesus. [13] Brethren, I count not myself to have apprehended: but this one thing I do, forgetting those things which are behind, and reaching forth unto those things which are before, [14] I press toward the mark for the prize of the high calling of God in Christ Jesus.

Colossians 1:21-23: And you, that were sometime alienated and enemies in your mind by wicked works, yet now hath he reconciled [22] In the body of his flesh through death, to present you holy and unblameable and unreproveable in his sight: [23] If ye continue in the faith grounded and settled, and be not moved away from the hope of the gospel, which ye have heard, and which was preached to every creature which is under heaven; whereof I Paul am made a minister;

1 Timothy 4:1: Now the Spirit speaketh expressly, that in the latter times some shall depart from the faith, giving heed to seducing spirits, and doctrines of devils;

1 Timothy 5:15: For some are already turned aside after Satan.

2 Timothy 2:12: If we suffer, we shall also reign with him: if we deny him, he also will deny us:

Hebrews 3:12-14: Take heed, brethren, lest there be in any of you an evil heart of unbelief, in departing from the living God. [13] But exhort one another daily, while it is called To day; lest any of you be hardened through the deceitfulness of sin. [14] For we are made partakers of Christ, if we hold the beginning of our confidence stedfast unto the end;

Hebrews 4:14: Seeing then that we have a great high priest, that is passed into the heavens, Jesus the Son of God, let us hold fast our profession.

Hebrews 6:4-6: For it is impossible for those who were once enlightened, and have tasted of the heavenly gift, and were made partakers of the Holy Ghost, [5] And have tasted the good word of God, and the powers of the world to come, [6] If they shall fall away, to renew them again unto repentance; seeing they crucify to themselves the Son of God afresh, and put him to an open shame. (RSV: "For it is impossible to restore again to repentance those who have once been enlightened, who have tasted the heavenly gift, and have become partakers of the Holy Spirit, and have tasted the goodness of the word of God, and the powers of the age to come, if they then commit apostasy")

Hebrews 6:15: And so, after he had patiently endured, he obtained the promise.

Hebrews 10:26, 29: For if we sin wilfully after that we have received the knowledge of the truth, there remaineth no more sacrifice for sins . . . [29] Of how much sorer punishment, suppose ye, shall he be thought worthy, who hath trodden under foot the Son of God, and hath counted the blood of the covenant, wherewith he was sanctified, an unholy thing, and hath done despite unto the Spirit of grace?

Hebrews 10:36-39: For ye have need of patience, that, after ye have done the will of God, ye might receive the promise.

[37] For yet a little while, and he that shall come will come, and will not tarry. [38] Now the just shall live by faith: but if any man draw back, my soul shall have no pleasure in him. [39] But we are not of them who draw back unto perdition; but of them that believe to the saving of the soul.

Hebrews 12:15: Looking diligently lest any man fail of the grace of God; lest any root of bitterness springing up trouble you, and thereby many be defiled;

James 1:25: But whoso looketh into the perfect law of liberty, and continueth therein, he being not a forgetful hearer, but a doer of the work, this man shall be blessed in his deed.

2 Peter 1:10: Wherefore the rather, brethren, give diligence to make your calling and election sure: for if ye do these things, ye shall never fall:

2 Peter 2:15, 20-21: Which have forsaken the right way, and are gone astray, following the way of Balaam the son of Bosor, who loved the wages of unrighteousness . . . [20] For if after they have escaped the pollutions of the world through the knowledge of the Lord and Saviour Jesus Christ, they are again entangled therein, and overcome, the latter end is worse with them than the beginning. [21] For it had been better for them not to have known the way of righteousness, than, after they have known it, to turn from the holy commandment delivered unto them.

Revelation 2:3-5: And hast borne, and hast patience, and for my name's sake hast laboured, and hast not fainted. [4] Nevertheless I have somewhat against thee, because thou hast left thy first love. [5] Remember therefore from whence thou art fallen, and repent, and do the first works; or else I will come unto thee quickly, and will remove thy candlestick out of his place, except thou repent.

Revelation 2:10-11: Fear none of those things which thou shalt suffer: behold, the devil shall cast some of you into prison, that ye may be tried; and ye shall have tribulation ten days: be thou faithful unto death, and I will give thee a crown of life.

[11] He that hath an ear, let him hear what the Spirit saith unto the churches; He that overcometh shall not be hurt of the second death.

Revelation 2:25-26: But that which ye have already hold fast till I come. [26] And he that overcometh, and keepeth my works unto the end, to him will I give power over the nations:

Revelation 3:3: Remember therefore how thou hast received and heard, and hold fast, and repent. If therefore thou shalt not watch, I will come on thee as a thief, and thou shalt not know what hour I will come upon thee.

Revelation 3:5: He that overcometh, the same shall be clothed in white raiment; and I will not blot out his name out of the book of life, but I will confess his name before my Father, and before his angels. (cf. "blot" motif: Exod. 17:14; 23:23; 32:32-33; Deut. 9:14; 25:19; 29:20; 2 Kings 14:27; Ps. 9:5; 69:28)

Revelation 3:11: Behold, I come quickly: hold that fast which thou hast, that no man take thy crown.

We may have a vigilant moral assurance
of salvation with perseverance, in hope

Romans 5:1-5: Therefore being justified by faith, we have peace with God through our Lord Jesus Christ: [2] By whom also we have access by faith into this grace wherein we stand, and rejoice in hope of the glory of God. [3] And not only so, but we glory in tribulations also: knowing that tribulation worketh patience;

[4] And patience, experience; and experience, hope: [5] And hope maketh not ashamed; because the love of God is shed abroad in our hearts by the Holy Ghost which is given unto us.

Romans 8:16-17: The Spirit itself beareth witness with our spirit, that we are the children of God: [17] And if children, then heirs; heirs of God, and joint-heirs with Christ; if so be that we suffer with him, that we may be also glorified together.

Romans 12:12: Rejoicing in hope; patient in tribulation; continuing instant in prayer;

Romans 15:4: For whatsoever things were written aforetime were written for our learning, that we through patience and comfort of the scriptures might have hope.

Romans 15:13: Now the God of hope fill you with all joy and peace in believing, that ye may abound in hope, through the power of the Holy Ghost.

1 Corinthians 13:13: And now abideth faith, hope, charity, these three; but the greatest of these is charity.

Galatians 5:5-6: For we through the Spirit wait for the hope of righteousness by faith. [6] For in Jesus Christ neither circumcision availeth anything, nor uncircumcision; but faith which worketh by love.

Ephesians 1:9-14, 18: Having made known unto us the mystery of his will, according to his good pleasure which he hath purposed in himself: [10] That in the dispensation of the fulness of times he might gather together in one all things in Christ, both which are in heaven, and which are on earth; even in him: [11] In whom also we have obtained an inheritance, being predestinated according to the purpose of him who worketh all things after the counsel of his own will: [12] That we should be to the praise of his glory, who first trusted in Christ. [13] In whom ye also trusted, after that ye heard the word of truth, the gospel of your salvation: in whom also after that ye believed, ye were sealed with that holy Spirit of promise, [14] Which is the earnest of our inheritance until the redemption of the purchased possession, unto the praise of his glory . . . [18] The eyes of your understanding being enlightened; that ye may know what is the hope of his calling, and what the riches of the glory of his inheritance in the saints,

Colossians 1:11-14: Strengthened with all might, according to his glorious power, unto all patience and longsuffering with joyfulness; [12] Giving thanks unto the Father, which hath made us meet to be partakers of the inheritance of the saints in light:

[13] Who hath delivered us from the power of darkness, and hath translated us into the kingdom of his dear Son: [14] In whom we have redemption through his blood, even the forgiveness of sins:

Colossians 3:24: Knowing that of the Lord ye shall receive the reward of the inheritance: for ye serve the Lord Christ.

1 Thessalonians 5:8: But let us, who are of the day, be sober, putting on the breastplate of faith and love; and for an helmet, the hope of salvation.

Titus 1:2: In hope of eternal life, which God, that cannot lie, promised before the world began;

Titus 3:7: That being justified by his grace, we should be made heirs according to the hope of eternal life.

Hebrews 3:6: But Christ as a son over his own house; whose house are we, if we hold fast the confidence and the rejoicing of the hope firm unto the end.

Hebrews 6:11-12: And we desire that every one of you do shew the same diligence to the full assurance of hope unto the end:

[12] That ye be not slothful, but followers of them who through faith and patience inherit the promises.

Hebrews 6:18-19: That by two immutable things, in which it was impossible for God to lie, we might have a strong consolation, who have fled for refuge to lay hold upon the hope set before us:

[19] Which hope we have as an anchor of the soul, both sure and stedfast, and which entereth into that within the veil;

Hebrews 10:23: Let us hold fast the profession of our faith without wavering; (for he is faithful that promised;)

Hebrews 11:1: Now faith is the substance of things hoped for, the evidence of things not seen.

1 Peter 1:3-7: Blessed be the God and Father of our Lord Jesus Christ, which according to his abundant mercy hath begotten us again unto a lively hope by the resurrection of Jesus Christ from the dead, [4] To an inheritance incorruptible, and undefiled, and that fadeth not away, reserved in heaven for you, [5] Who are kept by the power of God through faith unto salvation ready to be revealed in the last time. [6] Wherein ye greatly rejoice, though now for a season, if need be, ye are in heaviness through manifold temptations: [7] That the trial of your faith, being much more precious than of gold that perisheth, though it be tried with fire, might be found unto praise and honour and glory at the appearing of Jesus Christ:

1 Peter 1:13: Wherefore gird up the loins of your mind, be sober, and hope to the end for the grace that is to be brought unto you at the revelation of Jesus Christ . . . [21] Who by him do believe in God, that raised him up from the dead, and gave him glory; that your faith and hope might be in God.

1 Peter 3:15: But sanctify the Lord God in your hearts: and be ready always to give an answer to every man that asketh you a reason of the hope that is in you with meekness and fear:

1 John 3:3: And every man that hath this hope in him purifieth himself, even as he is pure.

Chapter Five

Purgatory

Perfect holiness requires purification

Numbers 31:23: Every thing that may abide the fire, ye shall make it go through the fire, and it shall be clean: nevertheless it shall be purified with the water of separation: and all that abideth not the fire ye shall make go through the water.

Deuteronomy 4:33-38: Did ever people hear the voice of God speaking out of the midst of the fire, as thou hast heard, and live?
[34] Or hath God assayed to go and take him a nation from the midst of another nation, by temptations, by signs, and by wonders, and by war, and by a mighty hand, and by a stretched out arm, and by great terrors, according to all that the LORD your God did for you in Egypt before your eyes? [35] Unto thee it was shewed, that thou mightest know that the LORD he is God; there is none else beside him. [36] Out of heaven he made thee to hear his voice, that he might instruct thee: and upon earth he shewed thee his great fire; and thou heardest his words out of the midst of the fire. [37] And because he loved thy fathers, therefore he chose their seed after them, and brought thee out in his sight with his mighty power out of Egypt; [38] To drive out nations from before thee greater and mightier than thou art, to bring thee in, to give thee their land for an inheritance, as it is this day.

Deuteronomy 8:5: Thou shalt also consider in thine heart, that, as a man chasteneth his son, so the LORD thy God chasteneth thee. (cf. 11:2)

Job 23:10: But he knoweth the way that I take: when he hath tried me, I shall come forth as gold. (cf. 4:17; 25:4)

Psalm 51:2, 7: Wash me throughly from mine iniquity, and cleanse me from my sin . . . Purge me with hyssop, and I shall be clean: wash me, and I shall be whiter than snow.

Psalm 66:10-12: For thou, O God, hast proved us: thou hast tried us, as silver is tried. [11] Thou broughtest us into the net; thou laidst affliction upon our loins. [12] Thou hast caused men to ride over our heads; we went through fire and through water: but thou broughtest us out into a wealthy place. (cf. 12:6)

Proverbs 3:11: My son, despise not the chastening of the LORD; neither be weary of his correction:

Proverbs 17:3: The fining pot is for silver, and the furnace for gold: but the LORD trieth the hearts.

Proverbs 20:30: The blueness of a wound cleanseth away evil: so do stripes the inward parts of the belly. (cf. 30:12)

Ecclesiastes 12:14: For God shall bring every work into judgment, with every secret thing, whether it be good, or whether it be evil.

Isaiah 1:25-26: And I will turn my hand upon thee, and purely purge away thy dross, and take away all thy tin: [26] And I will restore thy judges as at the first, and thy counsellers as at the beginning: afterward thou shalt be called, The city of righteousness, the faithful city.

Isaiah 4:4: When the Lord shall have washed away the filth of the daughters of Zion, and shall have purged the blood of Jerusalem from the midst thereof by the spirit of judgment, and by the spirit of burning.

Isaiah 48:10: Behold, I have refined thee, but not with silver; I have chosen thee in the furnace of affliction.

Jeremiah 9:7: Therefore thus saith the LORD of hosts, Behold, I will melt them, and try them; for how shall I do for the daughter of my people?

Jeremiah 30:11: For I am with thee, saith the LORD, to save thee: though I make a full end of all nations whither I have scattered thee, yet will I not make a full end of thee: but I will correct thee in measure, and will not leave thee altogether unpunished.

Jeremiah 33:8: And I will cleanse them from all their iniquity, whereby they have sinned against me; and I will pardon all their iniquities, whereby they have sinned, and whereby they have transgressed against me.

Ezekiel 22:18-22: Son of man, the house of Israel is to me become dross: all they are brass, and tin, and iron, and lead, in the midst of the furnace; they are even the dross of silver.
[19] Therefore thus saith the Lord GOD; Because ye are all become dross, behold, therefore I will gather you into the midst of Jerusalem. [20] As they gather silver, and brass, and iron, and lead, and tin, into the midst of the furnace, to blow the fire upon it, to melt it; so will I gather you in mine anger and in my fury, and I will leave you there, and melt you. [21] Yea, I will gather you, and blow upon you in the fire of my wrath, and ye shall be melted in the midst thereof. [22] As silver is melted in the midst of the furnace, so shall ye be melted in the midst thereof; and ye shall know that I the LORD have poured out my fury upon you.

Ezekiel 36:25, 33: Then will I sprinkle clean water upon you, and ye shall be clean: from all your filthiness, and from all your idols, will I cleanse you . . . Thus saith the Lord GOD; In the day that I shall have cleansed you from all your iniquities I will also cause you to dwell in the cities, and the wastes shall be builded. (cf. 37:23; Lam. 3:39; Dan. 11:35; 12:10)

Micah 7:8-9: Rejoice not against me, O mine enemy: when I fall, I shall arise; when I sit in darkness, the LORD shall be a light unto me. [9] I will bear the indignation of the LORD, because I have sinned against him, until he plead my cause, and execute judgment for me: he will bring me forth to the light, and I shall behold his righteousness.

Zechariah 9:11: As for thee also, by the blood of thy covenant I have sent forth thy prisoners out of the pit wherein is no water.

Zechariah 13:1, 9: On that day there shall be a fountain opened for the house of David and the inhabitants of Jerusalem to cleanse them from sin and uncleanness . . . [9] And I will put this third into the fire, and refine them as one refines silver, and test them as gold is tested. They will call on my name, and I will answer them. I will say, "They are my people"; and they will say, "The LORD is my God."

Malachi 3:2-4: But who may abide the day of his coming? and who shall stand when he appeareth? for he is like a refiner's fire, and like fullers' soap: [3] And he shall sit as a refiner and purifer of silver: and he shall purify the sons of Levi, and purge them as gold and silver, that they may offer unto the LORD an offering in righteousness. [4] Then shall the offering of Judah and Jerusalem be pleasant unto the LORD, as in the days of old, and as in former years.

Wisdom 3:1-7: But the souls of the righteous are in the hand of God, and there shall no torment touch them. [2] In the sight of the unwise they seemed to die: and their departure is taken for misery, [3] And their going from us to be utter destruction: but they are in peace. [4] For though they be punished in the sight of men, yet is their hope full of immortality. [5] And having been a little chastised, they shall be greatly rewarded: for God proved them, and found them worthy for himself. [6] As gold in the furnace hath he tried them, and received them as a burnt offering.

[7] And in the time of their visitation they shall shine, and run to and fro like sparks among the stubble.

Wisdom 11:9-10: For when they were tried albeit but in mercy chastised, they knew how the ungodly were judged in wrath and tormented, thirsting in another manner than the just. [10] For these thou didst admonish and try, as a father: but the other, as a severe king, thou didst condemn and punish.

Sirach 2:5: For gold is tried in the fire, and acceptable men in the furnace of adversity.

2 Maccabees 12:39-45: And upon the day following, as the use had been, Judas and his company came to take up the bodies of them that were slain, and to bury them with their kinsmen in their fathers' graves. [40] Now under the coats of every one that was slain they found things consecrated to the idols of the Jamnites, which is forbidden the Jews by the law. Then every man saw that this was the cause wherefore they were slain. [41] All men therefore praising the Lord, the righteous Judge, who had opened the things that were hid, [42] Betook themselves unto prayer, and besought him that the sin committed might wholly be put out of remembrance. Besides, that noble Judas exhorted the people to keep themselves from sin, forsomuch as they saw before their eyes the things that came to pass for the sins of those that were slain. [43] And when he had made a gathering throughout the company to the sum of two thousand drachms of silver, he sent it to Jerusalem to offer a sin offering, doing therein very well and honestly, in that he was mindful of the resurrection: [44] For if he had not hoped that they that were slain should have risen again, it had been superfluous and vain to pray for the dead. [45] And also in that he perceived that there was great favour laid up for those that died godly, it was an holy and good thought. Whereupon he made a reconciliation for the dead, that they might be delivered from sin.

Matthew 5:22: But I say unto you, That whosoever is angry with his brother without a cause shall be in danger of the judgment: and whosoever shall say to his brother, Raca, shall be in danger of the council: but whosoever shall say, Thou fool, shall be in danger of hell fire. (RSV: "whoever insults his brother shall be liable to the council")

Matthew 5:25-26: Agree with thine adversary quickly, whiles thou art in the way with him; lest at any time the adversary deliver thee to the judge, and the judge deliver thee to the officer, and thou be cast into prison. [26] Verily I say unto thee, Thou shalt by no means come out thence, till thou hast paid the uttermost farthing. (cf. Luke 12:58-59)

Matthew 12:32: And whosoever speaketh a word against the Son of man, it shall be forgiven him: but whosoever speaketh against the Holy Ghost, it shall not be forgiven him, neither in this world, neither in the world to come.

Luke 16:19-31: There was a certain rich man, which was clothed in purple and fine linen, and fared sumptuously every day:
[20] And there was a certain beggar named Lazarus, which was laid at his gate, full of sores, [21] And desiring to be fed with the crumbs which fell from the rich man's table: moreover the dogs came and licked his sores. [22] And it came to pass, that the beggar died, and was carried by the angels into Abraham's bosom: the rich man also died, and was buried; [23] And in hell he lift up his eyes, being in torments, and seeth Abraham afar off, and Lazarus in his bosom. [24] And he cried and said, Father Abraham, have mercy on me, and send Lazarus, that he may dip the tip of his finger in water, and cool my tongue; for I am tormented in this flame. [25] But Abraham said, Son, remember that thou in thy lifetime receivedst thy good things, and likewise Lazarus evil things: but now he is comforted, and thou art tormented. [26] And beside all this, between us and you there is a great gulf fixed: so that they which would pass from hence to you cannot; neither can they pass to us, that would come from thence.
[27] Then he said, I pray thee therefore, father, that thou wouldest send him to my father's house: [28] For I have five brethren; that he may testify unto them, lest they also come into this place of torment. [29] Abraham saith unto him, They have Moses and the prophets; let them hear them. [30] And he said, Nay, father Abraham: but if one went unto them from the dead, they will repent. [31] And he said unto him, If they hear not

Moses and the prophets, neither will they be persuaded, though one rose from the dead.

1 Corinthians 3:11-15: For other foundation can no man lay than that is laid, which is Jesus Christ. [12] Now if any man build upon this foundation gold, silver, precious stones, wood, hay, stubble; [13] Every man's work shall be made manifest: for the day shall declare it, because it shall be revealed by fire; and the fire shall try every man's work of what sort it is. [14] If any man's work abide which he hath built thereupon, he shall receive a reward. [15] If any man's work shall be burned, he shall suffer loss: but he himself shall be saved; yet so as by fire. (cf. Acts 15:9; 2 Cor. 7:1)

1 Corinthians 15:29: Else what shall they do which are baptized for the dead, if the dead rise not at all? why are they then baptized for the dead?

In Holy Scripture, baptism is often used in the sense of afflictions and penances ("baptism of fire"), as in Matthew 3:11, Mark 10:38-39, Luke 3:16, 12:50. If this is what Paul had in mind, the passage makes perfect sense: he is talking about penances on behalf of the dead. Compare 2 Maccabees 12:44 (RSV): "if he were not expecting that those who had fallen would rise again, it would have been superfluous and foolish to pray for the dead."

2 Corinthians 4:17: For our light affliction, which is but for a moment, worketh for us a far more exceeding and eternal weight of glory;

2 Corinthians 5:10: For we must all appear before the judgment seat of Christ; that every one may receive the things done in his body, according to that he hath done, whether it be good or bad.

Ephesians 4:8-10: Wherefore he saith, When he ascended up on high, he led captivity captive, and gave gifts unto men.

[9] (Now that he ascended, what is it but that he also descended first into the lower parts of the earth? [10] He that descended is the same also that ascended up far above all heavens, that he might fill all things.)

Ephesians 5:5: For this ye know, that no whoremonger, nor unclean person, nor covetous man, who is an idolater, hath any inheritance in the kingdom of Christ and of God.

Philippians 2:10-11: That at the name of Jesus every knee should bow, of things in heaven, and things in earth, and things under the earth; [11] And that every tongue should confess that Jesus Christ is Lord, to the glory of God the Father.

1 Thessalonians 2:4: . . . God, which trieth our hearts. (RSV: "God who tests our hearts")

1 Thessalonians 3:13: To the end he may stablish your hearts unblameable in holiness before God, even our Father, at the coming of our Lord Jesus Christ with all his saints. (cf. 4:7)

Hebrews 10:22: Let us draw near with a true heart in full assurance of faith, having our hearts sprinkled from an evil conscience, and our bodies washed with pure water.

Hebrews 12:5-14: And ye have forgotten the exhortation which speaketh unto you as unto children, My son, despise not thou the chastening of the Lord, nor faint when thou art rebuked of him:
[6] For whom the Lord loveth he chasteneth, and scourgeth every son whom he receiveth. [7] If ye endure chastening, God dealeth with you as with sons; for what son is he whom the father chasteneth not? [8] But if ye be without chastisement, whereof all are partakers, then are ye bastards, and not sons.
[9] Furthermore we have had fathers of our flesh which corrected us, and we gave them reverence: shall we not much rather be in subjection unto the Father of spirits, and live? [10] For they verily for a few days chastened us after their own pleasure; but he for our profit, that we might be partakers of his holiness. [11] Now no chastening for the present seemeth to be joyous, but grievous: nevertheless afterward it yieldeth the peaceable fruit of righteousness unto them which are exercised thereby.

[12] Wherefore lift up the hands which hang down, and the feeble knees; [13] And make straight paths for your feet, lest that which is lame be turned out of the way; but let it rather be healed. [14] Follow peace with all men, and holiness, without which no man shall see the Lord:

Hebrews 12:22-23: But ye are come unto mount Sion, and unto the city of the living God, the heavenly Jerusalem, and to an innumerable company of angels, [23] To the general assembly and church of the first-born, which are written in heaven, and to God the Judge of all, and to the spirits of just men made perfect,

1 Peter 1:6-7: Wherein ye greatly rejoice, though now for a season, if need be, ye are in heaviness through manifold temptations: [7] That the trial of your faith, being much more precious than of gold that perisheth, though it be tried with fire, might be found unto praise and honour and glory at the appearing of Jesus Christ:

1 Peter 3:19-20: By which also he went and preached unto the spirits in prison; [20] Which sometime were disobedient, when once the longsuffering of God waited in the days of Noah, while the ark was a preparing, wherein few, that is, eight souls were saved by water.

1 Peter 4:6: For for this cause was the gospel preached also to them that are dead, that they might be judged according to men in the flesh, but live according to God in the spirit.

2 Peter 1:9: . . . he was purged from his old sins. (RSV: "cleansed from his old sins")

1 John 1:7-9: But if we walk in the light, as he is in the light, we have fellowship one with another, and the blood of Jesus Christ his Son cleanseth us from all sin. [8] If we say that we have no sin, we deceive ourselves, and the truth is not in us. [9] If we confess our sins, he is faithful and just to forgive us our sins, and to cleanse us from all unrighteousness.

1 John 3:2-3: Beloved, now are we the sons of God, and it doth not yet appear what we shall be: but we know that, when he shall appear, we shall be like him; for we shall see him as he is. [3] And every man that hath this hope in him purifieth himself, even as he is pure.

Revelation 5:3, 13: And no man in heaven, nor in earth, neither under the earth, was able to open the book, neither to look thereon . . . And every creature which is in heaven, and on the earth, and under the earth, and such as are in the sea, and all that are in them, heard I saying, Blessing, and honour, and glory, and power, be unto him that sitteth upon the throne, and unto the Lamb for ever and ever.

Revelation 21:27: And there shall in no wise enter into it any thing that defileth, neither whatsoever worketh abomination, or maketh a lie: but they which are written in the Lamb's book of life.

We should pray for the dead

1 Kings 17:21-22: And he stretched himself upon the child three times, and cried unto the LORD, and said, O LORD my God, I pray thee, let this child's soul come into him again. [22] And the LORD heard the voice of Elijah; and the soul of the child came into him again, and he revived.

2 Maccabees 12:39-45: And upon the day following, as the use had been, Judas and his company came to take up the bodies of them that were slain, and to bury them with their kinsmen in their fathers' graves. [40] Now under the coats of every one that was slain they found things consecrated to the idols of the Jamnites, which is forbidden the Jews by the law. Then every man saw that this was the cause wherefore they were slain. [41] All men therefore praising the Lord, the righteous Judge, who had opened the things that were hid, [42] Betook themselves unto prayer, and besought him that the sin committed might wholly be put out of remembrance. Besides, that noble Judas exhorted the people to keep themselves from sin, forsomuch as they saw before their eyes the things that came to pass for the sins of those that were slain. [43] And when he had made a gathering throughout the company to the sum of two thousand drachms of silver, he sent it to Jerusalem to offer a sin offering, doing therein very well and honestly, in that he was mindful of the resurrection: [44] For if he had not hoped that they that were slain should have risen again, it had been superfluous and vain to pray for the dead. [45] And also in that he perceived that there was great favour laid up for those that died godly, it was an holy and good thought. Whereupon he made a reconciliation for the dead, that they might be delivered from sin.

Mark 5:35-42: While he yet spake, there came from the ruler of the synagogue's house certain which said, Thy daughter is dead: why troublest thou the Master any further? [36] As soon as Jesus heard the word that was spoken, he saith unto the ruler of the synagogue, Be not afraid, only believe. [37] And he suffered no man to follow him, save Peter, and James, and John the brother of James. [38] And he cometh to the house of the ruler of the synagogue, and seeth the tumult, and them that wept and wailed greatly. [39] And when he was come in, he saith unto them, Why make ye this ado, and weep? the damsel is not dead, but sleepeth.

[40] And they laughed him to scorn. But when he had put them all out, he taketh the father and the mother of the damsel, and them that were with him, and entereth in where the damsel was lying. [41] And he took the damsel by the hand, and said unto her, Talitha cumi; which is, being interpreted, Damsel, I say unto thee, arise. [42] And straightway the damsel arose, and walked; for she was of the age of twelve years. And they were astonished with a great astonishment.

Luke 7:11-15: And it came to pass the day after, that he went into a city called Nain; and many of his disciples went with him, and much people. [12] Now when he came nigh to the gate of the city, behold, there was a dead man carried out, the only son of his mother, and she was a widow: and much people of the city was with her. [13] And when the Lord saw her, he had compassion on her, and said unto her, Weep not. [14] And he came and touched the bier: and they that bare him stood still. And he said, Young man, I say unto thee, Arise. [15] And he that was dead sat up, and began to speak. And he delivered him to his mother.

John 11:39-44: Jesus said, Take ye away the stone. Martha, the sister of him that was dead, saith unto him, Lord, by this time he stinketh: for he hath been dead four days. [40] Jesus saith unto her, Said I not unto thee, that, if thou wouldest believe, thou shouldest see the glory of God? [41] Then they took away the stone from the place where the dead was laid. And Jesus lifted up his eyes, and said, Father, I thank thee that thou hast heard me.

[42] And I knew that thou hearest me always: but because of the people which stand by I said it, that they may believe that thou hast sent me. [43] And when he thus had spoken, he cried with a loud voice, Lazarus, come forth. [44] And he that was dead came forth, bound hand and foot with graveclothes: and his face was bound about with a napkin. Jesus saith unto them, Loose him, and let him go.

Acts 9:36-41: Now there was at Joppa a certain disciple named Tabitha, which by interpretation is called Dorcas: this woman was full of good works and almsdeeds which she did. [37] And it came to pass in those days, that she was sick, and died: whom when they had washed, they laid her in an upper chamber. [38] And forasmuch as Lydda was nigh to Joppa, and the disciples had heard that Peter was there, they sent unto him two men, desiring him that he would not delay to come to them. [39] Then Peter arose and went with them. When he was come, they brought him into the upper chamber: and all the widows stood by him weeping, and shewing the coats and garments which Dorcas made, while she was with them. [40] But Peter put them all forth, and kneeled down, and prayed; and turning him to the body said, Tabitha, arise. And she opened her eyes: and when she saw Peter, she sat up. [41] And he gave her his hand, and lifted her up, and when he had called the saints and widows, presented her alive.

The Bible informs us that the disciples raised people from the dead (Matt. 11:5; Luke 7:22) and that Jesus told them that they would be able to, and should, do so (Matt. 10:8). So they went out and did it, with (presumably) the use of prayer for that end. Thus, they prayed for the dead. We see above an example of St. Peter doing just that. In two examples of the dead being raised (Mark 5:35-42 and Luke 7:11-15), there is no recorded prayer, but Jesus does talk to the dead girl and the dead man, an act that is considered by many non-Catholics to be both an impossible and impermissible thing. He's "communicating with the dead," in other words, but in a proper manner (that is, not through mediums, séances, necromancy, etc.).

1 Corinthians 15:29: Else what shall they do which are baptized for the dead, if the dead rise not at all? why are they then baptized for the dead?

2 Timothy 1:16-18: The Lord give mercy unto the house of Onesiphorus; for he oft refreshed me, and was not ashamed of my chain: [17] But, when he was in Rome, he sought me out very diligently, and found me. [18] The Lord grant unto him that he may find mercy of the Lord in that day: and in how many things he ministered unto me at Ephesus, thou knowest very well. (RSV: "May the Lord grant mercy to the household of Onesiphorus . . . may the Lord grant him to find mercy from the Lord on that Day")

Chapter Six

The Holy Eucharist and the Sacrifice of the Mass

The Last Supper was the first Mass

Matthew 26:26-28: And as they were eating, Jesus took bread, and blessed it, and brake it, and gave it to the disciples, and said, Take, eat; this is my body. [27] And he took the cup, and gave thanks, and gave it to them, saying, Drink ye all of it; [28] For this is my blood of the new testament, which is shed for many for the remission of sins.

Mark 14:22-24: And as they did eat, Jesus took bread, and blessed, and brake it, and gave to them, and said, Take, eat: this is my body. [23] And he took the cup, and when he had given thanks, he gave it to them: and they all drank of it. [24] And he said unto them, This is my blood of the new testament, which is shed for many.

Luke 22:19-20: And he took bread, and gave thanks, and brake it, and gave unto them, saying, This is my body which is given for you: this do in remembrance of me. [20] Likewise also the cup after supper, saying, This cup is the new testament in my blood, which is shed for you.

1 Corinthians 10:14-22: Wherefore, my dearly beloved, flee from idolatry. [15] I speak as to wise men; judge ye what I say.

[16] The cup of blessing which we bless, is it not the communion of the blood of Christ? The bread which we break, is it not the communion of the body of Christ? [17] For we being many are one bread, and one body: for we are all partakers of that one bread. [18] Behold Israel after the flesh: are not they which eat of the sacrifices partakers of the alter? [19] What say I then?

that the idol is any thing, or that which is offered in sacrifice to idols is any thing? [20] But I say, that the things which the Gentiles sacrifice, they sacrifice to devils, and not to God: and I would not that ye should have fellowship with devils. [21] Ye cannot drink the cup of the Lord, and the cup of devils: ye cannot be partakers of the Lord's table, and of the table of devils. [22] Do we provoke the Lord to jealousy? are we stronger than he? (RSV: "Therefore, my beloved, shun the worship of idols. . . . The cup of blessing which we bless, is it not a participation in the blood of Christ? The bread which we break, is it not a participation in the body of Christ? Because there is one bread, we who are many are one body, for we all partake of the one bread. Consider the people of Israel; are not those who eat the sacrifices partners in the altar? . . . what pagans sacrifice they offer to demons and not to God. I do not want you to be partners with demons. You cannot drink the cup of the Lord and the cup of demons. You cannot partake of the table of the Lord and the table of demons")

St. Paul's entire thrust here is to contrast Christian eucharistic sacrifice with pagan sacrifice. As the Jewish sacrifices were literal and not symbolic, so is the Christian Sacrifice of the Mass. Following this line of analogical thought, Paul contrasts the pagan "sacrifice" to the Christian one (10:19-20), and the pagan "table of devils" (RSV: "demons") to the "Lord's table" (i.e., altar: 10:21). It's inescapable.

1 Corinthians 11:23-30: For I have received of the Lord that which also I delivered unto you, That the Lord Jesus the same night in which he was betrayed took bread: [24] And when he had given thanks, he brake it, and said, Take, eat: this is my body, which is broken for you: this do in remembrance of me. [25] After the same manner also he took the cup, when he had supped, saying, This cup is the new testament in my blood: this do ye, as oft as ye drink it, in remembrance of me. [26] For as often as ye eat this bread, and drink this cup, ye do shew the Lord's death till he come. [27] Wherefore whosoever shall eat this bread, and drink this cup of the Lord, unworthily, shall be guilty of the body and blood of the Lord. [28] But let a man examine himself, and so let him eat of that bread, and drink of that cup. [29] For he that eateth and drinketh unworthily, eateth and drinketh damnation to himself, not discerning the Lord's body. [30] For this cause many are weak and sickly among you, and many sleep. (RSV: "In the same way also the cup, after supper, saying, 'This cup is the new covenant in my blood' . . . Whoever, therefore, eats the bread or drinks the cup of the Lord in an unworthy manner will be guilty of profaning the body and blood of the Lord")

This is also intended quite literally. For how can one be guilty of profaning the body and blood of the Lord by engaging in a merely symbolic act?

Jesus teaches us about the Eucharist

John 6:47-66: Verily, verily, I say unto you, He that believeth on me hath everlasting life. [48] I am that bread of life.

[49] Your fathers did eat manna in the wilderness, and are dead.

[50] This is the bread which cometh down from heaven, that a man may eat thereof, and not die. [51] I am the living bread which came down from heaven: if any man eat of this bread, he shall live for ever: and the bread that I will give is my flesh, which I will give for the life of the world. [52] The Jews therefore strove among themselves, saying, How can this man give us his flesh to eat? [53] Then Jesus said unto them, Verily, verily, I say unto you, Except ye eat the flesh of the Son of man, and drink his blood, ye have no life in you. [54] Whoso eateth my flesh, and drinketh my blood, hath eternal life; and I will raise him up at the last day. [55] For my flesh is meat indeed, and my blood is drink indeed. [56] He that eateth my flesh, and drinketh my blood, dwelleth in me, and I in him. [57] As the living Father hath sent me, and I live by the Father: so he that eateth me, even he shall live by me. [58] This is that bread which came down from heaven: not as your fathers did eat manna, and are dead: he that eateth of this bread shall live for ever. [59] These things said he in the synagogue, as he taught in Capernaum. [60] Many therefore of his disciples, when they had heard this, said, This is an hard saying; who can hear it? [61] When Jesus knew in himself that his disciples murmured at it, he said unto them, Doth this offend you? [62] What and if ye shall see the Son of man ascend up where he was before? [63] It is the spirit that quickeneth; the flesh

profiteth nothing: the words that I speak unto you, they are spirit, and they are life. [64] But there are some of you that believe not. For Jesus knew from the beginning who they were that believed not, and who should betray him.

[65] And he said, Therefore said I unto you, that no man can come unto me, except it were given unto him of my Father.

[66] From that time many of his disciples went back, and walked no more with him.

One Protestant argument against the literal interpretation of John 6 is to claim that Jesus' contrast of "flesh" and "spirit" in 6:63 establishes the symbolic and metaphorical nature of the whole discourse. But when the words flesh *and* spirit *are opposed to each other in the New Testament, it is always a figurative use, in the sense of sinful human nature ("flesh") contrasted with humanity enriched by God's grace ("spirit"). (See Matt. 26:41; Rom. 7:5-6,25; 8:1-14; 1 Cor. 5:5; 2 Cor. 7:1; Gal. 3:3; 4:29; 5:13-26; and 1 Pet. 3:18; 4:6.) In other words, Jesus is saying that His words can be received only by men endowed with supernatural grace.*

Note also that Jesus did not explain or elaborate upon what He meant when some disciples "murmured" (6:61). It is the only recorded instance (other than Judas) of any of His disciples ceasing to follow Him. The plausible reason is because He knew that they were questioning and would not have accepted any further explanation anyway. We know this from the hard evidence of John 6:64: "there are some of you that believe not. For Jesus knew from the beginning who they were that believed not, and who should betray him." Jesus often noted hardness of heart leading to unbelief (e.g., Matt. 13:13, 19; Luke 5:21-22; John 8:27, 43-47; 12:37-40).

Despite this, the counter-argument to the straightforward Catholic interpretation of Real Presence in this passage is that it was purely a symbolic, metaphorical discourse, which the disciples misunderstood, causing some of them to forsake Jesus (6:66). But this makes no sense, because Jesus certainly would have explained what He meant in order to clear up the misunderstanding (and the abandonment), rather than simply reiterate and emphasize the same point more and more strongly, as the passage records.

Moreover, in many other places in Scripture, Jesus explains His meaning when someone merely is uncomprehending (as opposed to willfully disbelieving). A typical example of this occurs in John 3:1-15: the incident with Nicodemus regarding the meaning of "born again." Nicodemus asks (RSV): "How can a man be born when he is old? Can he enter a second time into his mother's womb and be born?" (3:4). Jesus explains his meaning (3:5-8). Nicodemus, still baffled, again asks: "How can this be?" (3:9). Jesus replied: "Are you a teacher of Israel, and yet you do not understand this?" (3:10, RSV) and then proceeds to explain some more (3:11-15). He explained because He knew that Nicodemus was truly seeking. When someone wasn't seeking or open in their spirit, he usually (if not always) would not do so, as in John 6. Here are further examples:

Matthew 13:36, 51: Then Jesus sent the multitude away, and went into the house: and his disciples came unto him, saying, Declare unto us the parable of the tares of the field . . . Jesus saith unto them, Have ye understood all these things? They say unto him, Yea, Lord.

Matthew 15:10-20: And he called the multitude, and said unto them, Hear, and understand: [11] Not that which goeth into the mouth defileth a man; but that which cometh out of the mouth, this defileth a man. [12] Then came his disciples, and said unto him, Knowest thou that the Pharisees were offended, after they heard this saying? [13] But he answered and said, Every plant, which my heavenly Father hath not planted, shall be rooted up.

[14] Let them alone: they be blind leaders of the blind. And if the blind lead the blind, both shall fall into the ditch. [15] Then answered Peter and said unto him, Declare unto us this parable. [16] And Jesus said, Are ye also yet without understanding? [17] Do not ye yet understand, that whatsoever entereth in at the mouth goeth into the belly, and is cast out into the draught? [18] But those things which proceed out of the mouth come forth from the heart; and they defile the man. [19] For out of the heart proceed evil thoughts, murders, adulteries, fornications, thefts, false witness,

blasphemies: [20] These are the things which defile a man: but to eat with unwashen hands defileth not a man. (cf. Mark 7:17-18)

Matthew 16:5-12: And when his disciples were come to the other side, they had forgotten to take bread. [6] Then Jesus said unto them, Take heed and beware of the leaven of the Pharisees and of the Sadducees. [7] And they reasoned among themselves, saying, It is because we have taken no bread. [8] Which when Jesus perceived, he said unto them, O ye of little faith, why reason ye among yourselves, because ye have brought no bread? [9] Do ye not yet understand, neither remember the five loaves of the five thousand, and how many baskets ye took up? [10] Neither the seven loaves of the four thousand, and how many baskets ye took up? [11] How is it that ye do not understand that I spake it not to you concerning bread, that ye should beware of the leaven of the Pharisees and of the Sadducees? [12] Then understood they how that he bade them not beware of the leaven of bread, but of the doctrine of the Pharisees and of the Sadducees.

Matthew 17:9-13: And as they came down from the mountain, Jesus charged them, saying, Tell the vision to no man, until the Son of man be risen again from the dead. [10] And his disciples asked him, saying, Why then say the scribes that Elias must first come? [11] And Jesus answered and said unto them, Elias truly shall first come, and restore all things. [12] But I say unto you, That Elias is come already, and they knew him not, but have done unto him whatsoever they listed. Likewise shall also the Son of man suffer of them. [13] Then the disciples understood that he spake unto them of John the Baptist.

Matthew 19:24-26: And again I say unto you, It is easier for a camel to go through the eye of a needle, than for a rich man to enter into the kingdom of God. [25] When his disciples heard it, they were exceedingly amazed, saying, Who then can be saved?

[26] But Jesus beheld them, and said unto them, With men this is impossible; but with God all things are possible.

Mark 4:33-34: And with many such parables spake he the word unto them, as they were able to hear it. [34] But without a parable spake he not unto them: and when they were alone, he expounded all things to his disciples. (RSV: "privately to his own disciples he explained everything")

Therefore, he would *have in John 6 if a misunderstanding were involved, rather than a hardhearted disbelief, brought on by the influence of Satan.*

Luke 8:9-11: And his disciples asked him, saying, What might this parable be? [10] And he said, Unto you it is given to know the mysteries of the kingdom of God: but to others in parables; that seeing they might not see, and hearing they might not understand. [11] Now the parable is this: The seed is the word of God.

Jesus continued explaining in 8:12-15.

Luke 9:46-48: Then there arose a reasoning among them, which of them should be greatest. [47] And Jesus, perceiving the thought of their heart, took a child, and set him by him,

[48] And said unto them, Whosoever shall receive this child in my name receiveth me: and whosoever shall receive me receiveth him that sent me: for he that is least among you all, the same shall be great.

Luke 24:13-27: And, behold, two of them went that same day to a village called Emmaus, which was from Jerusalem about threescore furlongs. [14] And they talked together of all these things which had happened. [15] And it came to pass, that, while they communed together and reasoned, Jesus himself drew near, and went with them. [16] But their eyes were holden that they should not know him. [17] And he said unto them, What manner of communications are these that ye have one to another, as ye walk, and are sad? [18] And the one of them, whose name was Cleopas, answering said unto him, Art thou only a stranger in Jerusalem, and hast not known the things which are come to pass therein these days? [19] And he said unto them, What things? And they said unto him, Concerning Jesus of Nazareth, which was a prophet mighty in deed and word before God and all the people: [20] And how the chief priests and our rulers delivered him to be condemned to death, and have crucified him. [21] But we trusted that it had been he which should have redeemed Israel: and beside all this, to day is the third day since these things were done. [22] Yea, and certain women also of our company made us astonished, which were early at the sepulchre; [23] And when they found not his body, they came, saying, that they had also seen a vision of angels, which said that he was alive.

[24] And certain of them which were with us went to the sepulchre, and found it even so as the women had said: but him they saw not. [25] Then he said unto them, O fools, and slow of heart to believe all that the prophets have spoken:

[26] Ought not Christ to have suffered these things, and to enter into his glory? [27] And beginning at Moses and all the prophets, he expounded unto them in all the scriptures the things concerning himself.

John 4:31-34: In the mean while his disciples prayed him, saying, Master, eat. [32] But he said unto them, I have meat to eat that ye know not of. [33] Therefore said the disciples one to another, Hath any man brought him ought to eat? [34] Jesus saith unto them, My meat is to do the will of him that sent me, and to finish his work.

John 8:21-32: Then said Jesus again unto them, I go my way, and ye shall seek me, and shall die in your sins: whither I go, ye cannot come. [22] Then said the Jews, Will he kill himself? because he saith, Whither I go, ye cannot come. [23] And he said unto them, Ye are from beneath; I am from above: ye are of this world; I am not of this world. [24] I said therefore unto you, that ye shall die in your sins: for if ye believe not that I am he, ye shall die in your sins. [25] Then said they unto him, Who art thou? And Jesus saith unto them, Even the same that I said unto you from the beginning. [26] I have many things to say and to judge of you: but he that sent me is true; and I speak to the world those things which I have heard of him. [27] They understood not that he spake to them of the Father. [28] Then said Jesus unto them, When ye have lifted up the Son of man, then shall ye know that I am he, and that I do nothing of myself; but as my Father hath taught me, I speak these things. [29] And he that sent me is with me: the Father hath not left me alone; for I do always those things that please him. [30] As he spake these words, many believed on him. [31] Then said Jesus to those Jews which believed on him, If ye continue in my word, then are ye my disciples indeed; [32] And ye shall know the truth, and the truth shall make you free.

In this instance, Jesus explained because He knew (in His omniscience) that some of the hearers would believe in Him, while others would not.

John 10:6-7: This parable spake Jesus unto them: but they understood not what things they were which he spake unto them.

[7] Then said Jesus unto them again, Verily, verily, I say unto you, I am the door of the sheep.

Jesus elaborated that he was the "door": key information that was not present in 10:1-5.

John 11:8-15: His disciples say unto him, Master, the Jews of late sought to stone thee; and goest thou thither again? [9] Jesus answered, Are there not twelve hours in the day? If any man walk in the day, he stumbleth not, because he seeth the light of this world. [10] But if a man walk in the night, he stumbleth, because there is no light in him. [11] These things said he: and after that he saith unto them, Our friend Lazarus sleepeth; but I go, that I may awake him out of sleep. [12] Then said his disciples, Lord, if he sleep, he shall do well. [13] Howbeit Jesus spake of his death: but they thought that he had spoken of taking of rest in sleep. [14] Then said Jesus unto them plainly, Lazarus is dead. [15] And I am glad for your sakes that I was not there, to the intent ye may believe; nevertheless let us go unto him.

John 16:17-19, 29-31: Then said some of his disciples among themselves, What is this that he saith unto us, A little while, and ye shall not see me: and again, a little while, and ye shall see me: and, Because I go to the Father? [18] They said therefore, What is this that he saith, A little while? we cannot tell what he saith.

[19] Now Jesus knew that they were desirous to ask him, and said unto them, Do ye inquire among yourselves of that I said, A little while, and ye shall not see me: and again, a little while, and ye shall see me? . . . His disciples said unto him, Lo, now speakest thou plainly, and speakest no proverb. [30] Now are we sure that thou knowest all things, and needest not that any man should ask thee: by this we believe that thou camest forth from God.

[31] Jesus answered them, Do ye now believe?

The Mass is a sacrifice

Genesis 14:18: And Melchizedek king of Salem brought forth bread and wine: and he was the priest of the most high God.

Exodus 29:39-41: The one lamb thou shalt offer in the morning; and the other lamb thou shalt offer at even: [40] And with the one lamb a tenth deal of flour mingled with the fourth part of an hin of beaten oil; and the fourth part of an hin of wine for a drink offering. [41] And the other lamb thou shalt offer at even, and shalt do thereto according to the meat offering of the morning, and according to the drink offering thereof, for a sweet savour, an offering made by fire unto the LORD.

Leviticus 2:1, 8: And when any will offer a meat offering unto the LORD, his offering shall be of fine flour; and he shall pour oil upon it, and put frankincense thereon: . . . And thou shalt bring the meat offering that is made of these things unto the LORD: and when it is presented unto the priest, he shall bring it unto the altar.

Leviticus 6:15: And he shall take of it his handful, of the flour of the meat offering, and of the oil thereof, and all the frankincense which is upon the meat offering, and shall burn it upon the altar for a sweet savour, even the memorial of it, unto the LORD.

Leviticus 10:12: And Moses spake unto Aaron, and unto Eleazar and unto Ithamar, his sons that were left, Take the meat offering that remaineth of the offerings of the LORD made by fire, and eat it without leaven beside the altar: for it is most holy:

An "altar" in heaven is repeatedly referred to in Revelation 6:9; 8:3; 9:13; 11:1; 14:18; 16:7.

Leviticus 23:13: And the meat offering thereof shall be two tenth deals of fine flour mingled with oil, an offering made by fire unto the LORD for a sweet savour: and the drink offering thereof shall be of wine, the fourth part of an hin.

Numbers 6:15: And a basket of unleavened bread, cakes of fine flour mingled with oil, and wafers of unleavened bread anointed with oil, and their meat offering, and their drink offerings.

Numbers 15:5: And the fourth part of an hin of wine for a drink offering shalt thou prepare with the burnt offering or sacrifice, for one lamb. (cf. 15:7, 10)

Numbers 28:9: And on the sabbath day two lambs of the first year without spot, and two tenth deals of flour for a meat offering, mingled with oil, and the drink offering thereof:

Psalm 110:4: The LORD hath sworn, and will not repent, Thou art a priest for ever after the order of Melchizedek. (cf. Heb. 5:6, 10; 6:20; 7:1-28)

Isaiah 53:7: He was oppressed, and he was afflicted, yet he opened not his mouth: he is brought as a lamb to the slaughter, and as a sheep before her shearers is dumb, so he openeth not his mouth. (cf. Jer. 11:19; Acts 8:32)

Isaiah 66:18, 21: For I know their works and their thoughts: it shall come, that I will gather all nations and tongues; and they shall come, and see my glory . . . And I will also take of them for priests and for Levites, saith the LORD.

Malachi 1:11: For from the rising of the sun even unto the going down of the same my name shall be great among the Gentiles; and in every place incense shall be offered unto my name, and a pure offering: for my name shall be great among the heathen, saith the LORD of hosts.

Sirach 50:14-15: And finishing the service at the altar, that he might adorn the offering of the most high Almighty, [15] He stretched out his hand to the cup, and poured of the blood of the grape, he poured out at the foot of the altar a sweetsmelling savour unto the most high King of all.

Matthew 26:17-19: Now the first day of the feast of unleavened bread the disciples came to Jesus, saying unto him, Where wilt thou that we prepare for thee to eat the passover? [18] And he said, Go into the city to such a man, and say unto him, The Master saith, My time is at hand; I will keep the passover at thy house with my disciples. [19] And the disciples did as Jesus had appointed them; and they made ready the passover. (cf. Mark 14:12-16; Luke 22:11-15)

Luke 22:15: And he said unto them, With desire I have desired to eat this passover with you before I suffer:

John 1:29: The next day John seeth Jesus coming unto him, and saith, Behold the Lamb of God, which taketh away the sin of the world. (cf. 1:36)

1 Corinthians 5:7: Purge out therefore the old leaven, that ye may be a new lump, as ye are unleavened. For even Christ our passover is sacrificed for us: (RSV: "For Christ, our paschal lamb, has been sacrificed")

1 Corinthians 10:18-22: Behold Israel after the flesh: are not they which eat of the sacrifices partakers of the alter? [19] What say I then? that the idol is any thing, or that which is offered in sacrifice to idols is any thing? [20] But I say, that the things which the Gentiles sacrifice, they sacrifice to devils, and not to God: and I would not that ye should have fellowship with devils. [21] Ye cannot drink the cup of the Lord, and the cup of devils: ye cannot be partakers of the Lord's table, and of the table of devils. [22] Do we provoke the Lord to jealousy? are we stronger than he? (RSV: "demons")

Hebrews 9:11-14: But Christ being come an high priest of good things to come, by a greater and more perfect tabernacle, not made with hands, that is to say, not of this building; [12] Neither by the blood of goats and calves, but by his own blood he entered in once into the holy place, having obtained eternal redemption for us. [13] For if the blood of bulls and of goats, and the ashes of an heifer sprinkling the unclean, sanctifieth to the purifying of the flesh: [14] How much more shall the blood of Christ, who through the eternal Spirit offered himself without spot to God, purge your conscience from dead works to serve the living God? (cf. 2:17; 3:1; 4:14-16; 5:1-10; 8:1-6; 10:19-22)

Hebrews 9:24-28: For Christ is not entered into the holy places made with hands, which are the figures of the true; but into heaven itself, now to appear in the presence of God for us: [25] Nor yet that he should offer himself often, as the high priest entereth into the holy place every year with blood of others; [26] For then must he often have suffered since the foundation of the world: but now once in the end of the world hath he appeared to put away sin by the sacrifice of himself. [27] And as it is appointed unto men once to die, but after this the judgment:

[28] So Christ was once offered to bear the sins of many; and unto them that look for him shall he appear the second time without sin unto salvation.not to deal with sin but to save those who are eagerly waiting for him.

Hebrews 13:10-12: We have an altar, whereof they have no right to eat which serve the tabernacle. [11] For the bodies of those beasts, whose blood is brought into the sanctuary by the high priest for sin, are burned without the camp. [12] Wherefore Jesus also, that he might sanctify the people with his own blood, suffered without the gate.

1 Peter 1:18-19: Forasmuch as ye know that ye were not redeemed with corruptible things, as silver and gold, from your vain conversation received by tradition from your fathers; [19] But with the precious blood of Christ, as of a lamb without blemish and without spot:

Revelation 5:6: And I beheld, and, lo, in the midst of the throne and of the four beasts, and in the midst of the elders, stood a Lamb as it had been slain, having seven horns and seven eyes, which are the seven Spirits of God sent forth into all the earth. (cf. 5:8,12-13; 6:1,16)

Revelation 7:14: And I said unto him, Sir, thou knowest. And he said to me, These are they which came out of great tribulation, and have washed their robes, and made them white in the blood of the Lamb. (cf. 7:9-10, 17; 8:1; 14:1, 4, 10; 15:3; 17:14; 19:7, 9; 21:9, 14, 22-23, 27; 22:1, 3)

Revelation 12:11: And they overcame him by the blood of the Lamb . . .

Revelation 13:8: And all that dwell upon the earth shall worship him, whose names are not written in the book of life of the Lamb slain from the foundation of the world.

Chapter Seven

The Sacrament of Baptism

Our sins are washed away in Baptism

Joshua 3:15-16: And as they that bare the ark were come unto Jordan, and the feet of the priests that bare the ark were dipped in the brim of the water, (for Jordan overfloweth all his banks all the time of harvest,) [16] That the waters which came down from above stood and rose up upon an heap very far from the city Adam, that is beside Zaretan: and those that came down toward the sea of the plain, even the salt sea, failed, and were cut off: and the people passed over right against Jericho.

2 Kings 2:7-11: And fifty men of the sons of the prophets went, and stood to view afar off: and they two stood by Jordan. [8] And Elijah took his mantle, and wrapped it together, and smote the waters, and they were divided hither and thither, so that they two went over on dry ground. [9] And it came to pass, when they were gone over, that Elijah said unto Elisha, Ask what I shall do for thee, before I be taken away from thee. And Elisha said, I pray thee, let a double portion of thy spirit be upon me. [10] And he said, Thou hast asked a hard thing: nevertheless, if thou see me when I am taken from thee, it shall be so unto thee; but if not, it shall not be so. [11] And it came to pass, as they still went on, and talked, that, behold, there appeared a chariot of fire, and horses of fire, and parted them both asunder; and Elijah went up by a whirlwind into heaven.

Ezekiel 36:25: Then will I sprinkle clean water upon you, and ye shall be clean: from all your filthiness, and from all your idols, will I cleanse you.

Matthew 28:19: Go ye therefore, and teach all nations, baptizing them in the name of the Father, and of the Son, and of the Holy Ghost: (cf. Luke 24:47)

Mark 1:4: John did baptize in the wilderness, and preach the baptism of repentance for the remission of sins. (RSV: "for the forgiveness of sins")

Mark 16:16: He that believeth and is baptized shall be saved; but he that believeth not shall be damned.

Luke 1:76-77: And thou, child, shalt be called the prophet of the Highest: for thou shalt go before the face of the Lord to prepare his ways; [77] To give knowledge of salvation unto his people by the remission of their sins, (cf. Mark 1:4; Luke 3:3; Acts 2:38)

Luke 3:3: And he came into all the country about Jordan, preaching the baptism of repentance for the remission of sins;

Luke 24:47: And that repentance and remission of sins should be preached in his name among all nations, beginning at Jerusalem. (cf. Matt. 28:19)

John 3:5: Jesus answered, Verily, verily, I say unto thee, Except a man be born of water and of the Spirit, he cannot enter into the kingdom of God.

Acts 2:38-41: Then Peter said unto them, Repent, and be baptized every one of you in the name of Jesus Christ for the remission of sins, and ye shall receive the gift of the Holy Ghost. [39] For the promise is unto you, and to your children, and to all that are afar off, even as many as the Lord our God shall call. [40] And with many other words did he testify and exhort, saying, Save yourselves from this untoward generation. [41] Then they that gladly received his word were baptized: and the same day there were added unto them about three thousand souls. (RSV: "for the forgiveness of your sins"; cf. 10:43-48))

Acts 22:16: And now why tarriest thou? arise, and be baptized, and wash away thy sins, calling on the name of the Lord.

Romans 6:3-4: Know ye not, that so many of us as were baptized into Jesus Christ were baptized into his death? [4] Therefore we are buried with him by baptism into death: that like as Christ was raised up from the dead by the glory of the Father, even so we also should walk in newness of life.

1 Corinthians 6:11: And such were some of you: but ye are washed, but ye are sanctified, but ye are justified in the name of the Lord Jesus, and by the Spirit of our God. (RSV: "But you were washed, you were sanctified, you were justified")

1 Corinthians 10:1-2: Moreover, brethren, I would not that ye should be ignorant, how that all our fathers were under the cloud, and all passed through the sea; [2] And were all baptized unto Moses in the cloud and in the sea; (cf. Exod. 15:19)

Galatians 3:26-27: For ye are all the children of God by faith in Christ Jesus. [27] For as many of you as have been baptized into Christ have put on Christ.

Ephesians 4:5: One Lord, one faith, one baptism,

Ephesians 5:26: That he might sanctify and cleanse it with the washing of water by the word,

Colossians 2:12: Buried with him in baptism, wherein also ye are risen with him through the faith of the operation of God, who hath raised him from the dead.

Titus 3:5: Not by works of righteousness which we have done, but according to his mercy he saved us, by the washing of regeneration, and renewing of the Holy Ghost;

Hebrews 10:22: Let us draw near with a true heart in full assurance of faith, having our hearts sprinkled from an evil conscience, and our bodies washed with pure water.

1 Peter 3:20-21: Which sometime were disobedient, when once the longsuffering of God waited in the days of Noah, while the ark was a preparing, wherein few, that is, eight souls were saved by water. [21] The like figure whereunto even baptism doth also now save us (not the putting away of the filth of the flesh, but the answer of a good conscience toward God,) by the resurrection of Jesus Christ:

Infants were baptized
even in the early Church

Acts 16:15: . . . she was baptized, and her household . . .

Acts 16:33: . . . and was baptized, he and all his . . . (RSV: "he was baptized at once, with all his family")

Acts 18:8: And Crispus, the chief ruler of the synagogue, believed on the Lord with all his house; and many of the Corinthians hearing believed, and were baptized.

1 Corinthians 1:16: And I baptized also the household of Stephanas . . .

Many biblical passages connect household *and* children:

Genesis 18:19: For I know him, that he will command his children and his household after him, and they shall keep the way of the LORD, to do justice and judgment; that the LORD may bring upon Abraham that which he hath spoken of him. (cf. 31:41)

Genesis 36:6: And Esau took his wives, and his sons, and his daughters, and all the persons of his house, and his cattle, and all his beasts, and all his substance, which he had got in the land of Canaan; and went into the country from the face of his brother Jacob.

Genesis 47:12: And Joseph nourished his father, and his brethren, and all his father's household, with bread, according to their families.

Numbers 18:11: And this is thine; the heave offering of their gift, with all the wave offerings of the children of Israel: I have given them unto thee, and to thy sons and to thy daughters with thee, by a statute for ever: every one that is clean in thy house shall eat of it.

1 Chronicles 10:6: So Saul died, and his three sons, and all his house died together.

Matthew 19:29: And every one that hath forsaken houses, or brethren, or sisters, or father, or mother, or wife, or children, or lands, for my name's sake, shall receive an hundredfold, and shall inherit everlasting life. (cf. Mark 10:30)

1 Timothy 3:12: Let the deacons be the husbands of one wife, ruling their children and their own houses well.

In other biblical passages, entire households are referred to as being saved:

Luke 19:9: And Jesus said unto him, This day is salvation come to this house, forsomuch as he also is a son of Abraham.

Acts 11:14: Who shall tell thee words, whereby thou and all thy house shall be saved.

Acts 16:31: And they said, Believe on the Lord Jesus Christ, and thou shalt be saved, and thy house.

Infants are part of the
covenant and salvation

Genesis 17:7: And I will establish my covenant between me and thee and thy seed after thee in their generations for an everlasting covenant, to be a God unto thee, and to thy seed after thee.

Deuteronomy 10:16: Circumcise therefore the foreskin of your heart, and be no more stiffnecked.

Deuteronomy 29:10-12: Ye stand this day all of you before the LORD your God; your captains of your tribes, your elders, and your officers, with all the men of Israel, [11] Your little ones, your wives, and thy stranger that is in thy camp, from the hewer of thy wood unto the drawer of thy water: [12] That thou shouldest enter into covenant with the LORD thy God, and into his oath, which the LORD thy God maketh with thee this day:

Deuteronomy 30:6: And the LORD thy God will circumcise thine heart, and the heart of thy seed, to love the LORD thy God with all thine heart, and with all thy soul, that thou mayest live.

Jeremiah 4:4: Circumcise yourselves to the LORD, and take away the foreskins of your heart, ye men of Judah and inhabitants of Jerusalem: lest my fury come forth like fire, and burn that none can quench it, because of the evil of your doings.

Jeremiah 9:25: Behold, the days come, saith the LORD, that I will punish all them which are circumcised with the uncircumcised;

Matthew 19:14: But Jesus said, Suffer little children, and forbid them not, to come unto me: for of such is the kingdom of heaven.

Romans 2:26-29: Therefore if the uncircumcision keep the righteousness of the law, shall not his uncircumcision be counted for circumcision? [27] And shall not uncircumcision which is by nature, if it fulfil the law, judge thee, who by the letter and circumcision dost transgress the law? [28] For he is not a Jew, which is one outwardly; neither is that circumcision, which is outward in the flesh: [29] But he is a Jew, which is one inwardly; and circumcision is that of the heart, in the spirit, and not in the letter; whose praise is not of men, but of God. (cf. 3:30; 4:9-12)

Philippians 3:3: For we are the circumcision, which worship God in the spirit, and rejoice in Christ Jesus, and have no confidence in the flesh. (cf. 1 Cor. 7:18-19)

Colossians 2:11-13: In whom also ye are circumcised with the circumcision made without hands, in putting off the body of the sins of the flesh by the circumcision of Christ: [12] Buried with him in baptism, wherein also ye are risen with him through the faith of the operation of God, who hath raised him from the dead. [13] And you, being dead in your sins and the uncircumcision of your flesh, hath he quickened together with him, having forgiven you all trespasses; (cf. Gal. 5:6)

Chapter Eight

The Sacrament of Confirmation

The Holy Spirit descends upon persons

Wisdom 9:17: And thy counsel who hath known, except thou give wisdom, and send thy Holy Spirit from above?

Matthew 3:16: And Jesus, when he was baptized, went up straightway out of the water: and, lo, the heavens were opened unto him, and he saw the Spirit of God descending like a dove, and lighting upon him: (cf. Isa. 11:2)

Luke 2:25: And, behold, there was a man in Jerusalem, whose name was Simeon; and the same man was just and devout, waiting for the consolation of Israel: and the Holy Ghost was upon him.

Luke 3:22: And the Holy Ghost descended in a bodily shape like a dove upon him . . . (RSV: "Holy Spirit" — as usual in these passages)

Luke 11:13: If ye then, being evil, know how to give good gifts unto your children: how much more shall your heavenly Father give the Holy Spirit to them that ask him?

John 1:33: And I knew him not: but he that sent me to baptize with water, the same said unto me, Upon whom thou shalt see the Spirit descending, and remaining on him, the same is he which baptizeth with the Holy Ghost.

John 20:22: And when he had said this, he breathed on them, and saith unto them, Receive ye the Holy Ghost:

Acts 1:8: But ye shall receive power, after that the Holy Ghost is come upon you . . .

Acts 2:1-3: And when the day of Pentecost was fully come, they were all with one accord in one place. [2] And suddenly there came a sound from heaven as of a rushing mighty wind, and it filled all the house where they were sitting. [3] And there appeared unto them cloven tongues like as of fire, and it sat upon each of them.

Acts 2:15-18: For these are not drunken, as ye suppose, seeing it is but the third hour of the day. [16] But this is that which was spoken by the prophet Joel; [17] And it shall come to pass in the last days, saith God, I will pour out of my Spirit upon all flesh: and your sons and your daughters shall prophesy, and your young men shall see visions, and your old men shall dream dreams: [18] And on my servants and on my handmaidens I will pour out in those days of my Spirit; and they shall prophesy:

Acts 2:33: Therefore being by the right hand of God exalted, and having received of the Father the promise of the Holy Ghost, he hath shed forth this, which ye now see and hear.

Acts 2:38: Then Peter said unto them, Repent, and be baptized every one of you in the name of Jesus Christ for the remission of sins, and ye shall receive the gift of the Holy Ghost.

Acts 5:32: . . . the Holy Ghost, whom God hath given to them that obey him.

Acts 8:14-16: Now when the apostles which were at Jerusalem heard that Samaria had received the word of God, they sent unto them Peter and John: [15] Who, when they were come down, prayed for them, that they might receive the Holy Ghost: [16] (For as yet he was fallen upon none of them: only they were baptized in the name of the Lord Jesus.)

Acts 10:44-47: While Peter yet spake these words, the Holy Ghost fell on all them which heard the word. [45] And they of the circumcision which believed were astonished, as many as came with Peter, because that on the Gentiles also was poured out the gift of the Holy Ghost. [46] For they heard them speak with tongues, and magnify God. Then answered Peter, [47] Can any man forbid water, that these should not be baptized, which have received the Holy Ghost as well as we?

Acts 11:15: And as I began to speak, the Holy Ghost fell on them, as on us at the beginning.

Acts 15:8: And God, which knoweth the hearts, bare them witness, giving them the Holy Ghost, even as he did unto us;

Acts 19:2: He said unto them, Have ye received the Holy Ghost since ye believed? And they said unto him, We have not so much as heard whether there be any Holy Ghost.

Romans 5:5: And hope maketh not ashamed; because the love of God is shed abroad in our hearts by the Holy Ghost which is given unto us.

1 Thessalonians 4:8: He therefore that despiseth, despiseth not man, but God, who hath also given unto us his holy Spirit.

Jesus baptizes with the Holy Spirit

Matthew 3:11: I indeed baptize you with water unto repentance: but he that cometh after me is mightier than I, whose shoes I am not worthy to bear: he shall baptize you with the Holy Ghost, and with fire:

Mark 1:8: I indeed have baptized you with water: but he shall baptize you with the Holy Ghost.

Luke 3:16: John answered, saying unto them all, I indeed baptize you with water; but one mightier than I cometh, the latchet of whose shoes I am not worthy to unloose: he shall baptize you with the Holy Ghost and with fire:

John 1:33: And I knew him not: but he that sent me to baptize with water, the same said unto me, Upon whom thou shalt see the Spirit descending, and remaining on him, the same is he which baptizeth with the Holy Ghost.

Acts 1:5: For John truly baptized with water; but ye shall be baptized with the Holy Ghost not many days hence.

Acts 11:16: Then remembered I the word of the Lord, how that he said, John indeed baptized with water; but ye shall be baptized with the Holy Ghost.

Persons may be "filled" with the Holy Spirit

Luke 1:15: For he shall be great in the sight of the Lord, and shall drink neither wine nor strong drink; and he shall be filled with the Holy Ghost, even from his mother's womb.

Luke 1:41: . . . and Elisabeth was filled with the Holy Ghost:

Luke 1:67: And his father Zacharias was filled with the Holy Ghost, and prophesied, saying,

Luke 4:1: And Jesus being full of the Holy Ghost . . .

Acts 2:4: And they were all filled with the Holy Ghost . . .

Acts 4:8: Then Peter, filled with the Holy Ghost . . .

Acts 4:31: And when they had prayed, the place was shaken where they were assembled together; and they were all filled with the Holy Ghost, and they spake the word of God with boldness.

Acts 6:5: . . . Stephen, a man full of faith and of the Holy Ghost . . .

Acts 7:55: But he, being full of the Holy Ghost, looked up stedfastly into heaven, and saw the glory of God, and Jesus standing on the right hand of God,

Acts 11:24: For he was a good man, and full of the Holy Ghost and of faith . . .

Acts 13:9: Then Saul, (who also is called Paul,) filled with the Holy Ghost, set his eyes on him,

Acts 13:52: And the disciples were filled with joy, and with the Holy Ghost.

Ephesians 5:18: And be not drunk with wine, wherein is excess; but be filled with the Spirit; (cf. Exod. 31:3; 35:31; Mic. 3:8; Sir. 48:12)

The Holy Spirit comes
through the laying on of hands

Acts 8:17-20: Then laid they their hands on them, and they received the Holy Ghost. [18] And when Simon saw that through laying on of the apostles' hands the Holy Ghost was given, he offered them money, [19] Saying, Give me also this power, that on whomsoever I lay hands, he may receive the Holy Ghost.

[20] But Peter said unto him, Thy money perish with thee, because thou hast thought that the gift of God may be purchased with money.

Acts 9:17: And Ananias went his way, and entered into the house; and putting his hands on him said, Brother Saul, the Lord, even Jesus, that appeared unto thee in the way as thou camest, hath sent me, that thou mightest receive thy sight, and be filled with the Holy Ghost.

Acts 13:2-4: As they ministered to the Lord, and fasted, the Holy Ghost said, Separate me Barnabas and Saul for the work whereunto I have called them. [3] And when they had fasted and prayed, and laid their hands on them, they sent them away. [4] So they, being sent forth by the Holy Ghost, departed unto Seleucia; and from thence they sailed to Cyprus.

Acts 19:6: And when Paul had laid his hands upon them, the Holy Ghost came on them; and they spake with tongues, and prophesied. (cf. 1 Tim. 4:14; 2 Tim. 1:6)

We are "sealed" with the Holy Spirit

2 Corinthians 1:22: Who hath also sealed us, and given the earnest of the Spirit in our hearts.

Ephesians 1:13-14: In whom ye also trusted, after that ye heard the word of truth, the gospel of your salvation: in whom also after that ye believed, ye were sealed with that holy Spirit of promise, [14] Which is the earnest of our inheritance until the redemption of the purchased possession, unto the praise of his glory.

Ephesians 4:30: And grieve not the holy Spirit of God, whereby ye are sealed unto the day of redemption.

Persons are anointed with oil for a sacred purpose or to receive the Holy Spirit

Exodus 28:41: And thou shalt put them upon Aaron thy brother, and his sons with him; and shalt anoint them, and consecrate them, and sanctify them, that they may minister unto me in the priest's office.

Leviticus 16:32: And the priest, whom he shall anoint, and whom he shall consecrate to minister in the priest's office in his father's stead, shall make the atonement, and shall put on the linen clothes, even the holy garments:

1 Samuel 10:1: Then Samuel took a vial of oil, and poured it upon his head, and kissed him, and said, Is it not because the LORD hath anointed thee to be captain over his inheritance?

1 Samuel 16:13: Then Samuel took the horn of oil, and anointed him in the midst of his brethren: and the Spirit of the LORD came upon David from that day forward. So Samuel rose up, and went to Ramah.

Isaiah 61:1: The Spirit of the Lord GOD is upon me; because the LORD hath anointed me to preach good tidings unto the meek; he hath sent me to bind up the brokenhearted, to proclaim liberty to the captives, and the opening of the prison to them that are bound;

Luke 4:18: The Spirit of the Lord is upon me, because he hath anointed me to preach the gospel to the poor; he hath sent me to heal the brokenhearted, to preach deliverance to the captives, and recovering of sight to the blind, to set at liberty them that are bruised,

Acts 10:38: . . . God anointed Jesus of Nazareth with the Holy Ghost and with power . . .

The Holy Spirit received through authoritative persons

Acts 4:31: And when they had prayed, the place was shaken where they were assembled together; and they were all filled with the Holy Ghost, and they spake the word of God with boldness.

Acts 8:17: Then laid they their hands on them, and they received the Holy Ghost.

Acts 10:44: While Peter yet spake these words, the Holy Ghost fell on all them which heard the word.

Acts 11:15: And as I began to speak, the Holy Ghost fell on them, as on us at the beginning.

Acts 13:2-4: As they ministered to the Lord, and fasted, the Holy Ghost said, Separate me Barnabas and Saul for the work whereunto I have called them. [3] And when they had fasted and prayed, and laid their hands on them, they sent them away. [4] So they, being sent forth by the Holy Ghost, departed unto Seleucia; and from thence they sailed to Cyprus.

Acts 19:6: And when Paul had laid his hands upon them, the Holy Ghost came on them; and they spake with tongues, and prophesied.

Thus, we see that all essential elements of the Catholic sacrament of Confirmation are present in Holy Scripture, and quite explicitly so. Also, the day of Pentecost (Acts 2) when the Holy Spirit came upon and into all Christians, was presided over by St. Peter, the leader of the Church and the first pope.

Chapter Nine

The Sacrament of Anointing

Priests anoint with oil to heal

Mark 6:12-13: And they went out, and preached that men should repent. [13] And they cast out many devils, and anointed with oil many that were sick, and healed them.

James 5:14-15: Is any sick among you? let him call for the elders of the church; and let them pray over him, anointing him with oil in the name of the Lord: [15] And the prayer of faith shall save the sick, and the Lord shall raise him up; and if he have committed sins, they shall be forgiven him.

The laying on of hands can bring healing

Mark 6:5: And he could there do no mighty work, save that he laid his hands upon a few sick folk, and healed them.

Luke 4:40: Now when the sun was setting, all they that had any sick with divers diseases brought them unto him; and he laid his hands on every one of them, and healed them.

Luke 22:51: And Jesus answered and said, Suffer ye thus far. And he touched his ear, and healed him.

John 9:6-7: When he had thus spoken, he spat on the ground, and made clay of the spittle, and he anointed the eyes of the blind man with the clay, [7] And said unto him, Go, wash in the pool of Siloam, (which is by interpretation, Sent.) He went his way therefore, and washed, and came seeing.

Acts 28:8: And it came to pass, that the father of Publius lay sick of a fever and of a bloody flux: to whom Paul entered in, and prayed, and laid his hands on him, and healed him.

Some who touched Christ were healed

Mark 3:10: For he had healed many; insomuch that they pressed upon him for to touch him, as many as had plagues.

Luke 6:19: And the whole multitude sought to touch him: for there went virtue out of him, and healed them all.

Spiritual benefit in healing (demoniacs)

Matthew 4:24: And his fame went throughout all Syria: and they brought unto him all sick people that were taken with divers diseases and torments, and those which were possessed with devils, and those which were lunatick, and those that had the palsy; and he healed them.

Matthew 8:16: When the even was come, they brought unto him many that were possessed with devils: and he cast out the spirits with his word, and healed all that were sick:

Matthew 10:1, 8: And when he had called unto him his twelve disciples, he gave them power against unclean spirits, to cast them out, and to heal all manner of sickness and all manner of disease . . . Heal the sick, cleanse the lepers, raise the dead, cast out devils: freely ye have received, freely give.

Matthew 12:22: Then was brought unto him one possessed with a devil, blind, and dumb: and he healed him, insomuch that the blind and dumb both spake and saw.

Mark 1:34: And he healed many that were sick of divers diseases, and cast out many devils; and suffered not the devils to speak, because they knew him.

Luke 8:2: And certain women, which had been healed of evil spirits and infirmities, Mary called Magdalene, out of whom went seven devils,

Luke 9:42: And as he was yet a coming, the devil threw him down, and tare him. And Jesus rebuked the unclean spirit, and healed the child, and delivered him again to his father.

Acts 5:16: There came also a multitude out of the cities round about unto Jerusalem, bringing sick folks, and them which were vexed with unclean spirits: and they were healed every one.

Acts 8:7: For unclean spirits, crying with loud voice, came out of many that were possessed with them: and many taken with palsies, and that were lame, were healed.

Chapter Ten

Sacramentals, Liturgy, and Devotional Practice

Formal prayer is not "vain repetition"

Psalm 136:1-5: O give thanks unto the LORD; for he is good: for his mercy endureth for ever.

[2] O give thanks unto the God of gods: for his mercy endureth for ever.

[3] O give thanks to the Lord of lords: for his mercy endureth for ever.

[4] To him who alone doeth great wonders: for his mercy endureth for ever.

[5] To him that by wisdom made the heavens: for his mercy endureth for ever.

The same phrase is repeated in twenty-six straight verses, for the entire psalm. Obviously, then, God is not opposed to all repetition whatsoever. Repetition is a device used throughout the Psalms and also in Proverbs and the prophets. For example, in Psalm 29 "voice of the Lord" is repeated seven times in as many verses. "Thou hast" is repeated in six straight verses in Psalm 44:9-14.

Instructions concerning the Mosaic Law in the first five books are extremely repetitious. Elaborate, painstaking instructions for the ark of the covenant (Exod. 25:1-22), the tabernacle (Exod. 25:23-40; chapters 26-27), and the Temple (1 Kings, chapters 6-7) illustrate the highly ritualistic nature of Hebrew worship (see also Lev.23:37-38 and 24:5-8). The four Gospels often repeat each other's sayings. Many other examples could be cited.

Matthew 6:7: But when ye pray, use not vain repetitions, as the heathen do: for they think that they shall be heard for their much speaking. (RSV: "And in praying do not heap up empty phrases as the Gentiles do; for they think that they will be heard for their many words")

Jesus is discussing "empty phrases." The Greek battalogeo here means "to repeat idly," or "meaningless and mechanically repeated phrases." So the Lord is condemning prayers uttered without the proper reverence or respect for God.

Revelation 4:8: And the four beasts had each of them six wings about him; and they were full of eyes within: and they rest not day and night, saying, Holy, holy, holy, Lord God Almighty, which was, and is, and is to come.

God is concerned with the inner dispositions and righteousness of the worshiper, and adherence to His commands (e.g., Isa. 56:6-7; Jer. 17:24-26; Mal. 1:11), not with outward appearance or how often something is repeated (which is contradicted by Psalm 136 and the passage above). This is a common theme in Scripture, and is seen in the following passages:

Isaiah 1:13-17: Bring no more vain oblations; incense is an abomination unto me; the new moons and sabbaths, the calling of assemblies, I cannot away with; it is iniquity, even the solemn meeting. [14] Your new moons and your appointed feasts my soul hateth: they are a trouble unto me; I am weary to bear them. [15] And when ye spread forth your hands, I will hide mine eyes from you: yea, when ye make many prayers, I will not hear: your hands are full of blood. [16] Wash you, make you clean; put away the evil of your doings from before mine eyes; cease to do evil; [17] Learn to do well; seek judgment, relieve the oppressed, judge the fatherless, plead for the widow.

Jeremiah 6:19-20: Hear, O earth: behold, I will bring evil upon this people, even the fruit of their thoughts, because they have not hearkened unto my words, nor to my law, but rejected it.

[20] To what purpose cometh there to me incense from Sheba, and the sweet cane from a far country? your burnt offerings are not acceptable, nor your sacrifices sweet unto me.

Amos 5:11-14, 21-24: Forasmuch therefore as your treading is upon the poor, and ye take from him burdens of wheat: ye have built houses of hewn stone, but ye shall not dwell in them; ye have planted pleasant vineyards, but ye shall not drink wine of them. [12] For I know your manifold transgressions and your mighty sins: they afflict the just, they take a bribe, and they turn aside the poor in the gate from their right. [13] Therefore the prudent shall keep silence in that time; for it is an evil time. [14] Seek good, and not evil, that ye may live: and so the LORD, the God of hosts, shall be with you, as ye have spoken . . . I hate, I despise your feast days, and I will not smell in your solemn assemblies. [22] Though ye offer me burnt offerings and your meat offerings, I will not accept them: neither will I regard the peace offerings of your fat beasts. [23] Take thou away from me the noise of thy songs; for I will not hear the melody of thy viols. [24] But let judgment run down as waters, and righteousness as a mighty stream. (cf. Prov. 15:8; 21:27; Mal. 1:6-14)

Matthew 15:7-9: Ye hypocrites, well did Esaias [Isaiah] prophesy of you, saying, [8] This people draweth nigh unto me with their mouth, and honoureth me with their lips; but their heart is far from me. [9] But in vain they do worship me, teaching for doctrines the commandments of men. (cf. Mark 7:6-7)

Matthew 23:23: Woe unto you, scribes and Pharisees, hypocrites! for ye pay tithe of mint and anise and cummin, and have omitted the weightier matters of the law, judgment, mercy, and faith: these ought ye to have done, and not to leave the other undone.

James 1:26-27: If any man among you seem to be religious, and bridleth not his tongue, but deceiveth his own heart, this man's religion is vain. [27] Pure religion and undefiled before God and the Father is this, To visit the fatherless and widows in their affliction, and to keep himself unspotted from the world.

Ritualistic, formal worship of God is described as taking place in heaven (Rev. 4:8-11; 5:8-14), complete with repetitious prayer (Rev. 4:8 above), and repeated chants or hymns (4:11; 5:9-10).

Holy water

Exodus 23:25: And ye shall serve the LORD your God, and he shall bless thy bread, and thy water; and I will take sickness away from the midst of thee.

Numbers 5:17: And the priest shall take holy water in an earthen vessel; and of the dust that is in the floor of the tabernacle the priest shall take, and put it into the water:

Numbers 19:9, 13-20: And a man that is clean shall gather up the ashes of the heifer, and lay them up without the camp in a clean place, and it shall be kept for the congregation of the children of Israel for a water of separation: it is a purification for sin ... [13] Whosoever toucheth the dead body of any man that is dead, and purifieth not himself, defileth the tabernacle of the LORD; and that soul shall be cut off from Israel: because the water of separation was not sprinkled upon him, he shall be unclean; his uncleanness is yet upon him. [14] This is the law, when a man dieth in a tent: all that come into the tent, and all that is in the tent, shall be unclean seven days. [15] And every open vessel, which hath no covering bound upon it, is unclean. [16] And whosoever toucheth one that is slain with a sword in the open fields, or a dead body, or a bone of a man, or a grave, shall be unclean seven days. [17] And for an unclean person they shall take of the ashes of the burnt heifer of purification for sin, and running water shall be put thereto in a vessel:

[18] And a clean person shall take hyssop, and dip it in the water, and sprinkle it upon the tent, and upon all the vessels, and upon the persons that were there, and upon him that touched a bone, or one slain, or one dead, or a grave: [19] And the clean person shall sprinkle upon the unclean on the third day, and on the seventh day: and on the seventh day he shall purify himself, and wash his clothes, and bathe himself in water, and shall be clean at even.

[20] But the man that shall be unclean, and shall not purify himself, that soul shall be cut off from among the congregation, because he hath defiled the sanctuary of the LORD: the water of separation hath not been sprinkled upon him; he is unclean.

2 Kings 2:19-22: And the men of the city said unto Elisha, Behold, I pray thee, the situation of this city is pleasant, as my lord seeth: but the water is naught, and the ground barren. [20] And he said, Bring me a new cruse, and put salt therein. And they brought it to him. [21] And he went forth unto the spring of the waters, and cast the salt in there, and said, Thus saith the LORD, I have healed these waters; there shall not be from thence any more death or barren land. [22] So the waters were healed unto this day, according to the saying of Elisha which he spake.

2 Kings 5:13-14: And his servants came near, and spake unto him, and said, My father, if the prophet had bid thee do some great thing, wouldest thou not have done it? how much rather then, when he saith to thee, Wash, and be clean? [14] Then went he down, and dipped himself seven times in Jordan, according to the saying of the man of God: and his flesh came again like unto the flesh of a little child, and he was clean.

John 9:6-7: When he had thus spoken, he spat on the ground, and made clay of the spittle, and he anointed the eyes of the blind man with the clay, [7] And said unto him, Go, wash in the pool of Siloam, (which is by interpretation, Sent.) He went his way therefore, and washed, and came seeing.

Water in scripture is utilized for cleansing *(Lev. 14:8-9, 50-52; 15:5-27; 17:15; Num. 8:7; 19:12,18-19; 2 Kings 5:12; Ps. 51:7; Ezek. 16:4; 36:25)* and purifying *(Exod. 29:4; 40:12, 30-32; Lev. 11:32; 16:4, 24, 26, 28; 22:6; Num. 19:7-8; 31:23; Deut. 23:10-11; 1 Kings 18:33-34; John 2:6; Heb. 9:19).*

Candles and incense

Incense or burning sacrifices, as an image of prayer or offering, along with the metaphorical smelling of the offering by God, is a common biblical motif:

Genesis 8:20-21: And Noah builded an altar unto the LORD; and took of every clean beast, and of every clean fowl, and offered burnt offerings on the altar. [21] And the LORD smelled a sweet savour; and the LORD said in his heart, I will not again curse the ground any more for man's sake; for the imagination of man's heart is evil from his youth; neither will I again smite any more every thing living, as I have done.

Leviticus 2:9: And the priest shall take from the meat offering a memorial thereof, and shall burn it upon the altar: it is an offering made by fire, of a sweet savour unto the LORD.

Leviticus 6:15, 21: And he shall take of it his handful, of the flour of the meat offering, and of the oil thereof, and all the frankincense which is upon the meat offering, and shall burn it upon the altar for a sweet savour, even the memorial of it, unto the LORD . . . [21] In a pan it shall be made with oil; and when it is baken, thou shalt bring it in: and the baken pieces of the meat offering shalt thou offer for a sweet savour unto the LORD.

Psalm 141:2: Let my prayer be set forth before thee as incense; and the lifting up of my hands as the evening sacrifice.

Luke 1:9-10: According to the custom of the priest's office, his lot was to burn incense when he went into the temple of the Lord. [10] And the whole multitude of the people were praying without at the time of incense.

Revelation 5:8: And when he had taken the book, the four beasts and four and twenty elders fell down before the Lamb, having every one of them harps, and golden vials full of odours, which are the prayers of saints.

Revelation 8:3-4: And another angel came and stood at the altar, having a golden censer; and there was given unto him much incense, that he should offer it with the prayers of all saints upon the golden altar which was before the throne. [4] And the smoke of the incense, which came with the prayers of the saints, ascended up before God out of the angel's hand.

The Bible even uses the symbolism of fragrance for the gospel, Jesus' redemptive sacrifice on the Cross, and charitable giving:

2 Corinthians 2:14: Now thanks be unto God, which always causeth us to triumph in Christ, and maketh manifest the savour of his knowledge by us in every place. (RSV: "fragrance of the knowledge of him")

Ephesians 5:2: And walk in love, as Christ also hath loved us, and hath given himself for us an offering and a sacrifice to God for a sweet-smelling savour.

Philippians 4:18: But I have all, and abound: I am full, having received of Epaphroditus the things which were sent from you, an odour of a sweet smell, a sacrifice acceptable, wellpleasing to God.

Explicit evidence for candles in the Bible is seen in the form of "lamps." The classic form of this is the menorah, *or seven-branched lampstand, which has often been used as a symbol of Judaism. The King James Bible often uses* candle *or* candlestick *in these passages and others (as did the American Standard Version of 1901). But the Greek* lychnos *and* lychnia *describe (technically) oil lamps, not candles per se (made of wax, as we know them today). These were containers filled with olive oil, with a wick of flax or hemp.*

Exodus 25:31-38: And thou shalt make a candlestick of pure gold: of beaten work shall the candlestick be made: his shaft, and his branches, his bowls, his knops, and his flowers, shall be of the same. [32] And six branches shall come out of the sides of it; three branches of the candlestick out of the one side, and three branches of the candlestick out of the other side: [33] Three bowls made like unto almonds, with a knop and a flower in one branch; and three bowls made like almonds in the other branch, with a knop and a flower: so in the six branches that come out of the candlestick. [34] And in the candlestick shall be four bowls made like unto almonds, with their knops and their flowers.

[35] And there shall be a knop under two branches of the same, and a knop under two branches of the same, and a knop under two branches of the same, according to the six branches that proceed out of the candlestick. [36] Their knops and their branches shall be of the same: all it shall be one beaten work of pure gold. [37] And thou shalt make the seven lamps thereof: and they shall light the lamps thereof, that they may give light over against it. [38] And the tongs thereof, and the snuffdishes thereof, shall be of pure gold. (cf. 26:35; Num. 3:31; 4:9; 8:2-4; 1 Sam. 3:3; 1 Kings 7:49; 1 Chron. 28:15; 2 Chron. 4:7, 2 0-21; Jer. 52:19; Zech. 4:2, 11)

Exodus 27:19-20: All the vessels of the tabernacle in all the service thereof, and all the pins thereof, and all the pins of the court, shall be of brass. [20] And thou shalt command the children of Israel, that they bring thee pure oil olive beaten for the light, to cause the lamp to burn always. (cf. Lev. 24:2-4)

Exodus 30:7-8: And Aaron shall burn thereon sweet incense every morning: when he dresseth the lamps, he shall burn incense upon it. [8] And when Aaron lighteth the lamps at even, he shall burn incense upon it, a perpetual incense before the LORD throughout your generations. (cf. 30:27; 31:8; 35:14; 37:17-23; 39:37; 40:4)

Exodus 40:24-25: And he put the candlestick in the tent of the congregation, over against the table, on the side of the tabernacle southward.

[25] And he lighted the lamps before the LORD; as the LORD commanded Moses.

2 Chronicles 13:11: And they burn unto the LORD every morning and every evening burnt sacrifices and sweet incense: the shewbread also set they in order upon the pure table; and the candlestick of gold with the lamps thereof, to burn every evening: for we keep the charge of the LORD our God; but ye have forsaken him.

2 Chronicles 29:7: Also they have shut up the doors of the porch, and put out the lamps, and have not burned incense nor offered burnt offerings in the holy place unto the God of Israel.

1 Maccabees 4:49-50: They made also new holy vessels, and into the temple they brought the candlestick, and the altar of burnt offerings, and of incense, and the table. [50] And upon the altar they burned incense, and the lamps that were upon the candlestick they lighted, that they might give light in the temple.

2 Maccabees 10:3: And having cleansed the temple they made another altar, and striking stones they took fire out of them, and offered a sacrifice after two years, and set forth incense, and lights, and shewbread.

Hebrews 9:2: For there was a tabernacle made; the first, wherein was the candlestick, and the table, and the shewbread; which is called the sanctuary.

Revelation 1:12-13, 20: And I turned to see the voice that spake with me. And being turned, I saw seven golden candlesticks;
[13] And in the midst of the seven candlesticks one like unto the Son of man, clothed with a garment down to the foot, and girt about the paps with a golden girdle . . . The mystery of the seven stars which thou sawest in my right hand, and the seven golden candlesticks. The seven stars are the angels of the seven churches: and the seven candlesticks which thou sawest are the seven churches.

Revelation 2:1, 5: Unto the angel of the church of Ephesus write; These things saith he that holdeth the seven stars in his right hand, who walketh in the midst of the seven golden candlesticks . . . Remember therefore from whence thou art fallen, and repent, and do the first works; or else I will come unto thee quickly, and will remove thy candlestick out of his place, except thou repent.

Revelation 4:5: And out of the throne proceeded lightnings and thunderings and voices: and there were seven lamps of fire burning before the throne, which are the seven Spirits of God.

Fasting, abstinence, and Lent

Exodus 24:18: And Moses went into the midst of the cloud, and gat him up into the mount: and Moses was in the mount forty days and forty nights.

Exodus 34:28: And he was there with the LORD forty days and forty nights; he did neither eat bread, nor drink water. And he wrote upon the tables the words of the covenant, the ten commandments.

Leviticus 10:9: Do not drink wine nor strong drink, thou, nor thy sons with thee, when ye go into the tabernacle of the congregation, lest ye die: it shall be a statute for ever throughout your generations:

Numbers 6:1-4: And the LORD spake unto Moses, saying, [2] Speak unto the children of Israel, and say unto them, When either man or woman shall separate themselves to vow a vow of a Nazarite, to separate themselves unto the LORD: [3] He shall separate himself from wine and strong drink, and shall drink no vinegar of wine, or vinegar of strong drink, neither shall he drink any liquor of grapes, nor eat moist grapes, or dried. [4] All the days of his separation shall he eat nothing that is made of the vine tree, from the kernels even to the husk.

Deuteronomy 9:9: When I was gone up into the mount to receive the tables of stone, even the tables of the covenant which the LORD made with you, then I abode in the mount forty days and forty nights, I neither did eat bread nor drink water:

Deuteronomy 9:25: Thus I fell down before the LORD forty days and forty nights, as I fell down at the first; because the LORD had said he would destroy you.

Deuteronomy 29:5-6: And I have led you forty years in the wilderness: your clothes are not waxen old upon you, and thy shoe is not waxen old upon thy foot. [6] Ye have not eaten bread, neither have ye drunk wine or strong drink: that ye might know that I am the LORD your God.

Judges 13:3-5: And the angel of the LORD appeared unto the woman, and said unto her, Behold now, thou art barren, and bearest not: but thou shalt conceive, and bear a son. [4] Now therefore beware, I pray thee, and drink not wine nor strong drink, and eat not any unclean thing: [5] For, lo, thou shalt conceive, and bear a son; and no rasor shall come on his head: for the child shall be a Nazarite unto God from the womb: and he shall begin to deliver Israel out of the hand of the Philistines. (cf. 13:14)

1 Samuel 1:15: And Hannah answered and said, No, my lord, I am a woman of a sorrowful spirit: I have drunk neither wine nor strong drink, but have poured out my soul before the LORD.

1 Samuel 31:13: And they took their bones, and buried them under a tree at Jabesh, and fasted seven days.

2 Samuel 1:12: And they mourned, and wept, and fasted until even, for Saul, and for Jonathan his son, and for the people of the LORD, and for the house of Israel; because they were fallen by the sword.

2 Samuel 12:16: David therefore besought God for the child; and David fasted, and went in, and lay all night upon the earth. (cf. 12:21-23)

1 Kings 19:8: And he arose, and did eat and drink, and went in the strength of that meat forty days and forty nights unto Horeb the mount of God.

1 Chronicles 10:12: They arose, all the valiant men, and took away the body of Saul, and the bodies of his sons, and brought them to Jabesh, and buried their bones under the oak in Jabesh, and fasted seven days.

2 Chronicles 20:3: And Jehoshaphat feared, and set himself to seek the LORD, and proclaimed a fast throughout all Judah.

Ezra 8:21-23: Then I proclaimed a fast there, at the river of Ahava, that we might afflict ourselves before our God, to seek of him a right way for us, and for our little ones, and for all our substance. [22] For I was ashamed to require of the king a band of soldiers and horsemen to help us against the enemy in the way: because we had spoken unto the king, saying, The hand of our God is upon all them for good that seek him; but his power and his wrath is against all them that forsake him. [23] So we fasted and besought our God for this: and he was intreated of us. (cf. 9:5)

Nehemiah 1:4: And it came to pass, when I heard these words, that I sat down and wept, and mourned certain days, and fasted, and prayed before the God of heaven,

Nehemiah 9:1: Now in the twenty and fourth day of this month the children of Israel were assembled with fasting, and with sackclothes, and earth upon them.

Esther 4:3: And in every province, whithersoever the king's commandment and his decree came, there was great mourning among the Jews, and fasting, and weeping, and wailing; and many lay in sackcloth and ashes.

Esther 4:16: Go, gather together all the Jews that are present in Shushan, and fast ye for me, and neither eat nor drink three days, night or day: I also and my maidens will fast likewise; and so will I go in unto the king, which is not according to the law: and if I perish, I perish.

Esther 9:31: To confirm these days of Purim in their times appointed, according as Mordecai the Jew and Esther the queen had enjoined them, and as they had decreed for themselves and for their seed, the matters of the fastings and their cry.

Psalm 35:13: But as for me, when they were sick, my clothing was sackcloth: I humbled my soul with fasting; and my prayer returned into mine own bosom.

Psalm 69:10: . . . I wept, and chastened my soul with fasting . . .

Psalm 109:24: My knees are weak through fasting; and my flesh faileth of fatness.

Jeremiah 36:9: And it came to pass in the fifth year of Jehoiakim the son of Josiah king of Judah, in the ninth month, that they proclaimed a fast before the LORD to all the people in Jerusalem, and to all the people that came from the cities of Judah unto Jerusalem.

Ezekiel 4:4-12: Lie thou also upon thy left side, and lay the iniquity of the house of Israel upon it: according to the number of the days that thou shalt lie upon it thou shalt bear their iniquity.

[5] For I have laid upon thee the years of their iniquity, according to the number of the days, three hundred and ninety days: so shalt thou bear the iniquity of the house of Israel. [6] And when thou hast accomplished them, lie again on thy right side, and thou shalt bear the iniquity of the house of Judah forty days: I have appointed thee each day for a year. [7] Therefore thou shalt set thy face toward the siege of Jerusalem, and thine arm shall be uncovered, and thou shalt prophesy against it. [8] And, behold, I will lay bands upon thee, and thou shalt not turn thee from one side to another, till thou hast ended the days of thy siege.

[9] Take thou also unto thee wheat, and barley, and beans, and lentiles, and millet, and fitches, and put them in one vessel, and make thee bread thereof, according to the number of the days that thou shalt lie upon thy side, three hundred and ninety days shalt thou eat thereof. [10] And thy meat which thou shalt eat shall be by weight, twenty shekels a day: from

time to time shalt thou eat it. [11] Thou shalt drink also water by measure, the sixth part of an hin: from time to time shalt thou drink. [12] And thou shalt eat it as barley cakes, and thou shalt bake it with dung that cometh out of man, in their sight.

Daniel 6:18: Then the king went to his palace, and spent the night fasting; no diversions were brought to him, and sleep fled from him.

Daniel 9:3: And I set my face unto the Lord God, to seek by prayer and supplication, with fasting, and sackcloth, and ashes:

Joel 1:14: Sanctify ye a fast, call a solemn assembly . . . (cf. 2:15)

Joel 2:12: Therefore also now, saith the LORD, turn ye even to me with all your heart, and with fasting, and with weeping, and with mourning:

Jonah 3:5: So the people of Nineveh believed God, and proclaimed a fast, and put on sackcloth, from the greatest of them even to the least of them.

Zechariah 8:19: Thus saith the LORD of hosts; The fast of the fourth month, and the fast of the fifth, and the fast of the seventh, and the fast of the tenth, shall be to the house of Judah joy and gladness, and cheerful feasts; therefore love the truth and peace. (cf. 7:3, 5)

Tobit 12:8: Prayer is good with fasting and alms and righteousness. A little with righteousness is better than much with unrighteousness. It is better to give alms than to lay up gold:

Judith 4:9, 13: Then every man of Israel cried to God with great fervency, and with great vehemency did they humble their souls . . . So God heard their prayers, and looked upon their afflictions: for the people fasted many days in all Judea and Jerusalem before the sanctuary of the Lord Almighty.

Judith 8:6: And she fasted all the days of her widowhood, save the eves of the sabbaths, and the sabbaths, and the eves of the new moons, and the new moons and the feasts and solemn days of the house of Israel.

Sirach 34:26: So is it with a man that fasteth for his sins, and goeth again, and doeth the same: who will hear his prayer? or what doth his humbling profit him?

2 Maccabees 13:12: So when they had all done this together, and besought the merciful Lord with weeping and fasting, and lying flat upon the ground three days long, Judas, having exhorted them, commanded they should be in a readiness. (cf. 1 Macc. 3:47; Bar. 1:5)

Matthew 4:2: And when he had fasted forty days and forty nights, he was afterward an hungred.

Matthew 6:16-18: Moreover when ye fast, be not, as the hypocrites, of a sad countenance: for they disfigure their faces, that they may appear unto men to fast. Verily I say unto you, They have their reward. [17] But thou, when thou fastest, anoint thine head, and wash thy face; [18] That thou appear not unto men to fast, but unto thy Father which is in secret: and thy Father, which seeth in secret, shall reward thee openly.

Matthew 9:14-15: Then came to him the disciples of John, saying, Why do we and the Pharisees fast oft, but thy disciples fast not? [15] And Jesus said unto them, Can the children of the bridechamber mourn, as long as the bridegroom is with them? but the days will come, when the bridegroom shall be taken from them, and then shall they fast. (cf. Mark 2:18-20; Luke 5:33-35; 18:12)

Luke 2:37: And she was a widow of about fourscore and four years, which departed not from the temple, but served God with fastings and prayers night and day.

Luke 7:33: For John the Baptist came neither eating bread nor drinking wine; and ye say, He hath a devil. (cf. Matt. 11:18; Luke 1:15)

Acts 13:2-3: As they ministered to the Lord, and fasted, the Holy Ghost said, Separate me Barnabas and Saul for the work whereunto I have called them. [3] And when they had fasted and prayed, and laid their hands on them, they sent them away.

Acts 14:23: And when they had ordained them elders in every church, and had prayed with fasting, they commended them to the Lord, on whom they believed.

Acts 15:20: But that we write unto them, that they abstain from pollutions of idols, and from fornication, and from things strangled, and from blood.

Acts 15:29: That ye abstain from meats offered to idols, and from blood, and from things strangled, and from fornication: from which if ye keep yourselves, ye shall do well. Fare ye well. (cf. 21:25)

Romans 14:3: Let not him that eateth despise him that eateth not; and let not him which eateth not judge him that eateth: for God hath received him.

Romans 14:6: He that regardeth the day, regardeth it unto the Lord; and he that regardeth not the day, to the Lord he doth not regard it. He that eateth, eateth to the Lord, for he giveth God thanks; and he that eateth not, to the Lord he eateth not, and giveth God thanks.

Romans 14:15, 21: But if thy brother be grieved with thy meat, now walkest thou not charitably. Destroy not him with thy meat, for whom Christ died . . . It is good neither to eat flesh, nor to drink wine, nor any thing whereby thy brother stumbleth, or is offended, or is made weak.

1 Corinthians 8:13: Wherefore, if meat make my brother to offend, I will eat no flesh while the world standeth, lest I make my brother to offend. (cf. 2 Cor. 6:4-5; 11:27)

The forty days of Lenten observance have several forty-day parallels in Scripture (all listed above): Moses' fasts on the holy mountain (Exod. 24:18; 34:28; Deut. 9:9) and his intercession for Israel (Deut. 9:25), Elijah's journey to Mt. Horeb (1 Kings 19:8), Ezekiel's lying on one side (Ezek. 4:6), and Christ's fast in the wilderness (Matt. 4:2).

We use ashes to show our penitence

Genesis 2:7: And the LORD God formed man of the dust of the ground, and breathed into his nostrils the breath of life; and man became a living soul.

Genesis 3:19: In the sweat of thy face shalt thou eat bread, till thou return unto the ground; for out of it wast thou taken: for dust thou art, and unto dust shalt thou return.

Genesis 18:27: And Abraham answered and said, Behold now, I have taken upon me to speak unto the Lord, which am but dust and ashes:

2 Samuel 13:19: And Tamar put ashes on her head, and rent her garment of divers colours that was on her, and laid her hand on her head, and went on crying.

Nehemiah 9:1: Now in the twenty and fourth day of this month the children of Israel were assembled with fasting, and with sackclothes, and earth upon them.

Esther 4:1-3: When Mordecai perceived all that was done, Mordecai rent his clothes, and put on sackcloth with ashes, and went out into the midst of the city, and cried with a loud and a bitter cry; [2] And came even before the king's gate: for none might enter into the king's gate clothed with sackcloth. [3] And in every province, whithersoever the king's commandment and his decree came, there was great mourning among the Jews, and fasting, and weeping, and wailing; and many lay in sackcloth and ashes.

Job 2:8: And he took him a potsherd to scrape himself withal; and he sat down among the ashes.

Job 34:15: All flesh shall perish together, and man shall turn again unto dust.

Job 42:6: Wherefore I abhor myself, and repent in dust and ashes.

Psalm 90:3: Thou turnest man to destruction; and sayest, Return, ye children of men. (RSV: "Thou turnest man back to the dust")

Isaiah 58:5: Is it such a fast that I have chosen? a day for a man to afflict his soul? is it to bow down his head as a bulrush, and to spread sackcloth and ashes under him? wilt thou call this a fast, and an acceptable day to the LORD?

Jeremiah 6:26: O daughter of my people, gird thee with sackcloth, and wallow thyself in ashes: make thee mourning, as for an only son, most bitter lamentation: for the spoiler shall suddenly come upon us.

Jeremiah 25:34: Howl, ye shepherds, and cry; and wallow yourselves in the ashes . . .

Ezekiel 27:30: And shall cause their voice to be heard against thee, and shall cry bitterly, and shall cast up dust upon their heads, they shall wallow themselves in the ashes:

Daniel 9:3: And I set my face unto the Lord God, to seek by prayer and supplication, with fasting, and sackcloth, and ashes:

Jonah 3:6: For word came unto the king of Nineveh, and he arose from his throne, and he laid his robe from him, and covered him with sackcloth, and sat in ashes.

Judith 4:11, 15: Thus every man and women, and the little children, and the inhabitants of Jerusalem, fell before the temple, and cast ashes upon their heads, and spread out their sackcloth before the face of the

Lord: also they put sackcloth about the altar . . . And had ashes on their mitres, and cried unto the Lord with all their power, that he would look upon all the house of Israel graciously.

Sirach 17:32: He vieweth the power of the height of heaven; and all men are but earth and ashes. (RSV: "dust and ashes")

Sirach 40:3: From him that sitteth on a throne of glory, unto him that is humbled in earth and ashes; (RSV: "dust and ashes")

1 Maccabees 3:47: Then they fasted that day, and put on sackcloth, and cast ashes upon their heads, and rent their clothes, (cf. 4:39)

Matthew 11:21: Woe unto thee, Chorazin! woe unto thee, Bethsaida! for if the mighty works, which were done in you, had been done in Tyre and Sidon, they would have repented long ago in sackcloth and ashes. (cf. Luke 10:13)

1 Corinthians 15:47: The first man is of the earth, earthy: the second man is the Lord from heaven. (RSV: "The first man was from the earth, a man of dust": cf. 15:48-49)

Revelation 18:19: And they cast dust on their heads, and cried, weeping and wailing . . .

We must examine our consciences

1 Corinthians 9:24-27: Know ye not that they which run in a race run all, but one receiveth the prize? So run, that ye may obtain. [25] And every man that striveth for the mastery is temperate in all things. Now they do it to obtain a corruptible crown; but we an incorruptible. [26] I therefore so run, not as uncertainly; so fight I, not as one that beateth the air: [27] But I keep under my body, and bring it into subjection: lest that by any means, when I have preached to others, I myself should be a castaway.

1 Corinthians 11:28: But let a man examine himself, and so let him eat of that bread, and drink of that cup.

2 Corinthians 13:5: Examine yourselves, whether ye be in the faith; prove your own selves. Know ye not your own selves, how that Jesus Christ is in you, except ye be reprobates?

This sort of self-examination (usually prior to confession) is sometimes critiqued and scorned as "uncertainty of salvation," as if it were a bondage or something undesirable, or altogether lacking in the hope, joy, and peace we have in Christ. It's not that at all. St. Paul clearly had a robust confidence in God's mercy and of the moral assurance of salvation. But he was also very aware of human sin and self-delusion.

The Greek word for examine in 1 Corinthians 11:28 and prove in 2 Corinthians 13:5 is dokimazo. In KJV it is translated variously as "examine," "discern," "prove," "try," and "approve." Examine in 2 Corinthians 13:5 is a different word: pirazo, usually translated as "tempt" or "tempted." Dokimazo appears elsewhere in the New Testament in similar fashion:

Romans 12:2: And be not conformed to this world: but be ye transformed by the renewing of your mind, that ye may prove what is that good, and acceptable, and perfect, will of God.

2 Corinthians 8:7-8: Therefore, as ye abound in every thing, in faith, and utterance, and knowledge, and in all diligence, and in your love to us, see that ye abound in this grace also. [8] I speak not by commandment, but by occasion of the forwardness of others, and to prove the sincerity of your love.

2 Corinthians 8:22: And we have sent with them our brother, whom we have oftentimes proved diligent in many things, but now much more diligent, upon the great confidence which I have in you.

Galatians 6:4: But let every man prove his own work, and then shall he have rejoicing in himself alone, and not in another.

1 Thessalonians 5:21: Prove all things; hold fast that which is good.

1 Timothy 3:10: And let these also first be proved; then let them use the office of a deacon, being found blameless.

Almsgiving is more than mere tithing

Luke 3:11: He answereth and saith unto them, He that hath two coats, let him impart to him that hath none; and he that hath meat, let him do likewise.

Luke 19:8-9: And Zacchaeus stood, and said unto the Lord; Behold, Lord, the half of my goods I give to the poor; and if I have taken any thing from any man by false accusation, I restore him fourfold. [9] And Jesus said unto him, This day is salvation come to this house, forsomuch as he also is a son of Abraham.

Acts 2:44-45: And all that believed were together, and had all things common; [45] And sold their possessions and goods, and parted them to all men, as every man had need.

Acts 4:34-37: Neither was there any among them that lacked: for as many as were possessors of lands or houses sold them, and brought the prices of the things that were sold, [35] And laid them down at the apostles' feet: and distribution was made unto every man according as he had need. [36] And Joses, who by the apostles was surnamed Barnabas, (which is, being interpreted, The son of consolation,) a Levite, and of the country of Cyprus,

[37] Having land, sold it, and brought the money, and laid it at the apostles' feet.

Acts 10:2: A devout man, and one that feared God with all his house, which gave much alms to the people, and prayed to God alway.

Acts 11:29: Then the disciples, every man according to his ability, determined to send relief unto the brethren which dwelt in Judaea:

Romans 12:8: Or he that exhorteth, on exhortation: he that giveth, let him do it with simplicity; he that ruleth, with diligence; he that sheweth mercy, with cheerfulness.

1 Corinthians 16:1-2: Now concerning the collection for the saints, as I have given order to the churches of Galatia, even so do ye. [2] Upon the first day of the week let every one of you lay by him in store, as God hath prospered him, that there be no gatherings when I come.

2 Corinthians 8:3-14: For to their power, I bear record, yea, and beyond their power they were willing of themselves; [4] Praying us with much intreaty that we would receive the gift, and take upon us the fellowship of the ministering to the saints. [5] And this they did, not as we hoped, but first gave their own selves to the Lord, and unto us by the will of God. [6] Insomuch that we desired Titus, that as he had begun, so he would also finish in you the same grace also. [7] Therefore, as ye abound in every thing, in faith, and utterance, and knowledge, and in all diligence, and in your love to us, see that ye abound in this grace also. [8] I speak not by commandment, but by occasion of the forwardness of others, and to prove the sincerity of your love. [9] For ye know the grace of our Lord Jesus Christ, that, though he was rich, yet for your sakes he became poor, that ye through his poverty might be rich. [10] And herein I give my advice: for this is expedient for you, who have begun before, not only to do, but also to be forward a year ago. [11] Now therefore perform the doing of it; that as there was a readiness to will, so there may be a performance also out of that which ye have. [12] For if there be first a willing mind, it is accepted according to that a man hath, and not according to that he hath not. [13] For I mean not that other men be eased, and ye burdened: [14] But by an equality, that now at this time your abundance may be a supply for their want, that their abundance also may be a supply for your want: that there may be equality:

2 Corinthians 9:6-8: But this I say, He which soweth sparingly shall reap also sparingly; and he which soweth bountifully shall reap also bountifully. [7] Every man according as he purposeth in his heart, so let him give; not grudgingly, or of necessity: for God loveth a cheerful giver. [8] And God is able to make all grace abound toward you; that ye, always having all sufficiency in all things, may abound to every good work:

1 Timothy 6:17-18: Charge them that are rich in this world, that they be not highminded, nor trust in uncertain riches, but in the living God, who giveth us richly all things to enjoy; [18] That they do good, that they be rich in good works, ready to distribute, willing to communicate;

Hebrews 13:16: But to do good and to communicate forget not: for with such sacrifices God is well pleased.

We show reverence by genuflecting and kneeling in God's presence

Genesis 18:1-2: And the LORD appeared unto him in the plains of Mamre: and he sat in the tent door in the heat of the day; [2] And he lift up his eyes and looked, and, lo, three men stood by him: and when he saw them, he ran to meet them from the tent door, and bowed himself toward the ground,

Genesis 24:52: And it came to pass, that, when Abraham's servant heard their words, he worshipped the LORD, bowing himself to the earth.

1 Kings 8:54: And it was so, that when Solomon had made an end of praying all this prayer and supplication unto the LORD, he arose from before the altar of the LORD, from kneeling on his knees with his hands spread up to heaven.

2 Chronicles 6:13: For Solomon had made a brasen scaffold, of five cubits long, and five cubits broad, and three cubits high, and had set it in the midst of the court: and upon it he stood, and kneeled down upon his knees before all the congregation of Israel, and spread forth his hands toward heaven,

2 Chronicles 7:3: And when all the children of Israel saw how the fire came down, and the glory of the LORD upon the house, they bowed themselves with their faces to the ground upon the pavement, and worshipped, and praised the LORD, saying, For he is good; for his mercy endureth for ever.

2 Chronicles 20:18: And Jehoshaphat bowed his head with his face to the ground: and all Judah and the inhabitants of Jerusalem fell before the LORD, worshipping the LORD.

Ezra 9:5: And at the evening sacrifice I arose up from my heaviness; and having rent my garment and my mantle, I fell upon my knees, and spread out my hands unto the LORD my God.

Nehemiah 8:6: And Ezra blessed the LORD, the great God. And all the people answered, Amen, Amen, with lifting up their hands: and they bowed their heads, and worshipped the LORD with their faces to the ground.

Psalm 95:6: O come, let us worship and bow down: let us kneel before the LORD our maker.

Ezekiel 11:13: And it came to pass, when I prophesied, that Pelatiah the son of Benaiah died. Then fell I down upon my face, and cried with a loud voice, and said, Ah Lord GOD! wilt thou make a full end of the remnant of Israel?

Daniel 6:10: Now when Daniel knew that the writing was signed, he went into his house; and his windows being open in his chamber toward Jerusalem, he kneeled upon his knees three times a day, and prayed, and gave thanks before his God, as he did aforetime.

Judith 13:17: Then all the people were wonderfully astonished, and bowed themselves and worshipped God, and said with one accord, Blessed be thou, O our God, which hast this day brought to nought the enemies of thy people.

Sirach 50:17: Then all the people together hasted, and fell down to the earth upon their faces to worship their Lord God Almighty, the most High.

2 Maccabees 3:15: But the priests, prostrating themselves before the altar in their priests' vestments, called unto heaven upon him that made a law concerning things given to he kept, that they should safely be preserved for such as had committed them to be kept.

2 Maccabees 10:4: When that was done, they fell flat down, and besought the Lord that they might come no more into such troubles; but if they sinned any more against him, that he himself would chasten them with mercy, and that they might not be delivered unto the blasphemous and barbarous nations.

Matthew 2:11: And when they were come into the house, they saw the young child with Mary his mother, and fell down, and worshipped him: and when they had opened their treasures, they presented unto him gifts; gold, and frankincense, and myrrh.

Matthew 8:2: And, behold, there came a leper and worshipped him, saying, Lord, if thou wilt, thou canst make me clean. (RSV: "knelt before him")

Matthew 9:18: While he spake these things unto them, behold, there came a certain ruler, and worshipped him, saying, My daughter is even now dead: but come and lay thy hand upon her, and she shall live. (RSV: "a ruler came in and knelt before him")

Matthew 15:25: Then came she and worshipped him, saying, Lord, help me. (RSV: "knelt before him")

Matthew 28:9: And as they went to tell his disciples, behold, Jesus met them, saying, All hail. And they came and held him by the feet, and worshipped him.

Mark 1:40: And there came a leper to him, beseeching him, and kneeling down to him, and saying unto him, If thou wilt, thou canst make me clean.

Romans 14:11: For it is written, As I live, saith the Lord, every knee shall bow to me, and every tongue shall confess to God.

Ephesians 3:14: For this cause I bow my knees unto the Father of our Lord Jesus Christ,

Philippians 2:10: That at the name of Jesus every knee should bow, of things in heaven, and things in earth, and things under the earth;

Revelation 1:17: And when I saw him, I fell at his feet as dead. And he laid his right hand upon me, saying unto me, Fear not; I am the first and the last:

Revelation 5:14: And the four beasts said, Amen. And the four and twenty elders fell down and worshipped him that liveth for ever and ever.

Revelation 7:11: And all the angels stood round about the throne, and about the elders and the four beasts, and fell before the throne on their faces, and worshipped God,

Revelation 11:16: And the four and twenty elders, which sat before God on their seats, fell upon their faces, and worshipped God,

Revelation 19:4: And the four and twenty elders and the four beasts fell down and worshipped God that sat on the throne, saying, Amen; Alleluia.

Priests may impart blessings

Exodus 39:43: And Moses did look upon all the work, and, behold, they have done it as the LORD had commanded, even so had they done it: and Moses blessed them. (cf. Gen. 27:28-30; 28:1-6; 31:55; 47:7, 10; 48:14-20; 49:26, 28; Num. 24:10; 2 Sam. 19:39)

Leviticus 9:22-23: And Aaron lifted up his hand toward the people, and blessed them, and came down from offering of the sin offering, and the burnt offering, and peace offerings. [23] And Moses and Aaron went into the tabernacle of the congregation, and came out, and blessed the people: and the glory of the LORD appeared unto all the people.

Deuteronomy 33:1: And this is the blessing, wherewith Moses the man of God blessed the children of Israel before his death. (cf. 33:13, 20, 24)

Joshua 14:13: And Joshua blessed him, and gave unto Caleb the son of Jephunneh Hebron for an inheritance.

Joshua 22:6-7: So Joshua blessed them, and sent them away: and they went unto their tents. [7] Now to the one half of the tribe of Manasseh Moses had given possession in Bashan: but unto the other half thereof gave Joshua among their brethren on this side Jordan westward. And when Joshua sent them away also unto their tents, then he blessed them,

1 Kings 8:14: And the king turned his face about, and blessed all the congregation of Israel: (and all the congregation of Israel stood;) (cf. 8:55)

1 Chronicles 16:2: And when David had made an end of offering the burnt offerings and the peace offerings, he blessed the people in the name of the LORD.

2 Chronicles 6:3: And the king turned his face, and blessed the whole congregation of Israel: and all the congregation of Israel stood.

2 Chronicles 30:27: Then the priests the Levites arose and blessed the people: and their voice was heard, and their prayer came up to his holy dwelling place, even unto heaven.

Sirach 3:9: For the blessing of the father establisheth the houses of children; but the curse of the mother rooteth out foundations.

Sirach 36:17: O Lord, hear the prayer of thy servants, according to the blessing of Aaron over thy people, that all they which dwell upon the earth may know that thou art the Lord, the eternal God.

Sirach 50:19-21: And the people besought the Lord, the most High, by prayer before him that is merciful, till the solemnity of the Lord was ended, and they had finished his service. [20] Then he went down, and lifted up his hands over the whole congregation of the children of Israel, to give the blessing of the Lord with his lips, and to rejoice in his name. [21] And they bowed themselves down to worship the second time, that they might receive a blessing from the most High.

Luke 24:50-51: And he led them out as far as to Bethany, and he lifted up his hands, and blessed them. [51] And it came to pass, while he blessed them, he was parted from them, and carried up into heaven.

Hebrews 7:1: For this Melchisedec, king of Salem, priest of the most high God, who met Abraham returning from the slaughter of the kings, and blessed him;

Hebrews 11:20-21: By faith Isaac blessed Jacob and Esau concerning things to come. [21] By faith Jacob, when he was a dying, blessed both the sons of Joseph; and worshipped, leaning upon the top of his staff.

Hebrews 12:17: For ye know how that afterward, when he would have inherited the blessing, he was rejected: for he found no place of repentance, though he sought it carefully with tears.

Relics can be channels of grace and healing

Exodus 29:37: Seven days thou shalt make an atonement for the altar, and sanctify it; and it shall be an altar most holy: whatsoever toucheth the altar shall be holy.

Exodus 30:28-29: And the altar of burnt offering with all his vessels, and the laver and his foot. [29] And thou shalt sanctify them, that they may be most holy: whatsoever toucheth them shall be holy.

Leviticus 6:27: Whatsoever shall touch the flesh thereof shall be holy . . . (cf. 6:18)

2 Kings 2:11-14: And it came to pass, as they still went on, and talked, that, behold, there appeared a chariot of fire, and horses of fire, and parted them both asunder; and Elijah went up by a whirlwind into heaven. [12] And Elisha saw it, and he cried, My father, my father, the chariot of Israel, and the horsemen thereof. And he saw him no more: and he took hold of his own clothes, and rent them in two pieces. [13] He took up also the mantle of Elijah that fell from him, and went back, and stood by the bank of Jordan; [14] And he took the mantle of Elijah that fell from him, and smote the waters, and said, Where is the LORD God of Elijah? and when he also had smitten the waters, they parted hither and thither: and Elisha went over.

Elijah's mantle is an example of a "second-class" relic: items that have power because they were connected with a holy person.

2 Kings 13:20-21: And Elisha died, and they buried him. And the bands of the Moabites invaded the land at the coming in of the year. [21] And it came to pass, as they were burying a man, that, behold, they spied a band of men; and they cast the man into the sepulchre of Elisha: and when the man was let down, and touched the bones of Elisha, he revived, and stood up on his feet.

The bones or relics of Elisha had so much supernatural power or "grace" in them that they could even cause a man to be raised from the dead. His bones were a "first-class" relic: from the person himself or herself.

Mark 5:25-30: And a certain woman, which had an issue of blood twelve years, [26] And had suffered many things of many physicians, and had spent all that she had, and was nothing bettered, but rather grew worse, [27] When she had heard of Jesus, came in the press behind, and touched his garment. [28] For she said, If I may touch but his clothes, I shall be whole.

[29] And straightway the fountain of her blood was dried up; and she felt in her body that she was healed of that plague. [30] And Jesus, immediately knowing in himself that virtue had gone out of him, turned him about in the press, and said, Who touched my clothes?

Luke 8:43-48: And a woman having an issue of blood twelve years, which had spent all her living upon physicians, neither could be healed of any, [44] Came behind him, and touched the border of his garment: and immediately her issue of blood stanched. [45] And Jesus said, Who touched me? When all denied, Peter and they that were with him said, Master, the multitude throng thee and press thee, and sayest thou, Who touched me? [46] And Jesus said, Somebody hath touched me: for I perceive that virtue is gone out of me. [47] And when the woman saw that she was not hid, she came trembling, and falling down before him, she declared unto him before all the people for what cause she had touched him and how she was healed immediately. [48] And he said unto her, Daughter, be of good comfort: thy faith hath made thee whole; go in peace.

Jesus did say that the woman's faith made her well, yet the instrumentality of a physical object in contact with Jesus was also a factor: as indicated precisely by its effect of causing "power" to go "forth from him." God used the physical object for spiritual (and supernatural physical) purposes: a healing. We see it again, when Jesus heals the blind man:

John 9:6-7: When he had thus spoken, he spat on the ground, and made clay of the spittle, and he anointed the eyes of the blind man with the clay, [7] And said unto him, Go, wash in the pool of Siloam, (which is by interpretation, Sent.) He went his way therefore, and washed, and came seeing.

Jesus could have simply declared him healed, with no material object used. But, interestingly enough, Jesus didn't do that. He used a bodily fluid (his own), and also clay, or dirt, and then the water of the pool, and rubbed the man's eyes, to effect the miracle (two liquids, solid matter, and physical anointing action of fingers). The Bible thus teaches that physical things related to a holy person in some fashion can be channels to bring about miracles. This is exactly how Catholics view relics. There are several other examples of the same thing, with touch or matter of some sort being utilized to heal:

Matthew 8:14-15: And when Jesus was come into Peter's house, he saw his wife's mother laid, and sick of a fever. [15] And he touched her hand, and the fever left her: and she arose, and ministered unto them.

Matthew 9:28-30: And when he was come into the house, the blind men came to him: and Jesus saith unto them, Believe ye that I am able to do this? They said unto him, Yea, Lord. [29] Then touched he their eyes, saying, According to your faith be it unto you. [30] And their eyes were opened; and Jesus straitly charged them, saying, See that no man know it.

Mark 1:30-31: But Simon's wife's mother lay sick of a fever, and anon they tell him of her. [31] And he came and took her by the hand, and lifted her up; and immediately the fever left her, and she ministered unto them.

Mark 7:33-35: And he took him aside from the multitude, and put his fingers into his ears, and he spit, and touched his tongue; [34] And looking up to heaven, he sighed, and saith unto him, Ephphatha, that is, Be opened. [35] And straightway his ears were opened, and the string of his tongue was loosed, and he spake plain.

Mark 8:22-25: And he cometh to Bethsaida; and they bring a blind man unto him, and besought him to touch him. [23] And he took the blind man by the hand, and led him out of the town; and when he had spit on his eyes, and put his hands upon him, he asked him if he saw ought. [24] And he looked up, and said, I see men as trees, walking. [25] After that he put his hands again upon his eyes, and made him look up: and he was restored, and saw every man clearly.

Mark 9:26-27: And the spirit cried, and rent him sore, and came out of him: and he was as one dead; insomuch that many said, He is dead. [27] But Jesus took him by the hand, and lifted him up; and he arose.

Luke 13:12-13: And when Jesus saw her, he called her to him, and said unto her, Woman, thou art loosed from thine infirmity. [13] And he laid his hands on her: and immediately she was made straight, and glorified God.

Luke 14:2-4: And, behold, there was a certain man before him which had the dropsy. [3] And Jesus answering spake unto the lawyers and Pharisees, saying, Is it lawful to heal on the sabbath day? [4] And they held their peace. And he took him, and healed him, and let him go;

See also the examples of lepers healed by Jesus' touch (Matt. 8:2; Mark 1:40-41; Luke 5:13), and touch used to raise the dead (Matt. 9:24-25; Mark 5:40-42; 8:53-55), and further similar examples in chapter 9. One of these miracles is particularly interesting:

Luke 7:13-15: And when the Lord saw her, he had compassion on her, and said unto her, Weep not. [14] And he came and touched the bier: and they that bare him stood still. And he said, Young man, I say unto thee, Arise. [15] And he that was dead sat up, and began to speak. And he delivered him to his mother.

Note that Jesus merely touched the bier *that the coffin was being carried on, not even the* person himself. *Luke thought that this was important enough to mention. The implication is that grace was indirectly channeled by touch through the bier (an inanimate object) to the dead man, for the purpose of raising him.*

Acts 5:15-16: Insomuch that they brought forth the sick into the streets, and laid them on beds and couches, that at the least the shadow of Peter passing by might overshadow some of them. [16] There came also a multitude out of the cities round about unto Jerusalem, bringing sick folks, and them which were vexed with unclean spirits: and they were healed every one.

St. Peter's shadow is another example of a "second-class" relic. Jesus' garments and saliva are also in this category.

Acts 19:11-12: And God wrought special miracles by the hands of Paul: [12] So that from his body were brought unto the sick handkerchiefs or aprons, and the diseases departed from them, and the evil spirits went out of them. (cf. Matt. 9:20-22)

This is a third-class relic: a thing that has merely touched a holy person or a first-class relic (St. Paul's handkerchiefs and aprons).

Physical objects can aid us in worship

For background on the prohibition of graven images, see Exodus 2:3-5; Leviticus 26:1; Deuteronomy 5:8-9; Micah 5:13. The objects listed below include the burning bush, pillars of cloud and fire, Mt. Sinai, smoke, fire, the ark of the covenant and carved cherubim on top of it, the Temple, carved cherubim on the Temple walls, altars in the Temple, Jerusalem, the Holy Land, Mt. Carmel, sacred priestly clothes, the sanctuary of the Temple, bodies of Christians, the gate to Jerusalem, God's throne and the altar in heaven, and crowns.

Exodus 3:2-5: And the angel of the LORD appeared unto him in a flame of fire out of the midst of a bush: and he looked, and, behold, the bush burned with fire, and the bush was not consumed. [3] And Moses said, I will now turn aside, and see this great sight, why the bush is not burnt. [4] And when the LORD saw that he turned aside to see, God called unto him out of the midst of the bush, and said, Moses, Moses. And he said, Here am I. [5] And he said, Draw not nigh hither: put off thy shoes from off thy feet, for the place whereon thou standest is holy ground. (cf. Acts 7:30)

Exodus 13:21-22: And the LORD went before them by day in a pillar of a cloud, to lead them the way; and by night in a pillar of fire, to give them light; to go by day and night: [22] He took not away the pillar of the cloud by day, nor the pillar of fire by night, from before the people. (cf. 14:24; Num. 14:14; Neh. 9:12, 19)

Exodus 19:17-20: And Moses brought forth the people out of the camp to meet with God; and they stood at the nether part of the mount. [18] And mount Sinai was altogether on a smoke, because the LORD descended upon it in fire: and the smoke thereof ascended as the smoke of a furnace, and the whole mount quaked greatly. [19] And when the voice of the trumpet sounded long, and waxed louder and louder, Moses spake, and God answered him by a voice. [20] And the LORD came down upon mount Sinai, on the top of the mount: and the LORD called Moses up to the top of the mount; and Moses went up.

Exodus 25:22: And there I will meet with thee, and I will commune with thee from above the mercy seat, from between the two cherubims which are upon the ark of the testimony, of all things which I will give thee in commandment unto the children of Israel.

Exodus 30:6: And thou shalt put it before the vail that is by the ark of the testimony, before the mercy seat that is over the testimony, where I will meet with thee. (cf. Lev. 16:2)

Numbers 7:89: And when Moses was gone into the tabernacle of the congregation to speak with him, then he heard the voice of one speaking unto him from off the mercy seat that was upon the ark of testimony, from between the two cherubims: and he spake unto him. (cf. 1 Sam. 4:4; 2 Sam. 6:2; 2 Kings 19:15; 1 Chron. 13:6; Ps. 80:1; 99:1; Isa. 37:16; Ezek. 10:4; Heb. 9:5)

Deuteronomy 10:8: At that time the LORD separated the tribe of Levi, to bear the ark of the covenant of the LORD, to stand before the LORD to minister unto him, and to bless in his name, unto this day. (cf. 1 Kings 3:15; 8:5; 2 Chron. 5:6)

Joshua 7:6-8: And Joshua rent his clothes, and fell to the earth upon his face before the ark of the LORD until the eventide, he and the elders of Israel, and put dust upon their heads. [7] And Joshua said, Alas, O Lord

GOD, wherefore hast thou at all brought this people over Jordan, to deliver us into the hand of the Amorites, to destroy us? would to God we had been content, and dwelt on the other side Jordan! [8] O Lord, what shall I say, when Israel turneth their backs before their enemies!

1 Kings 6:23-35: And within the oracle he made two cherubims of olive tree, each ten cubits high. [24] And five cubits was the one wing of the cherub, and five cubits the other wing of the cherub: from the uttermost part of the one wing unto the uttermost part of the other were ten cubits. [25] And the other cherub was ten cubits: both the cherubims were of one measure and one size. [26] The height of the one cherub was ten cubits, and so was it of the other cherub. [27] And he set the cherubims within the inner house: and they stretched forth the wings of the cherubims, so that the wing of the one touched the one wall, and the wing of the other cherub touched the other wall; and their wings touched one another in the midst of the house. [28] And he overlaid the cherubims with gold. [29] And he carved all the walls of the house round about with carved figures of cherubims and palm trees and open flowers, within and without.

[30] And the floor of the house he overlaid with gold, within and without. [31] And for the entering of the oracle he made doors of olive tree: the lintel and side posts were a fifth part of the wall. [32] The two doors also were of olive tree; and he carved upon them carvings of cherubims and palm trees and open flowers, and overlaid them with gold, and spread gold upon the cherubims, and upon the palm trees. [33] So also made he for the door of the temple posts of olive tree, a fourth part of the wall. [34] And the two doors were of fir tree: the two leaves of the one door were folding, and the two leaves of the other door were folding.

[35] And he carved thereon cherubims and palm trees and open flowers: and covered them with gold fitted upon the carved work.

1 Kings 8:22: And Solomon stood before the altar of the LORD in the presence of all the congregation of Israel, and spread forth his hands toward heaven:

1 Kings 8:44, 48: If thy people go out to battle against their enemy, whithersoever thou shalt send them, and shall pray unto the LORD toward the city which thou hast chosen, and toward the house that I have built for thy name . . . [48] And so return unto thee with all their heart, and with all their soul, in the land of their enemies, which led them away captive, and pray unto thee toward their land, which thou gavest unto their fathers, the city which thou hast chosen, and the house which I have built for thy name: (cf. 2 Chron. 6:34, 38)

1 Kings 8:54: And it was so, that when Solomon had made an end of praying all this prayer and supplication unto the LORD, he arose from before the altar of the LORD, from kneeling on his knees with his hands spread up to heaven.

1 Kings 18:42: So Ahab went up to eat and to drink. And Elijah went up to the top of Carmel; and he cast himself down upon the earth, and put his face between his knees,

1 Chronicles 16:4: And he appointed certain of the Levites to minister before the ark of the LORD, and to record, and to thank and praise the LORD God of Israel:

1 Chronicles 16:29: Give unto the LORD the glory due unto his name: bring an offering, and come before him: worship the LORD in the beauty of holiness.

2 Chronicles 3:7: He overlaid also the house, the beams, the posts, and the walls thereof, and the doors thereof, with gold; and graved cherubims on the walls. (cf. Ezek. 41:20, 25)

2 Chronicles 6:12-14: And he stood before the altar of the LORD in the presence of all the congregation of Israel, and spread forth his hands: [13] For Solomon had made a brasen scaffold, of five cubits long, and five cubits broad, and three cubits high, and had set it in the midst of the court: and upon it he stood, and kneeled down upon his knees before all the congregation of Israel, and spread forth his hands toward heaven, [14] And said, O LORD God of Israel, there is no God like thee in the heaven, nor in the earth; which keepest covenant, and shewest mercy unto thy servants, that walk before thee with all their hearts:

2 Chronicles 6:20: That thine eyes may be open upon this house day and night, upon the place whereof thou hast said that thou wouldest put thy name there; to hearken unto the prayer which thy servant prayeth toward this place.

2 Chronicles 6:21: Hearken therefore unto the supplications of thy servant, and of thy people Israel, which they shall make toward this place: hear thou from thy dwelling place, even from heaven; and when thou hearest, forgive.

2 Chronicles 6:22: If a man sin against his neighbour, and an oath be laid upon him to make him swear, and the oath come before thine altar in this house;

2 Chronicles 6:26-27: When the heaven is shut up, and there is no rain, because they have sinned against thee; yet if they pray toward this place, and confess thy name, and turn from their sin, when thou dost afflict them; [27] Then hear thou from heaven, and forgive the sin of thy servants, and of thy people Israel, when thou hast taught them the good way, wherein they should walk; and send rain upon thy land, which thou hast given unto thy people for an inheritance.

2 Chronicles 6:29-30: Then what prayer or what supplication soever shall be made of any man, or of all thy people Israel, when every one shall know his own sore and his own grief, and shall spread forth his hands in this house: [30] Then hear thou from heaven thy dwelling place, and forgive, and render unto every man according unto all his ways, whose heart thou knowest; (for thou only knowest the hearts of the children of men:)

2 Chronicles 6:32-33: Moreover concerning the stranger, which is not of thy people Israel, but is come from a far country for thy great name's sake, and thy mighty hand, and thy stretched out arm; if they come and pray in this house; [33] Then hear thou from the heavens, even from thy dwelling place, and do according to all that the stranger calleth to thee for; that all people of the earth may know thy name, and fear thee, as doth thy people Israel, and may know that this house which I have built is called by thy name. (cf. 1 Kings 29-30, 35, 42)

2 Chronicles 7:3: And when all the children of Israel saw how the fire came down, and the glory of the LORD upon the house, they bowed themselves with their faces to the ground upon the pavement, and worshipped, and praised the LORD, saying, For he is good; for his mercy endureth for ever.

Psalm 5:7: But as for me, I will come into thy house in the multitude of thy mercy: and in thy fear will I worship toward thy holy temple.

Psalm 28:2: Hear the voice of my supplications, when I cry unto thee, when I lift up my hands toward thy holy oracle.

Psalm 29:2: Give unto the LORD the glory due unto his name; worship the LORD in the beauty of holiness.

Psalm 96:9: O worship the LORD in the beauty of holiness: fear before him, all the earth.

Psalm 99:9: Exalt the LORD our God, and worship at his holy hill; for the LORD our God is holy.

Psalm 134:2: Lift up your hands in the sanctuary, and bless the LORD.

Psalm 138:2: I will worship toward thy holy temple, and praise thy name for thy lovingkindness and for thy truth: for thou hast magnified thy word above all thy name.

Isaiah 27:13: And it shall come to pass in that day, that the great trumpet shall be blown, and they shall come which were ready to perish in the land of Assyria, and the outcasts in the land of Egypt, and shall worship the LORD in the holy mount at Jerusalem.

Ezekiel 46:3: Likewise the people of the land shall worship at the door of this gate before the LORD in the sabbaths and in the new moons.

Daniel 6:10: Now when Daniel knew that the writing was signed, he went into his house; and his windows being open in his chamber toward Jerusalem, he kneeled upon his knees three times a day, and prayed, and gave thanks before his God, as he did aforetime.

Romans 12:1: I beseech you therefore, brethren, by the mercies of God, that ye present your bodies a living sacrifice, holy, acceptable unto God, which is your reasonable service.

Philippians 1:20: According to my earnest expectation and my hope, that in nothing I shall be ashamed, but that with all boldness, as always, so now also Christ shall be magnified in my body, whether it be by life, or by death.

Revelation 4:10: The four and twenty elders fall down before him that sat on the throne, and worship him that liveth for ever and ever, and cast their crowns before the throne, saying,

Revelation 7:11: And all the angels stood round about the throne, and about the elders and the four beasts, and fell before the throne on their faces, and worshipped God,

Revelation 8:3: And another angel came and stood at the altar, having a golden censer; and there was given unto him much incense, that he should offer it with the prayers of all saints upon the golden altar which was before the throne.

Chapter Eleven

Penance, Redemptive Suffering, and Atonement on Behalf of Others

We may make atonement

Exodus 32:30-32: And it came to pass on the morrow, that Moses said unto the people, Ye have sinned a great sin: and now I will go up unto the LORD; peradventure I shall make an atonement for your sin. [31] And Moses returned unto the LORD, and said, Oh, this people have sinned a great sin, and have made them gods of gold. [32] Yet now, if thou wilt forgive their sin — ; and if not, blot me, I pray thee, out of thy book which thou hast written. (cf. 29:36-37; 30:10, 15-16)

Leviticus 4:20: . . . and the priest shall make an atonement for them, and it shall be forgiven them. (cf. 4:26, 31, 35; 5:6, 10, 13, 16, 18; 6:7, 30)

Leviticus 9:7: And Moses said unto Aaron, Go unto the altar, and offer thy sin offering, and thy burnt offering, and make an atonement for thyself, and for the people: and offer the offering of the people, and make an atonement for them; as the LORD commanded.

Leviticus 10:17: Wherefore have ye not eaten the sin offering in the holy place, seeing it is most holy, and God hath given it you to bear the iniquity of the congregation, to make atonement for them before the LORD?

Leviticus 16:6: And Aaron shall offer his bullock of the sin offering, which is for himself, and make an atonement for himself, and for his house.

Leviticus 16:16: And he shall make an atonement for the holy place, because of the uncleanness of the children of Israel, and because of their transgressions in all their sins: and so shall he do for the tabernacle of the congregation, that remaineth among them in the midst of their uncleanness. (cf. 16:17-18, 24, 30, 32-33)

Leviticus 16:34: And this shall be an everlasting statute unto you, to make an atonement for the children of Israel for all their sins once a year. And he did as the LORD commanded Moses.

Numbers 16:46-48: And Moses said unto Aaron, Take a censer, and put fire therein from off the altar, and put on incense, and go quickly unto the congregation, and make an atonement for them: for there is wrath gone out from the LORD; the plague is begun. [47] And Aaron took as Moses commanded, and ran into the midst of the congregation; and, behold, the plague was begun among the people: and he put on incense, and made an atonement for the people. [48] And he stood between the dead and the living; and the plague was stayed.

Numbers 25:11-13: Phinehas, the son of Eleazar, the son of Aaron the priest, hath turned my wrath away from the children of Israel, while he was zealous for my sake among them, that I consumed not the children of Israel in my jealousy.

[12] Wherefore say, Behold, I give unto him my covenant of peace: [13] And he shall have it, and his seed after him, even the covenant of an everlasting priesthood; because he was zealous for his God, and made an atonement for the children of Israel.

2 Chronicles 29:24: And the priests killed them, and they made reconciliation with their blood upon the altar, to make an atonement for all Israel: for the king commanded that the burnt offering and the sin offering should be made for all Israel.

Proverbs 16:6: By mercy and truth iniquity is purged: and by the fear of the LORD men depart from evil.

Sirach 3:3: Whoso honoureth his father maketh an atonement for his sins: (cf. 45:16, 23)

Our sufferings can be
penitential and redemptive

Matthew 10:38: And he that taketh not his cross, and followeth after me, is not worthy of me.

Matthew 16:24: Then said Jesus unto his disciples, If any man will come after me, let him deny himself, and take up his cross, and follow me. (cf. Mark 8:34-35)

Romans 8:17: And if children, then heirs; heirs of God, and joint-heirs with Christ; if so be that we suffer with him, that we may be also glorified together.

Romans 15:1-2: We then that are strong ought to bear the infirmities of the weak, and not to please ourselves. [2] Let every one of us please his neighbour for his good to edification.

1 Corinthians 12:26: And whether one member suffer, all the members suffer with it; or one member be honoured, all the members rejoice with it.

1 Corinthians 15:29: Else what shall they do which are baptized for the dead, if the dead rise not at all? why are they then baptized for the dead? (RSV: "Otherwise, what do people mean by being baptized on behalf of the dead? If the dead are not raised at all, why are people baptized on their behalf?")

2 Corinthians 1:5-7: For as the sufferings of Christ abound in us, so our consolation also aboundeth by Christ. [6] And whether we be afflicted, it is for your consolation and salvation, which is effectual in the enduring of the same sufferings which we also suffer: or whether we be comforted, it is for your consolation and salvation. [7] And our hope of you is stedfast, knowing, that as ye are partakers of the sufferings, so shall ye be also of the consolation.

2 Corinthians 4:8-12, 15: We are troubled on every side, yet not distressed; we are perplexed, but not in despair; [9] Persecuted, but not forsaken; cast down, but not destroyed; [10] Always bearing about in the body the dying of the Lord Jesus, that the life also of Jesus might be made manifest in our body. [11] For we which live are alway delivered unto death for Jesus' sake, that the life also of Jesus might be made manifest in our mortal flesh. [12] So then death worketh in us, but life in you . . . [15] For all things are for your sakes, that the abundant grace might through the thanksgiving of many redound to the glory of God. (cf. 5:12-13)

2 Corinthians 12:15, 19: And I will very gladly spend and be spent for you; though the more abundantly I love you, the less I be loved . . . [19] Again, think ye that we excuse ourselves unto you? we speak before God in Christ: but we do all things, dearly beloved, for your edifying. (RSV: "be spent for your souls")

Galatians 2:20: I am crucified with Christ: nevertheless I live; yet not I, but Christ liveth in me: and the life which I now live in the flesh I live by the faith of the Son of God, who loved me, and gave himself for me.

Galatians 6:2: Bear ye one another's burdens, and so fulfil the law of Christ.

Galatians 6:17: From henceforth let no man trouble me: for I bear in my body the marks of the Lord Jesus.

The Greek word for marks *here is* stigma, *from which Catholics derive the term* stigmata.

Ephesians 3:1: For this cause I Paul, the prisoner of Jesus Christ for you Gentiles,

Ephesians 3:13: Wherefore I desire that ye faint not at my tribulations for you, which is your glory.

Philippians 1:7, 12-14: Even as it is meet for me to think this of you all, because I have you in my heart; inasmuch as both in my bonds, and in the defence and confirmation of the gospel, ye all are partakers of my grace . . . [12] But I would ye should understand, brethren, that the things which happened unto me have fallen out rather unto the furtherance of the gospel;

[13] So that my bonds in Christ are manifest in all the palace, and in all other places; [14] And many of the brethren in the Lord, waxing confident by my bonds, are much more bold to speak the word without fear.

Philippians 1:29-30: For unto you it is given in the behalf of Christ, not only to believe on him, but also to suffer for his sake; [30] Having the same conflict which ye saw in me, and now hear to be in me.

Philippians 2:17: Yea, and if I be offered upon the sacrifice and service of your faith, I joy, and rejoice with you all.

Philippians 3:10: That I may know him, and the power of his resurrection, and the fellowship of his sufferings, being made conformable unto his death;

Colossians 1:24: Who now rejoice in my sufferings for you, and fill up that which is behind of the afflictions of Christ in my flesh for his body's sake, which is the church: (RSV: "Now I rejoice in my sufferings for your sake, and in my flesh I complete what is lacking in Christ's afflictions for the sake of his body, that is, the church,")

2 Thessalonians 1:4-5: So that we ourselves glory in you in the churches of God for your patience and faith in all your persecutions and tribulations that ye endure: [5] Which is a manifest token of the righteous judgment of God, that ye may be counted worthy of the kingdom of God, for which ye also suffer: (cf. 1 Thess. 1:5)

2 Timothy 2:10: Therefore I endure all things for the elect's sakes, that they may also obtain the salvation which is in Christ Jesus with eternal glory.

2 Timothy 4:6: For I am now ready to be offered, and the time of my departure is at hand. (RSV: "For I am already on the point of being sacrificed")

1 Peter 2:19-21: For this is thankworthy, if a man for conscience toward God endure grief, suffering wrongfully. [20] For what glory is it, if, when ye be buffeted for your faults, ye shall take it patiently? but if, when ye do well, and suffer for it, ye take it patiently, this is acceptable with God. [21] For even hereunto were ye called: because Christ also suffered for us, leaving us an example, that ye should follow his steps:

1 Peter 4:12-14: Beloved, think it not strange concerning the fiery trial which is to try you, as though some strange thing happened unto you: [13] But rejoice, inasmuch as ye are partakers of Christ's sufferings; that, when his glory shall be revealed, ye may be glad also with exceeding joy. [14] If ye be reproached for the name of Christ, happy are ye; for the spirit of glory and of God resteth upon you: on their part he is evil spoken of, but on your part he is glorified. (cf. 4:1)

1 John 3:16: Hereby perceive we the love of God, because he laid down his life for us: and we ought to lay down our lives for the brethren.

Chapter Twelve

Angels and the Communion of Saints

Dead saints have returned to earth

1 Samuel 28:7-20: Then said Saul unto his servants, Seek me a woman that hath a familiar spirit, that I may go to her, and inquire of her. And his servants said to him, Behold, there is a woman that hath a familiar spirit at Endor. [8] And Saul disguised himself, and put on other raiment, and he went, and two men with him, and they came to the woman by night: and he said, I pray thee, divine unto me by the familiar spirit, and bring me him up, whom I shall name unto thee. [9] And the woman said unto him, Behold, thou knowest what Saul hath done, how he hath cut off those that have familiar spirits, and the wizards, out of the land: wherefore then layest thou a snare for my life, to cause me to die? [10] And Saul sware to her by the LORD, saying, As the LORD liveth, there shall no punishment happen to thee for this thing. [11] Then said the woman, Whom shall I bring up unto thee? And he said, Bring me up Samuel. [12] And when the woman saw Samuel, she cried with a loud voice: and the woman spake to Saul, saying, Why hast thou deceived me? for thou art Saul. [13] And the king said unto her, Be not afraid: for what sawest thou? And the woman said unto Saul, I saw gods ascending out of the earth. [14] And he said unto her, What form is he of? And she said, An old man cometh up; and he is covered with a mantle. And Saul perceived that it was Samuel, and he stooped with his face to the ground, and bowed himself. [15] And Samuel said to Saul, Why hast thou disquieted me, to bring me up? And Saul answered, I am sore distressed; for the Philistines make war against me, and God is departed from me, and answereth me no more, neither by prophets, nor by dreams: therefore I have called thee, that thou mayest make known unto me what I shall do. [16] Then said Samuel, Wherefore then dost thou ask of me, seeing the LORD is departed from thee, and is become thine enemy? [17] And the LORD hath done to him, as he spake by me: for the LORD hath rent the kingdom out of thine hand, and given it to thy neighbour, even to David: [18] Because thou obeyedst not the voice of the LORD, nor executedst his fierce wrath upon Amalek, therefore hath the LORD done this thing unto thee this day. [19] Moreover the LORD will also deliver Israel with thee into the hand of the Philistines: and to morrow shalt thou and thy sons be with me: the LORD also shall deliver the host of Israel into the hand of the Philistines.

[20] Then Saul fell straightway all along on the earth, and was sore afraid, because of the words of Samuel: and there was no strength in him; for he had eaten no bread all the day, nor all the night.

Sirach 46:19-20: And before his long sleep he made protestations in the sight of the Lord and his anointed, I have not taken any man's goods, so much as a shoe: and no man did accuse him. [20] And after his death he prophesied, and shewed the king his end, and lifted up his voice from the earth in prophecy, to blot out the wickedness of the people.

Matthew 17:1-4: And after six days Jesus taketh Peter, James, and John his brother, and bringeth them up into an high mountain apart, [2] And was transfigured before them: and his face did shine as the sun, and his raiment was white as the light.

[3] And, behold, there appeared unto them Moses and Elias talking with him. [4] Then answered Peter, and said unto Jesus, Lord, it is good for us to be here: if thou wilt, let us make here three tabernacles; one for thee, and one for Moses, and one for Elias. (cf. Mark 9:2-5; Luke 9:29-33)

Matthew 27:50-53: Jesus, when he had cried again with a loud voice, yielded up the ghost. [51] And, behold, the veil of the temple was rent in twain from the top to the bottom; and the earth did quake, and the rocks rent; [52] And the graves were opened; and many bodies of the saints which slept arose, [53] And came out of the graves after his resurrection, and went into the holy city, and appeared unto many.

Revelation 11:3-12: And I will give power unto my two witnesses, and they shall prophesy a thousand two hundred and threescore days, clothed in sackcloth. [4] These are the two olive trees, and the two candlesticks standing before the God of the earth. [5] And if any man will hurt them, fire proceedeth out of their mouth, and devoureth their enemies: and if any man will hurt them, he must in this manner be killed. [6] These have power to shut heaven, that it rain not in the days of their prophecy: and have power over waters to turn them to blood, and to smite the earth with all plagues, as often as they will. [7] And when they shall have finished their testimony, the beast that ascendeth out of the bottomless pit shall make war against them, and shall overcome them, and kill them. [8] And their dead bodies shall lie in the street of the great city, which spiritually is called Sodom and Egypt, where also our Lord was crucified. [9] And they of the people and kindreds and tongues and nations shall see their dead bodies three days and an half, and shall not suffer their dead bodies to be put in graves. [10] And they that dwell upon the earth shall rejoice over them, and make merry, and shall send gifts one to another; because these two prophets tormented them that dwelt on the earth. [11] And after three days and an half the Spirit of life from God entered into them, and they stood upon their feet; and great fear fell upon them which saw them.

[12] And they heard a great voice from heaven saying unto them, Come up hither. And they ascended up to heaven in a cloud; and their enemies beheld them.

The actions of the two witnesses echo those of Moses before Pharaoh, and Elijah — especially the turning of water into blood, and the plagues (cf. Mal. 4:4-6; Matt. 17:11, Transfiguration accounts). As for the stopping of the rain, that was done by Elijah (James 5:16-18). Elijah also went up to heaven in a whirlwind (2 Kings 2:1, 11). Many Church fathers thought the two witnesses were Enoch and Elijah, because Enoch, like Elijah, also never died (Gen. 5:24; Sir. 44:16; 49:14; Heb. 11:5)

In any event, they were killed and rose again, and so "came back to earth." There are also four more individuals who were raised from the dead by Elijah, Jesus, and Peter (see chapter 5: "We should pray for the dead"), and others who were raised as a result of disciples' prayers (Matt. 11:5; Luke 7:22). Thus, there is no impenetrable divide between life on the earth and life after death. Hence the dead saints can also love us and intercede for us.

We should venerate saints and angels

Psalm 89:7: God is greatly to be feared in the assembly of the saints, and to be had in reverence of all them that are about him.

1 Corinthians 4:16: Wherefore I beseech you, be ye followers of me.

Philippians 3:17: Brethren, be followers together of me, and mark them which walk so as ye have us for an ensample.

Philippians 4:9: Those things, which ye have both learned, and received, and heard, and seen in me, do: and the God of peace shall be with you.

2 Thessalonians 3:7-9: For yourselves know how ye ought to follow us: for we behaved not ourselves disorderly among you; [8] Neither did we eat any man's bread for nought; but wrought with labour and travail night and day, that we might not be chargeable to any of you: [9] Not because we have not power, but to make ourselves an ensample unto you to follow us.
St. Paul, in turn, imitates Christ: 1 Corinthians 11:1; 1 Thessalonians 1:6.

Hebrews 6:12: That ye be not slothful, but followers of them who through faith and patience inherit the promises.

Hebrews 11:32-38: And what shall I more say? for the time would fail me to tell of Gedeon, and of Barak, and of Samson, and of Jephthae; of David also, and Samuel, and of the prophets: [33] Who through faith subdued kingdoms, wrought righteousness, obtained promises, stopped the mouths of lions, [34] Quenched the violence of fire, escaped the edge of the sword, out of weakness were made strong, waxed valiant in fight, turned to flight the armies of the aliens. [35] Women received their dead raised to life again: and others were tortured, not accepting deliverance; that they might obtain a better resurrection: [36] And others had trial of cruel mockings and scourgings, yea, moreover of bonds and imprisonment: [37] They were stoned, they were sawn asunder, were tempted, were slain with the sword: they wandered about in sheepskins and goatskins; being destitute, afflicted, tormented; [38] (Of whom the world was not worthy:) they wandered in deserts, and in mountains, and in dens and caves of the earth.

Hebrews 13:7: Remember them which have the rule over you, who have spoken unto you the word of God: whose faith follow, considering the end of their conversation. (RSV: "consider the outcome of their life, and imitate their faith")

James 5:10-11: Take, my brethren, the prophets, who have spoken in the name of the Lord, for an example of suffering affliction, and of patience. [11] Behold, we count them happy which endure. Ye have heard of the patience of Job, and have seen the end of the Lord; that the Lord is very pitiful, and of tender mercy.

By analogy, it is altogether proper to venerate and honor saints, who have more perfectly attained God's likeness (Matt. 22:30; 1 Cor. 13:9-12; 2 Cor. 3:18; Phil. 3:21; Heb. 11:40; 1 John 3:2; Rev. 21:27; 22:14), in light of the example of how "heroes of the faith" are regarded (Heb. 11) and also the biblical injunctions to honor all sorts of people:

Matthew 13:57: And they were offended in him. But Jesus said unto them, A prophet is not without honour, save in his own country, and in his own house. (cf. Mark 6:4; John 4:44)

Romans 12:10: Be kindly affectioned one to another with brotherly love; in honour preferring one another;

Romans 13:6-7: For for this cause pay ye tribute also: for they are God's ministers, attending continually upon this very thing. [7] Render therefore to all their dues: tribute to whom tribute is due; custom to whom custom; fear to whom fear; honour to whom honour.

1 Corinthians 12:23-26: And those members of the body, which we think to be less honourable, upon these we bestow more abundant honour; and our uncomely parts have more abundant comeliness. [24] For our comely parts have no need: but God hath tempered the body together, having given more abundant honour to that part which lacked: [25] That there should be no schism in the body; but that the members should have the same care one for another. [26] And whether one member suffer, all the members suffer with it; or one member be honoured, all the members rejoice with it.

2 Corinthians 8:21: Providing for honest things, not only in the sight of the Lord, but also in the sight of men.

Ephesians 6:2: Honour thy father and mother; (which is the first commandment with promise;) (cf. Exod. 20:12; Deut. 5:16)

1 Timothy 5:3: Honour widows that are widows indeed.

1 Timothy 5:17: Let the elders that rule well be counted worthy of double honour, especially they who labour in the word and doctrine.

Hebrews 13:18: Pray for us: for we trust we have a good conscience, in all things willing to live honestly.

1 Peter 2:17: Honour all men. Love the brotherhood. Fear God. Honour the king.

1 Peter 3:7: Likewise, ye husbands, dwell with them according to knowledge, giving honour unto the wife, as unto the weaker vessel, and as being heirs together of the grace of life; that your prayers be not hindered. (cf. Gen. 30:20)

Thus, we find that the angel of the LORD was honored (i.e., venerated):

Numbers 22:31: Then the LORD opened the eyes of Balaam, and he saw the angel of the LORD standing in the way, and his sword drawn in his hand: and he bowed down his head, and fell flat on his face.

Judges 13:17: And Manoah said unto the angel of the LORD, What is thy name, that when thy sayings come to pass we may do thee honour?

King Asa was honored after his death:

2 Chronicles 16:14: And they buried him in his own sepulchres, which he had made for himself in the city of David, and laid him in the bed which was filled with sweet odours and divers kinds of spices prepared by the apothecaries' art: and they made a very great burning for him. (RSV: "they made a very great fire in his honor"; cf. 21:19)

King Hezekiah was also so honored:

2 Chronicles 32:33: And Hezekiah slept with his fathers, and they buried him in the chiefest of the sepulchres of the sons of David: and all Judah and the inhabitants of Jerusalem did him honour at his death. And Manasseh his son reigned in his stead.

God even said he would honor those who honor him:

1 Samuel 2:30: Wherefore the LORD God of Israel saith, I said indeed that thy house, and the house of thy father, should walk before me for ever: but now the LORD saith, Be it far from me; for them that honour me I will honour, and they that despise me shall be lightly esteemed. (cf. 2 Chron. 26:18; Ps. 62:7; 71:21; 84:11; Eccles. 6:2; Rom. 2:9-11; 2 Cor. 8:21)

God the Father honors those who serve His Son Jesus:

John 12:26: If any man serve me, let him follow me; and where I am, there shall also my servant be: if any man serve me, him will my Father honour.

So how is it that we are told that we cannot honor and venerate fellow human saints, since they are dead? Just because they no longer walk the earth, it doesn't follow at all (per Heb.11) that they are no longer worthy of honor and veneration.

Saints and angels intercede for us

Jeremiah 15:1: Then said the LORD unto me, Though Moses and Samuel stood before me, yet my mind could not be toward this people: cast them out of my sight, and let them go forth.

Zechariah 1:12: Then the angel of the LORD answered and said, O LORD of hosts, how long wilt thou not have mercy on Jerusalem and on the cities of Judah, against which thou hast had indignation these threescore and ten years?

Tobit 12:12, 15: Now therefore, when thou didst pray, and Sara thy daughter in law, I did bring the remembrance of your prayers before the Holy One: and when thou didst bury the dead, I was with thee likewise . . . [15] I am Raphael, one of the seven holy angels, which present the prayers of the saints, and which go in and out before the glory of the Holy One.

2 Maccabees 15:11-16: Thus he armed every one of them, not so much with defence of shields and spears, as with comfortable and good words: and beside that, he told them a dream worthy to be believed, as if it had been so indeed, which did not a little rejoice them. [12] And this was his vision: That Onias, who had been high priest, a virtuous and a good man, reverend in conversation, gentle in condition, well spoken also, and exercised from a child in all points of virtue, holding up his hands prayed for the whole body of the Jews. [13] This done, in like manner there appeared a man with gray hairs, and exceeding glorious, who was of a wonderful and excellent majesty. [14] Then Onias answered, saying, This is a lover of the brethren, who prayeth much for the people, and for the holy city, to wit, Jeremias the prophet of God. [15] Whereupon Jeremias holding forth his right hand gave to Judas a sword of gold, and in giving it spake thus, [16] Take this holy sword, a gift from God, with the which thou shalt wound the adversaries.

Luke 15:10: Likewise, I say unto you, there is joy in the presence of the angels of God over one sinner that repenteth.

1 Corinthians 4:9: For I think that God hath set forth us the apostles last, as it were appointed to death: for we are made a spectacle unto the world, and to angels, and to men.

Hebrews 12:1: Wherefore seeing we also are compassed about with so great a cloud of witnesses, let us lay aside every weight, and the sin which doth so easily beset us, and let us run with patience the race that is set before us,

Revelation 1:4: John to the seven churches which are in Asia: Grace be unto you, and peace, from him which is, and which was, and which is to come; and from the seven Spirits which are before his throne;

Revelation 5:8: And when he had taken the book, the four beasts and four and twenty elders fell down before the Lamb, having every one of them harps, and golden vials full of odours, which are the prayers of saints.

Revelation 6:9-11: And when he had opened the fifth seal, I saw under the altar the souls of them that were slain for the word of God, and for the testimony which they held: [10] And they cried with a loud voice, saying, How long, O Lord, holy and true, dost thou not judge and avenge our blood on them that dwell on the earth? [11] And white robes were given unto every one of them; and it was said unto them, that they should rest yet for a little season, until their fellowservants also and their brethren, that should be killed as they were, should be fulfilled.

Revelation 8:3-4: And another angel came and stood at the altar, having a golden censer; and there was given unto him much incense, that he should offer it with the prayers of all saints upon the golden altar which was before the throne. [4] And the smoke of the incense, which came with the prayers of the saints, ascended up before God out of the angel's hand.

Straightforward deductions from the above passages and others lead to the following argument in favor of asking saints and angels to intercede for us:

• *We ought to pray for each other (much biblical proof).*

• *The intercessory prayer of a righteous man has great power in its effects (James 5:16-18).*

• *Dead saints are more alive than we ourselves are (e.g., Matt. 22:32; Luke 20:37-38).*

• *Dead saints are aware of what happens on the earth (Heb. 12:1 etc.), and indeed, are portrayed as praying for us in heaven (Rev. 6:9-10).*

• *Dead saints are exceptionally, if not wholly, righteous and holy, since they have been delivered from sin and are present with God (Rev. 21:27, 22:14).*

• *Therefore, it is perfectly sensible, permissible, and wise to ask them to pray on our behalf to God.*

Guardian angels watch over us

Genesis 24:7: The LORD God of heaven, which took me from my father's house, and from the land of my kindred, and which spake unto me, and that sware unto me, saying, Unto thy seed will I give this land; he shall send his angel before thee. . .

Exodus 23:20: Behold, I send an Angel before thee, to keep thee in the way, and to bring thee into the place which I have prepared.

Psalm 34:7: The angel of the LORD encampeth round about them that fear him, and delivereth them.

Psalm 91:9-12: Because thou hast made the LORD, which is my refuge, even the most High, thy habitation; [10] There shall no evil befall thee, neither shall any plague come nigh thy dwelling.

[11] For he shall give his angels charge over thee, to keep thee in all thy ways. [12] They shall bear thee up in their hands, lest thou dash thy foot against a stone.

Isaiah 63:9: In all their affliction he was afflicted, and the angel of his presence saved them: in his love and in his pity he redeemed them; and he bare them, and carried them all the days of old.

Daniel 6:22: My God hath sent his angel, and hath shut the lions' mouths, that they have not hurt me . . .

Tobit 5:21: For the good angel will keep him company, and his journey shall be prosperous, and he shall return safe.

Tobit 12:12-15: Now therefore, when thou didst pray, and Sara thy daughter in law, I did bring the remembrance of your prayers before the Holy One: and when thou didst bury the dead, I was with thee likewise. [13] And when thou didst not delay to rise up, and leave thy dinner, to go and cover the dead, thy good deed was not hid from me: but I was with thee. [14] And now God hath sent me to heal thee and Sara thy daughter in law.

[15] I am Raphael, one of the seven holy angels, which present the prayers of the saints, and which go in and out before the glory of the Holy One.

Matthew 18:10: Take heed that ye despise not one of these little ones; for I say unto you, That in heaven their angels do always behold the face of my Father which is in heaven.

Luke 4:10: For it is written, He shall give his angels charge over thee, to keep thee: (cf. Matt. 26:53)

Acts 12:5-16: Peter therefore was kept in prison: but prayer was made without ceasing of the church unto God for him. [6] And when Herod would have brought him forth, the same night Peter was sleeping between two soldiers, bound with two chains: and the keepers before the door kept the prison. [7] And, behold, the angel of the Lord came upon him, and a light shined in the prison: and he smote Peter on the side, and raised him up, saying, Arise up quickly. And his chains fell off from his hands.

[8] And the angel said unto him, Gird thyself, and bind on thy sandals. And so he did. And he saith unto him, Cast thy garment about thee, and follow me. [9] And he went out, and followed him; and wist not that it was true which was done by the angel; but thought he saw a vision. [10] When they were past the first and the second ward, they came unto the iron gate that leadeth unto the city; which opened to them of his own accord: and they went out, and passed on through one street; and forthwith the angel departed from him. [11] And when Peter was come to himself, he said, Now I know of a surety, that the Lord hath sent his angel, and hath

delivered me out of the hand of Herod, and from all the expectation of the people of the Jews. [12] And when he had considered the thing, he came to the house of Mary the mother of John, whose surname was Mark; where many were gathered together praying. [13] And as Peter knocked at the door of the gate, a damsel came to hearken, named Rhoda. [14] And when she knew Peter's voice, she opened not the gate for gladness, but ran in, and told how Peter stood before the gate.

[15] And they said unto her, Thou art mad. But she constantly affirmed that it was even so. Then said they, It is his angel.

[16] But Peter continued knocking: and when they had opened the door, and saw him, they were astonished.

Hebrews 1:14: Are they not all ministering spirits, sent forth to minister for them who shall be heirs of salvation?

Moreover, each of the seven churches in Revelation are said to have "an angel" (Rev. 1:20; 2:1, 8, 12, 18; 3:1, 7, 14).

Men have spoken to angels
(analogy to intercession of the saints)

Genesis 19:1-2: And there came two angels to Sodom at even; and Lot sat in the gate of Sodom: and Lot seeing them rose up to meet them; and he bowed himself with his face toward the ground; [2] And he said, Behold now, my lords, turn in, I pray you, into your servant's house, and tarry all night, and wash your feet, and ye shall rise up early, and go on your ways. And they said, Nay; but we will abide in the street all night.

Genesis 19:15, 18-21: And when the morning arose, then the angels hastened Lot, saying, Arise, take thy wife, and thy two daughters, which are here; lest thou be consumed in the iniquity of the city. . . . [18] And Lot said unto them, Oh, not so, my Lord:
[19] Behold now, thy servant hath found grace in thy sight, and thou hast magnified thy mercy, which thou hast shewed unto me in saving my life; and I cannot escape to the mountain, lest some evil take me, and I die: [20] Behold now, this city is near to flee unto, and it is a little one: Oh, let me escape thither, (is it not a little one?) and my soul shall live. [21] And he said unto him, See, I have accepted thee concerning this thing also, that I will not overthrow this city, for the which thou hast spoken.

Genesis 32:24-29: And Jacob was left alone; and there wrestled a man with him until the breaking of the day. [25] And when he saw that he prevailed not against him, he touched the hollow of his thigh; and the hollow of Jacob's thigh was out of joint, as he wrestled with him. [26] And he said,

Let me go, for the day breaketh. And he said, I will not let thee go, except thou bless me. [27] And he said unto him, What is thy name? And he said, Jacob. [28] And he said, Thy name shall be called no more Jacob, but Israel: for as a prince hast thou power with God and with men, and hast prevailed. [29] And Jacob asked him, and said, Tell me, I pray thee, thy name. And he said, Wherefore is it that thou dost ask after my name? And he blessed him there. (cf. 48:14-16)

Numbers 22:34-35: And Balaam said unto the angel of the LORD, I have sinned; for I knew not that thou stoodest in the way against me: now therefore, if it displease thee, I will get me back again. [35] And the angel of the LORD said unto Balaam, Go with the men: but only the word that I shall speak unto thee, that thou shalt speak. So Balaam went with the princes of Balak.

Psalm 103:20: Bless the LORD, ye his angels, that excel in strength, that do his commandments, hearkening unto the voice of his word. (cf. 148:2)

Zechariah 1:9, 13-14, 19: Then said I, O my lord, what are these? And the angel that talked with me said unto me, I will shew thee what these be . . . [13] And the LORD answered the angel that talked with me with good words and comfortable words. [14] So the angel that communed with me said unto me, Cry thou, saying, Thus saith the LORD of hosts; I am jealous for Jerusalem and for Zion with a great jealousy . . . [19] And I said unto the angel that talked with me, What be these? And he answered me, These are the horns which have scattered Judah, Israel, and Jerusalem.

Zechariah 2:1-3: I lifted up mine eyes again, and looked, and behold a man with a measuring line in his hand. [2] Then said I, Whither goest thou? And he said unto me, To measure Jerusalem, to see what is the breadth thereof, and what is the length thereof. [3] And, behold, the angel that talked with me went forth, and another angel went out to meet him,

Zechariah 4:1-5: And the angel that talked with me came again, and waked me, as a man that is wakened out of his sleep,

[2] And said unto me, What seest thou? And I said, I have looked, and behold a candlestick all of gold, with a bowl upon the top of it, and his seven lamps thereon, and seven pipes to the seven lamps, which are upon the top thereof: [3] And two olive trees by it, one upon the right side of the bowl, and the other upon the left side thereof. [4] So I answered and spake to the angel that talked with me, saying, What are these, my lord? [5] Then the angel that talked with me answered and said unto me, Knowest thou not what these be? And I said, No, my lord. (cf. 5:5, 10; 6:4-5)

Luke 1:18-19: And Zacharias said unto the angel, Whereby shall I know this? for I am an old man, and my wife well stricken in years. [19] And the angel answering said unto him, I am Gabriel, that stand in the presence of God; and am sent to speak unto thee, and to shew thee these glad tidings.

Luke 1:30, 34, 38: And the angel said unto her, Fear not, Mary: for thou hast found favour with God . . ." [34] Then said Mary unto the angel, How shall this be, seeing I know not a man? . . . [38] And Mary said, Behold the handmaid of the Lord; be it unto me according to thy word. And the angel departed from her.

Acts 27:23-24: For there stood by me this night the angel of God, whose I am, and whom I serve, [24] Saying, Fear not, Paul; thou must be brought before Caesar: and, lo, God hath given thee all them that sail with thee.

Revelation 10:8-9: And the voice which I heard from heaven spake unto me again, and said, Go and take the little book which is open in the hand of the angel which standeth upon the sea and upon the earth. [9] And I went unto the angel, and said unto him, Give me the little book. And he said unto me, Take it, and eat it up; and it shall make thy belly bitter, but it shall be in thy mouth sweet as honey.

Also, in Genesis 21:17-18, an angel speaks to Hagar from heaven, thus showing that a two-way communication is not ruled out. Furthermore, Scripture provides instances of angels communicating to men in dreams (Matt. 1:20; 2:13, 19-20). St. Paul even had a "vision" in which a "man of Macedonia" communicated with him (Acts 16:9-10, RSV). The analogy to the intercession of angels, then, works as follows (all plainly deduced from scriptural evidences):

• Men talk to angels, and even to dead men on several occasions (ten examples above).

• It makes no difference whether they are in heaven or on earth when this happens. Angels are not spatial, dimensional creatures in the first place.

• Angels (according to agreed Christian theology across the board based on biblical proofs) are extremely intelligent and can deduce our thoughts and follow our actions, and they intensely care about us and are able to help us (e.g., Luke 15:10).

• We know for certain that they pray for us (Zech. 1:12; Tob. 12:12, 15; Rev. 8:3-4) and that there are guardian angels (see the previous section above), and that part of the angelic mission is to aid human beings; also that they (excepting the rebellious demons) are holy and sinless, have never fallen.

• Angels even participate in giving grace (Tob. 12:12, 15; Rev. 1:4).

• Therefore we can ask angels to intercede and pray to God for us or for others, since this is essentially no different from talking to them, or being instructed what to do by them.

Chapter Thirteen

The Blessed Virgin Mary

Jesus was Mary's only child

The word brother *as used in the New Testament (Greek, adelphos), has a wide range of meaning, including those of the same nationality (Rom. 9:3), neighbors or any man (Matt. 5:22; 7:3; Luke 10:29), mankind (Matt. 25:40; Heb. 2:17), Christian believers (Acts 1:15), etc.*

Neither Hebrew nor Aramaic had a word for cousin. *Greek did have such a word, but since ancient Israel was a Semitic culture, they still used the equivalent of* brother *to signify a cousin. Jesus himself used the word in this way. He described the "crowds" and His "disciples" as his "brethren" (RSV: Matt. 23:8; cf. 12:49-50). We see this wider usage of* brother *even in English today. Here are some plain examples of the wider (non-sibling) usage of adelphos:*

Acts 3:12, 17, 22: And when Peter saw it, he answered unto the people, Ye men of Israel . . . [17] And now, brethren, I wot that through ignorance ye did it, as did also your rulers . . . [22] For Moses truly said unto the fathers, A prophet shall the Lord your God raise up unto you of your brethren, like unto me . . .

Acts 7:23-27: And when he was full forty years old, it came into his heart to visit his brethren the children of Israel. [24] And seeing one of them suffer wrong, he defended him, and avenged him that was oppressed, and smote the Egyptian: [25] For he supposed his brethren would have understood how that God by his hand would deliver them: but they understood not. [26] And the next day he shewed himself unto them as they strove, and would have set them at one again, saying, Sirs, ye are brethren;

why do ye wrong one to another? [27] But he that did his neighbour wrong thrust him away, saying, Who made thee a ruler and a judge over us?

Romans 1:7, 13: To all that be in Rome, beloved of God, called to be saints . . . [13] Now I would not have you ignorant, brethren . . .

I Thessalonians 1:1, 4: Paul, and Silvanus, and Timotheus, unto the church of the Thessalonians . . . [4] Knowing, brethren beloved, your election of God.

Hebrews 7:5: And verily they that are of the sons of Levi, who receive the office of the priesthood, have a commandment to take tithes of the people according to the law, that is, of their brethren, though they come out of the loins of Abraham:

Revelation 22:9: . . . thy brethren the prophets . . .

St. Paul uses adelphos 138 times, and it seems clear that in virtually every case, the meaning is in the wider "non-sibling" sense. Thus, when he refers to "James the Lord's brother" in Galatians 1:19, it is altogether sensible to interpret it in the same way. Keeping this usage in mind, let's look specifically at several related passages that mention Jesus' "brothers":

Matthew 13:55-56: Is not this the carpenter's son? is not his mother called Mary? and his brethren, James, and Joses, and Simon, and Judas? [56] And his sisters, are they not all with us? Whence then hath this man all these things?

Matthew 27:56: Among which was Mary Magdalene, and Mary the mother of James and Joses, and the mother of Zebedee's children.

Matthew 27:61: And there was Mary Magdalene, and the other Mary, sitting over against the sepulchre.

Matthew 28:1: In the end of the sabbath, as it began to dawn toward the first day of the week, came Mary Magdalene and the other Mary to see the sepulchre.

Mark 6:3: Is not this the carpenter, the son of Mary, the brother of James, and Joses, and of Juda, and Simon? and are not his sisters here with us? And they were offended at him.

Mark 15:40: There were also women looking on afar off: among whom was Mary Magdalene, and Mary the mother of James the less and of Joses, and Salome;

John 19:25: Now there stood by the cross of Jesus his mother, and his mother's sister, Mary the wife of Cleophas, and Mary Magdalene.

James and Joseph, who are described as Jesus' "brethren" or "brothers" (Matt. 13:55; Mark 6:3), are also called sons of Mary, wife of Cleophas or (RSV) Clopas (Matt. 27:56; Mark 15:40; cf. John 19:25). Thus, they were either Jesus' cousins or fellow Israelites — not literally siblings. This same "other Mary" (Matt. 27:61; 28:1) is called the Blessed Virgin Mary's "sister" (adelphe) in John 19:25.

Since it is unlikely that there were two Marys in one family, again the text must be referring to the Virgin Mary's cousin or more distant relative. By quite plausible deduction, then, Simon, Jude, and "sisters" (Matt. 13:55-56; Mark 6:3) are also Jesus' cousins or more remote relatives.

We may have a bit more biblical information about the "brother" Judas. Many scholars believe he could very well be the same person as the "Jude" who wrote the New Testament book of the same name. Granting this for the sake of argument, note that he describes himself as "a servant of Jesus Christ and brother of James" (1:1, RSV). It strains credulity to think that if he were Jesus' blood brother, or sibling, that he would describe himself as James's brother. Therefore, it is far more reasonable to believe that he is James's sibling and Jesus' cousin or more distant relative; just as we have seen is the case with James himself, from direct exegetical indications.

We also believe that Jesus was Mary's only child because, in the account of his visiting the Temple with his parents for the yearly passover observance when he was twelve, no siblings are mentioned (Luke 2:41-51), and also because, on the

Cross, he committed his mother to the care of St. John (John 19:26-27). It was unthinkable in that culture (as in most cultures) to do that if indeed Jesus had siblings.

Lastly, some think it is telling that sungenis (Greek for cousin) isn't used in direct reference to Jesus "brothers." Apart from the cultural considerations already discussed, there is at least one plausible indirect argument from cross-referencing, where this association does occur:

Mark 6:4: But Jesus said unto them, A prophet is not without honour, but in his own country, and among his own kin [*sungenis*], and in his own house.

John 7:3-5: His brethren therefore said unto him, Depart hence, and go into Judaea, that thy disciples also may see the works that thou doest. [4] For there is no man that doeth any thing in secret, and he himself seeketh to be known openly. If thou do these things, shew thyself to the world. [5] For neither did his brethren believe in him.

The two passages seem to be describing the same thing. If so, then this would be an equation of those who are called "brothers" in John 5, with "kin" (sungenis) in Mark 6:4; thus confirming the traditional Catholic interpretation yet again: that these "brothers" and "sisters" of Jesus are not siblings. Therefore, the doctrine of Mary's perpetual virginity is perfectly consistent with all of the biblical data, closely examined (which is why Luther, Calvin, and many Protestants throughout history have accepted this truth alongside Catholics and Orthodox).

Mary was free from sin
from the moment of conception

Luke 1:26-28: And in the sixth month the angel Gabriel was sent from God unto a city of Galilee, named Nazareth, [27] To a virgin espoused to a man whose name was Joseph, of the house of David; and the virgin's name was Mary. [28] And the angel came in unto her, and said, Hail, thou that art highly favoured, the Lord is with thee: blessed art thou among women. (RSV, Catholic edition: "Hail, full of grace"; non-Catholic RSV: "O favored one")

The Greek word for "full of grace" or "highly favored" is kecharitomene: *perfect passive participle of* charitoo, *which means "endowed with grace." Charis (the Greek word for* grace) *is translated in the KJV, as "grace" 129 times out of about 150 appearances. This passage teaches the sinlessness of Mary — itself the root assumption of the developed doctrine of the Immaculate Conception. With additional cross-referencing of a lot of scriptural material concerning grace, the striking "Catholic" conclusion becomes a lot clearer than it is at first glance. For St. Paul, grace (*charis) *is the antithesis and overcomer of sin:*

Romans 5:17, 20-21: For if by one man's offence death reigned by one; much more they which receive abundance of grace and of the gift of righteousness shall reign in life by one, Jesus Christ.) . . . [20] Moreover the law entered, that the offence might abound. But where sin abounded, grace did much more abound: [21] That as sin hath reigned unto death, even so might grace reign through righteousness unto eternal life by Jesus Christ our Lord.

Romans 6:14: For sin shall not have dominion over you: for ye are not under the law, but under grace. (cf. similar "zero-sum game" notions in 1 John 1:7, 9; 3:6, 9; 5:18)

2 Corinthians 1:12: For our rejoicing is this, the testimony of our conscience, that in simplicity and godly sincerity, not with fleshly wisdom, but by the grace of God, we have had our conversation in the world, and more abundantly to you-ward [toward you].

2 Corinthians 12:9: And he said unto me, My grace is sufficient for thee: for my strength is made perfect in weakness. Most gladly therefore will I rather glory in my infirmities, that the power of Christ may rest upon me.

2 Timothy 1:9: Who hath saved us, and called us with an holy calling, not according to our works, but according to his own purpose and grace, which was given us in Christ Jesus before the world began,

We are saved, of course, by grace, and grace alone:

Acts 15:11: But we believe that through the grace of the Lord Jesus Christ we shall be saved, even as they.

Romans 3:24: Being justified freely by his grace through the redemption that is in Christ Jesus: (cf. 11:5)

Ephesians 2:5: Even when we were dead in sins, hath quickened us together with Christ, (by grace ye are saved;)

Ephesians 2:8-9: For by grace are ye saved through faith; and that not of yourselves: it is the gift of God: [9] Not of works, lest any man should boast.

Titus 2:11: For the grace of God that bringeth salvation hath appeared to all men,

Titus 3:7: That being justified by his grace, we should be made heirs according to the hope of eternal life. (cf. 1 Pet. 1:10)

The implications of all this for Luke 1:28 and the Immaculate Conception of Mary now start to become more apparent. From this data we learn that two things are biblically certain:

- *Grace saves us.*
- *Grace gives us the power to be holy and righteous and without sin.*

Therefore, for a person to be full of grace is to both be saved and to be exceptionally, completely holy. The Bible also teaches that people can have different levels of grace (Acts 4:33; Rom. 5:20; 6:1; Eph. 4:7; James 4:6; 1 Pet. 5:5; 2 Pet. 1:2; 3:18). And Mary, as we know from Luke 1:28, was "full of grace." Thus, we can restate the above two propositions with Mary in mind, as follows:

- *To be full of the grace which saves is to surely be saved.*
- *To be full of the grace which gives us the power to be holy and righteous and without sin is to be fully without sin, by that same grace.*

Or, we could make the following deductive argument, with premises (the first two statements) derived directly from Scripture:

- *The Bible teaches that we are saved by God's grace.*
- *The Bible teaches that we need God's grace to live a holy life, above sin.*
- *To be "full of" God's grace, then, is to be saved.*
- *Therefore, Mary is saved.*
- *To be "full of" God's grace is also to be so holy that one is sinless.*
- *Therefore, Mary is holy and sinless.*
- *The essence of the Immaculate Conception is sinlessness.*
- *Therefore, the Immaculate Conception, in its essence, is directly deduced from the strong evidence of many biblical passages, which teach the doctrines of the two premises.*

The logic follows inexorably from unquestionable biblical principles. The only way out of it would be to deny one of the two premises, and hold that either grace doesn't save, or that grace isn't that power which enables one to be sinless and holy. In this fashion, the entire essence of the Immaculate Conception is proven from explicit biblical statements, and principles and doctrines that every orthodox

Protestant holds. All of this follows straightforwardly from Luke 1:28 and the (primarily Pauline) exegesis of charis *elsewhere in the New Testament.*

Luke 1:35: And the angel answered and said unto her, The Holy Ghost shall come upon thee, and the power of the Highest shall overshadow thee: therefore also that holy thing which shall be born of thee shall be called the Son of God.

The Greek word for overshadow *is* episkiasei, *which describes a bright, glorious cloud. It is used with reference to the cloud of transfiguration of Jesus (Matt. 17:5; Mark 9:7; Luke 9:34) and also has a connection to the shekinah glory of God in the Old Testament (Exod. 24:15-16; 40:34-38; 1 Kings 8:10). Mary is, therefore, in effect, the new temple and holy of holies, where God was present in a special fashion. In fact, scripture draws many parallels between Mary, the "ark of the new covenant" and the ark of the (old) covenant:*

Exodus 40:34-35: Then a cloud covered the tent of the congregation, and the glory of the LORD filled the tabernacle. [35] And Moses was not able to enter into the tent of the congregation, because the cloud abode thereon, and the glory of the LORD filled the tabernacle.

The Greek Septuagint translation uses the same word, episkiasei, *in this passage.*

1 Kings 8:6-11: And the priests brought in the ark of the covenant of the LORD unto his place, into the oracle of the house, to the most holy place, even under the wings of the cherubims. [7] For the cherubims spread forth their two wings over the place of the ark, and the cherubims covered the ark and the staves thereof above. [8] And they drew out the staves, that the ends of the staves were seen out in the holy place before the oracle, and they were not seen without: and there they are unto this day. [9] There was nothing in the ark save the two tables of stone, which Moses put there at Horeb, when the LORD made a covenant with the children of Israel, when they came out of the land of Egypt. [10] And it came to pass, when the priests were come out of the holy place, that the cloud filled the house of the LORD, [11] So that the priests could not stand to minister because of the cloud: for the glory of the LORD had filled the house of the LORD.

More direct parallels occur as well:

2 Samuel 6:9: And David was afraid of the LORD that day, and said, How shall the ark of the LORD come to me?

Luke 1:43: And whence is this to me, that the mother of my Lord should come to me?

2 Samuel 6:15: So David and all the house of Israel brought up the ark of the LORD with shouting, and with the sound of the trumpet.

Luke 1:42: And she spake out with a loud voice, and said, Blessed art thou among women, and blessed is the fruit of thy womb.

2 Samuel 6:14, 16: And David danced before the LORD with all his might; and David was girded with a linen ephod . . . [16] king David leaping and dancing before the LORD . . .

1 Chronicles 15:29: And it came to pass, as the ark of the covenant of the LORD came to the city of David, that Michal the daughter of Saul looking out at a window saw king David dancing and playing: and she despised him in her heart.

Luke 1:44: For, lo, as soon as the voice of thy salutation sounded in mine ears, the babe leaped in my womb for joy.

2 Samuel 6:10-11: So David would not remove the ark of the LORD unto him into the city of David: but David carried it aside into the house of Obed-edom the Gittite. [11] And the ark of the LORD continued in the house of Obed-edom the Gittite three months . . .

Luke 1:39, 56: And Mary arose in those days, and went into the hill country with haste, into a city of Juda . . . [56] And Mary abode with her about three months, and returned to her own house.

Further reflection on "holy places" and "holy items" (see chapter 2) brings out the meaning of the striking parallel symbolism. The Temple and Tabernacle were holy, and this was especially the case with the Holy of Holies, where the ark was kept. God was said to dwell above the ark, between the two cherubim (Exod. 25:22). The presence of God always imparted holiness (Deut. 7:6; 26:19; Jer. 2:3). The furnishings of the Tabernacle could not be touched by any- one, save a few priests, on pain of death (Num. 1:51-53; 2:17; 4:15).

This was true of the holiest things, associated with God and worship of God. The high priest entered the holy of holies only once a year, on the Day of Atone- ment (Num. 29:8). The Jews would tie a rope to his leg in case he perished from improper behavior (Lev. 16:2, 13), so they could pull him out. This was true of the ark itself. Uzziah merely reached out to steady it when it was toppling over, and was struck dead (2 Sam. 6:2-7). Others died when they simply looked inside of it (1 Sam. 6:19; cf. Exod. 33:20).

This is how God regards people and even inanimate objects that are in close prox- imity to Him. Thus, Mary, as the ark of the new covenant, Theotokos ("bearer of God") — the one who had the sublime honor of carrying God incarnate in her womb — had to be exceptionally holy to do so. This is indicated by both Luke 1:28, understood in its full implications, and the ark parallels noted above.

Thus, her sinlessness is strongly indicated, and this is the premise of her Im- maculate Conception, meaning that God miraculously preserved her free from the stain of Original Sin, from the moment of her conception. It was a free act of grace, obviously having nothing to do with Mary's will. Hence, "full of grace" and all its implications.

It's not as if being without sin is completely unimaginable. Adam and Eve were originally created without sin. The angels also were, and the ones who did not rebel have never sinned. There will eventually be no sin in heaven, when all things are redeemed. Prophets were exceptionally holy, and some (like Jeremiah and John the Baptist) were even sanctified from the womb:

Jeremiah 1:5: Before I formed thee in the belly I knew thee; and before thou camest forth out of the womb I sanctified thee, and I ordained thee a prophet unto the nations. (cf. Isa. 49:1, 5)

Sirach 49:7: For they entreated him evil, who nevertheless was a prophet, sanctified in his mother's womb, that he might root out, and afflict, and destroy; and that he might build up also, and plant.

Luke 1:15: For he shall be great in the sight of the Lord, and shall drink neither wine nor strong drink; and he shall be filled with the Holy Ghost, even from his mother's womb.

The Immaculate Conception and Mary's sinlessness are, therefore, concepts that are perfectly harmonious with what was taught in the Bible from the beginning, and even some explicit scriptural proofs on their behalf exist, as shown above.

Mary was assumed, body and soul, into heaven

No direct biblical indications of Mary's assumption are to be found. But (as always with Catholic doctrine), there are indirect, deductive arguments from things that are clear in Scripture, and nothing in Scripture that would contradict *the possibility of this happening. There were, for example, several instances of bodily resurrection or of persons going bodily to heaven recorded in Scripture that bear some similarity to the Catholic belief in Mary's bodily assumption:*

Genesis 5:24: And Enoch walked with God: and he was not; for God took him.

2 Kings 2:1, 11: And it came to pass, when the LORD would take up Elijah into heaven by a whirlwind, that Elijah went with Elisha from Gilgal . . . [11] And it came to pass, as they still went on, and talked, that, behold, there appeared a chariot of fire, and horses of fire, and parted them both asunder; and Elijah went up by a whirlwind into heaven.

Matthew 27:52-53: And the graves were opened; and many bodies of the saints which slept arose, [53] And came out of the graves after his resurrection, and went into the holy city, and appeared unto many.

Acts 1:9: And when he had spoken these things, while they beheld, he was taken up; and a cloud received him out of their sight.

2 Corinthians 12:2-3: I knew a man in Christ above fourteen years ago, (whether in the body, I cannot tell; or whether out of the body, I cannot tell: God knoweth;) such an one caught up to the third heaven. [3] And I knew such a man, (whether in the body, or out of the body, I cannot tell: God knoweth;)

1 Thessalonians 4:15-17: For this we say unto you by the word of the Lord, that we which are alive and remain unto the coming of the Lord shall not prevent them which are asleep. [16] For the Lord himself shall descend from heaven with a shout, with the voice of the archangel, and with the trump of God: and the dead in Christ shall rise first: [17] Then we which are alive and remain shall be caught up together with them in the clouds, to meet the Lord in the air: and so shall we ever be with the Lord.

Hebrews 11:5: By faith Enoch was translated that he should not see death; and was not found, because God had translated him: for before his translation he had this testimony, that he pleased God.

Revelation 11:9-12: And they of the people and kindreds and tongues and nations shall see their dead bodies three days and an half, and shall not suffer their dead bodies to be put in graves. [10] And they that dwell upon the earth shall rejoice over them, and make merry, and shall send gifts one to another; because these two prophets tormented them that dwelt on the earth. [11] And after three days and an half the Spirit of life from God entered into them, and they stood upon their feet; and great fear fell upon them which saw them. [12] And they heard a great voice from heaven saying unto them, Come up hither. And they ascended up to heaven in a cloud; and their enemies beheld them.

If one accepts Mary's Immaculate Conception, the Assumption follows from the fact of absence of sin. Bodily death and decay, after all, come about as a result of sin and the fall:

Genesis 3:14, 19: And the LORD God said unto the serpent, Because thou hast done this, thou art cursed above all cattle, and above every beast of the field; upon thy belly shalt thou go, and dust shalt thou eat all the days of thy life . . . [19] In the sweat of thy face shalt thou eat bread, till thou return unto the ground; for out of it wast thou taken: for dust thou art, and unto dust shalt thou return. (cf. Ps. 16:10)

Romans 5:12, 17: Wherefore, as by one man sin entered into the world, and death by sin; and so death passed upon all men, for that all have sinned . . . [17] For if by one man's offence death reigned by one; much more they which receive abundance of grace and of the gift of righteousness shall reign in life by one, Jesus Christ.)

The Blessed Virgin Mary was the "first fruits" (after Jesus) of what will eventually be a general resurrection:

1 Corinthians 15:12-26: Now if Christ be preached that he rose from the dead, how say some among you that there is no resurrection of the dead? [13] But if there be no resurrection of the dead, then is Christ not risen: [14] And if Christ be not risen, then is our preaching vain, and your faith is also vain. [15] Yea, and we are found false witnesses of God; because we have testified of God that he raised up Christ: whom he raised not up, if so be that the dead rise not. [16] For if the dead rise not, then is not Christ raised: [17] And if Christ be not raised, your faith is vain; ye are yet in your sins. [18] Then they also which are fallen asleep in Christ are perished. [19] If in this life only we have hope in Christ, we are of all men most miserable. [20] But now is Christ risen from the dead, and become the firstfruits of them that slept. [21] For since by man came death, by man came also the resurrection of the dead. [22] For as in Adam all die, even so in Christ shall all be made alive. [23] But every man in his own order: Christ the firstfruits; afterward they that are Christ's at his coming. [24] Then cometh the end, when he shall have delivered up the kingdom to God, even the Father; when he shall have put down all rule and all authority and power. [25] For he must reign, till he hath put all enemies under his feet. [26] The last enemy that shall be destroyed is death. (cf. Matt. 27:52-53)

Mary was preserved from sin in order to bear God incarnate. Because of this, she didn't have to undergo the bodily decay that is the lot of all fallen human beings. What more appropriate person should be made the "Second Eve": like Eve was before the fall? It makes perfect sense. The Assumption goes hand-in-hand with the general resurrection and the Immaculate Conception, and the latter goes hand-in-hand with the Incarnation itself. In biblical thinking, all things have a relationship to each other. Thus we see Mary being greatly exalted and venerated in heaven:

Revelation 12:1-5: And there appeared a great wonder in heaven; a woman clothed with the sun, and the moon under her feet, and upon her head a crown of twelve stars: [2] And she being with child cried, travailing in birth, and pained to be delivered. [3] And there appeared another wonder in heaven; and behold a great red dragon, having seven heads and ten horns, and seven crowns upon his heads. [4] And his tail drew the third part of the stars of heaven, and did cast them to the earth: and the dragon stood before the woman which was ready to be delivered, for to devour her child as soon as it was born. [5] And she brought forth a man child, who was to rule all nations with a rod of iron: and her child was caught up unto God, and to his throne.

Chapter Fourteen

Marriage and Sexuality

Matrimony reflects the relationship between Christ and his Church

Genesis 1:26-28: And God said, Let us make man in our image, after our likeness: and let them have dominion over the fish of the sea, and over the fowl of the air, and over the cattle, and over all the earth, and over every creeping thing that creepeth upon the earth. [27] So God created man in his own image, in the image of God created he him; male and female created he them. [28] And God blessed them, and God said unto them, Be fruitful, and multiply, and replenish the earth, and subdue it: and have dominion over the fish of the sea, and over the fowl of the air, and over every living thing that moveth upon the earth.

Genesis 2:18-25: And the LORD God said, It is not good that the man should be alone; I will make him an help meet for him. [19] And out of the ground the LORD God formed every beast of the field, and every fowl of the air; and brought them unto Adam to see what he would call them: and whatsoever Adam called every living creature, that was the name thereof. [20] And Adam gave names to all cattle, and to the fowl of the air, and to every beast of the field; but for Adam there was not found an help meet for him. [21] And the LORD God caused a deep sleep to fall upon Adam and he slept: and he took one of his ribs, and closed up the flesh instead thereof; [22] And the rib, which the LORD God had taken from man, made he a woman, and brought her unto the man. [23] And Adam said, This is now bone of my bones, and flesh of my flesh: she shall be called Woman,

because she was taken out of Man. [24] Therefore shall a man leave his father and his mother, and shall cleave unto his wife: and they shall be one
flesh. [25] And they were both naked, the man and his wife, and were not
ashamed.

The Song of Solomon (The entire book is regarded by most commen-
tators as a parable of God and His Church.)

Isaiah 61:10: I will greatly rejoice in the LORD, my soul shall be joyful
in my God; for he hath clothed me with the garments of salvation, he hath
covered me with the robe of righteousness, as a bridegroom decketh himself with ornaments, and as a bride adorneth herself with her jewels.

Isaiah 62:4-5: Thou shalt no more be termed Forsaken; neither shall
thy land any more be termed Desolate: but thou shalt be called Hephzi-
bah, and thy land Beulah: for the LORD delighteth in thee, and thy land
shall be married. [5] For as a young man marrieth a virgin, so shall thy sons
marry thee: and as the bridegroom rejoiceth over the bride, so shall thy
God rejoice over thee.

Jeremiah 2:2: Go and cry in the ears of Jerusalem, saying, Thus saith
the LORD; I remember thee, the kindness of thy youth, the love of thine es-
pousals, when thou wentest after me in the wilderness, in a land that was
not sown.

Jeremiah 2:32: Can a maid forget her ornaments, or a bride her attire?
yet my people have forgotten me days without number.

Matthew 25:10: And while they went to buy, the bridegroom came;
and they that were ready went in with him to the marriage: and the door
was shut.

Luke 5:34: And he said unto them, Can ye make the children of the
bridechamber fast, while the bridegroom is with them? (cf. Mark 2:19-20;
Matt. 9:15; John 2:1-11)

Luke 12:36: And ye yourselves like unto men that wait for their lord, when he will return from the wedding; that when he cometh and knocketh, they may open unto him immediately.

John 3:27-29: John answered and said, A man can receive nothing, except it be given him from heaven. [28] Ye yourselves bear me witness, that I said, I am not the Christ, but that I am sent before him. [29] He that hath the bride is the bridegroom: but the friend of the bridegroom, which standeth and heareth him, rejoiceth greatly because of the bridegroom's voice: this my joy therefore is fulfilled.

1 Corinthians 7:2, 7, 17: Nevertheless, to avoid fornication, let every man have his own wife, and let every woman have her own husband . . . [7] For I would that all men were even as I myself. But every man hath his proper gift of God, one after this manner, and another after that . . . [17] But as God hath distributed to every man, as the Lord hath called every one, so let him walk. And so ordain I in all churches.

1 Corinthians 7:38: So then he that giveth her in marriage doeth well; but he that giveth her not in marriage doeth better.

2 Corinthians 11:2: For I am jealous over you with godly jealousy: for I have espoused you to one husband, that I may present you as a chaste virgin to Christ.

Ephesians 5:22-32: Wives, submit yourselves unto your own husbands, as unto the Lord. [23] For the husband is the head of the wife, even as Christ is the head of the church: and he is the saviour of the body. [24] Therefore as the church is subject unto Christ, so let the wives be to their own husbands in every thing. [25] Husbands, love your wives, even as Christ also loved the church, and gave himself for it; [26] That he might sanctify and cleanse it with the washing of water by the word, [27] That he might present it to himself a glorious church, not having spot, or wrinkle, or any such thing; but that it should be holy and without blemish. [28] So ought men to love their wives as their own bodies. He that loveth his wife loveth himself. [29] For no man ever yet hated his own flesh; but nourisheth and cherisheth it, even as the Lord the church: [30] For we are members of his body, of his flesh, and of his bones. [31] For this cause shall a man leave his father and mother, and shall be joined unto his wife, and they two shall be one flesh. [32] This is a great mystery: but I speak concerning Christ and the church. (cf. 1 Pet. 3:1-9)

1 Timothy 4:1-3: Now the Spirit speaketh expressly, that in the latter times some shall depart from the faith, giving heed to seducing spirits, and doctrines of devils; [2] Speaking lies in hypocrisy; having their conscience seared with a hot iron; [3] Forbidding to marry, and commanding to abstain from meats, which God hath created to be received with thanksgiving of them which believe and know the truth.

Revelation 19:7-9: Let us be glad and rejoice, and give honour to him: for the marriage of the Lamb is come, and his wife hath made herself ready. [8] And to her was granted that she should be arrayed in fine linen, clean and white: for the fine linen is the righteousness of saints. [9] And he saith unto me, Write, Blessed are they which are called unto the marriage supper of the Lamb. And he saith unto me, These are the true sayings of God.

Revelation 21:2,9: And I John saw the holy city, new Jerusalem, coming down from God out of heaven, prepared as a bride adorned for her husband . . . [9] And there came unto me one of the seven angels which had the seven vials full of the seven last plagues, and talked with me, saying, Come hither, I will shew thee the bride, the Lamb's wife.

Revelation 22:17: And the Spirit and the bride say, Come. And let him that heareth say, Come. And let him that is athirst come. And whosoever will, let him take the water of life freely.

Marriage is indissoluble

Exodus 20:14: Thou shalt not commit adultery. (cf. Deut. 5:18; Lev. 20:10; Matt. 19:18; Mark 10:19; Luke 18:20; Rom. 13:9; James 2:11).

Proverbs 6:32: But whoso committeth adultery with a woman lacketh understanding: he that doeth it destroyeth his own soul. (cf. 6:26; 30:20)

Jeremiah 3:1: If a man divorces his wife and she goes from him and becomes another man's wife, will he return to her? Would not that land be greatly polluted? . . .

Jeremiah 7:9: They say, If a man put away his wife, and she go from him, and become another man's, shall he return unto her again? shall not that land be greatly polluted? but thou hast played the harlot with many lovers; yet return again to me, saith the LORD. (cf. 9:2)

Ezekiel 44:22: Neither shall they take for their wives a widow, nor her that is put away: but they shall take maidens of the seed of the house of Israel, or a widow that had a priest before.

Hosea 4:14: I will not punish your daughters when they commit whoredom, nor your spouses when they commit adultery: for themselves are separated with whores, and they sacrifice with harlots: therefore the people that doth not understand shall fall.

Malachi 2:16: For the LORD, the God of Israel, saith that he hateth putting away: for one covereth violence with his garment, saith the LORD of hosts: therefore take heed to your spirit, that ye deal not treacherously.

Malachi 3:5: And I will come near to you to judgment; and I will be a swift witness against the sorcerers, and against the adulterers, and against false swearers, and against those that oppress the hireling in his wages, the widow, and the fatherless, and that turn aside the stranger from his right, and fear not me, saith the LORD of hosts.

Wisdom 14:26: Disquieting of good men, forgetfulness of good turns, defiling of souls, changing of kind, disorder in marriages, adultery, and shameless uncleanness.

Sirach 23:23: For first, she hath disobeyed the law of the most High; and secondly, she hath trespassed against her own husband; and thirdly, she hath played the whore in adultery, and brought children by another man. (cf. 25:2)

Matthew 5:27-28: Ye have heard that it was said by them of old time, Thou shalt not commit adultery: [28] But I say unto you, That whosoever looketh on a woman to lust after her hath committed adultery with her already in his heart.

Matthew 5:31-32: It hath been said, Whosoever shall put away his wife, let him give her a writing of divorcement: [32] But I say unto you, That whosoever shall put away his wife, saving for the cause of fornication, causeth her to commit adultery: and whosoever shall marry her that is divorced committeth adultery. (RSV: "But I say to you that every one who divorces his wife, except on the ground of unchastity, makes her an adulteress")

Matthew 15:19: For out of the heart proceed evil thoughts, murders, adulteries, fornications, thefts, false witness, blasphemies:

Matthew 19:3-11: The Pharisees also came unto him, tempting him, and saying unto him, Is it lawful for a man to put away his wife for every cause? [4] And he answered and said unto them, Have ye not read, that he which made them at the beginning made them male and female, [5] And said, For this cause shall a man leave father and mother, and shall cleave to his wife: and they twain shall be one flesh? [6] Wherefore they are no more twain, but one flesh. What therefore God hath joined together, let not man put asunder. [7] They say unto him, Why did Moses then command to give a writing of divorcement, and to put her away?

[8] He saith unto them, Moses because of the hardness of your hearts suffered you to put away your wives: but from the beginning it was not so. [9] And I say unto you, Whosoever shall put away his wife, except it be for fornication, and shall marry another, committeth adultery: and whoso marrieth her which is put away doth commit adultery. [10] His disciples say unto him, If the case of the man be so with his wife, it is not good to marry.

[11] But he said unto them, All men cannot receive this saying, save they to whom it is given.

The Greek word for fornication *(RSV: "unchastity") in Matthew 5:32 and 19:9 is* porneia, *defined in standard Greek lexicons as "unlawful sexual intercourse." Jesus is contrasting a true marriage, with a cohabitation, concubinage, or some other illicit union (cf. 1 Cor. 5:1). If there is not truly a marriage present, then a separation can take place, but it is no "divorce" because it was no marriage to begin with.*

These passages can't be used to justify divorce as a result of an occurrence of adultery of the partner, because the usual Greek word for adultery (moicheia) is not used, as it is in many other places (thirty-five times in one of its forms).

The Greek word porneia *and its cognates are never translated in the KJV New Testament as "adultery" but as "fornication" or "fornicator" (thirty-nine times), "harlot" (eight times), "whore" (four times), and "whoremonger" (five times). Likewise, every variant of the English* fornication *in the KJV is always a translation of some form of* porneia.

*The same holds true for adultery and its variants; they are always transla-
tions of some form of moicheia (and these are never translated as anything other
than "adultery"). We also find the two Greek words distinguished from each
other in the same verse (Matt. 5:19; Mark 7:21; Gal. 5:19).*

Mark 10:2-12: And the Pharisees came to him, and asked him, Is it
lawful for a man to put away his wife? tempting him. [3] And he answered
and said unto them, What did Moses command you?

[4] And they said, Moses suffered to write a bill of divorcement, and to
put her away. [5] And Jesus answered and said unto them, For the hardness
of your heart he wrote you this precept. [6] But from the beginning of the
creation God made them male and female. [7] For this cause shall a man
leave his father and mother, and cleave to his wife; [8] And they twain
shall be one flesh: so then they are no more twain, but one flesh. [9] What
therefore God hath joined together, let not man put asunder. [10] And in
the house his disciples asked him again of the same matter.

[11] And he saith unto them, Whosoever shall put away his wife, and
marry another, committeth adultery against her. [12] And if a woman shall
put away her husband, and be married to another, she committeth adultery.

Luke 16:18: Whosoever putteth away his wife, and marrieth another,
committeth adultery: and whosoever marrieth her that is put away from
her husband committeth adultery.

Romans 2:22: Thou that sayest a man should not commit adultery,
dost thou commit adultery? thou that abhorrest idols, dost thou commit
sacrilege?

Romans 7:1-3: Know ye not, brethren, (for I speak to them that know
the law,) how that the law hath dominion over a man as long as he liveth?
[2] For the woman which hath an husband is bound by the law to her husband so long as he liveth; but if the husband be dead, she is loosed from the
law of her husband. [3] So then if, while her husband liveth, she be married
to another man, she shall be called an adulteress: but if her husband be

dead, she is free from that law; so that she is no adulteress, though she be married to another man.

1 Corinthians 6:9: Know ye not that the unrighteous shall not inherit the kingdom of God? Be not deceived: neither fornicators, nor idolaters, nor adulterers, nor effeminate, nor abusers of themselves with mankind,

1 Corinthians 7:3-15: Let the husband render unto the wife due benevolence: and likewise also the wife unto the husband. [4] The wife hath not power of her own body, but the husband: and likewise also the husband hath not power of his own body, but the wife. [5] Defraud ye not one the other, except it be with consent for a time, that ye may give yourselves to fasting and prayer; and come together again, that Satan tempt you not for your incontinency. [6] But I speak this by permission, and not of commandment. [7] For I would that all men were even as I myself. But every man hath his proper gift of God, one after this manner, and another after that. [8] I say therefore to the unmarried and widows, It is good for them if they abide even as I. [9] But if they cannot contain, let them marry: for it is better to marry than to burn. [10] And unto the married I command, yet not I, but the Lord, Let not the wife depart from her husband:

[11] But and if she depart, let her remain unmarried, or be reconciled to her husband: and let not the husband put away his wife. [12] But to the rest speak I, not the Lord: If any brother hath a wife that believeth not, and she be pleased to dwell with him, let him not put her away. [13] And the woman which hath an husband that believeth not, and if he be pleased to dwell with her, let her not leave him. [14] For the unbelieving husband is sanctified by the wife, and the unbelieving wife is sanctified by the husband: else were your children unclean; but now are they holy. [15] But if the unbelieving depart, let him depart. A brother or a sister is not under bondage in such cases: but God hath called us to peace.

1 Corinthians 7:27, 39: Art thou bound unto a wife? seek not to be loosed. Art thou loosed from a wife? seek not a wife . . . [39] The wife is bound by the law as long as her husband liveth; but if her husband be dead, she is at liberty to be married to whom she will; only in the Lord.

Hebrews 13:4: Marriage is honourable in all, and the bed undefiled: but whoremongers and adulterers God will judge.

2 Peter 2:14: Having eyes full of adultery, and that cannot cease from sin; beguiling unstable souls: an heart they have exercised with covetous practices; cursed children:

Premarital sex and cohabitation
are not permissible

Exodus 22:16: And if a man entice a maid that is not betrothed, and lie with her, he shall surely endow her to be his wife.

Leviticus 21:13-15: And he shall take a wife in her virginity. [14] A widow, or a divorced woman, or profane, or an harlot, these shall he not take: but he shall take a virgin of his own people to wife. [15] Neither shall he profane his seed among his people: for I the LORD do sanctify him.

Deuteronomy 22:28-29: If a man find a damsel that is a virgin, which is not betrothed, and lay hold on her, and lie with her, and they be found; [29] Then the man that lay with her shall give unto the damsel's father fifty shekels of silver, and she shall be his wife; because he hath humbled her, he may not put her away all his days.

Hosea 4:14: I will not punish your daughters when they commit whoredom, nor your spouses when they commit adultery: for themselves are separated with whores, and they sacrifice with harlots: therefore the people that doth not understand shall fall.

Sirach 23:17-19: All bread is sweet to a whoremonger, he will not leave off till he die. [18] A man that breaketh wedlock, saying thus in his heart, Who seeth me? I am compassed about with darkness, the walls cover me, and no body seeth me; what need I to fear? the most High will not remember my sins: [19] Such a man only feareth the eyes of men, and knoweth not that the eyes of the Lord are ten thousand times brighter than the sun, beholding all the ways of men, and considering the most secret parts.

Mark 7:21: For from within, out of the heart of men, proceed evil thoughts, adulteries, fornications, murders,

1 Corinthians 6:18: Flee fornication. Every sin that a man doeth is without the body; but he that committeth fornication sinneth against his own body.

1 Corinthians 7:1-2, 9: Now concerning the things whereof ye wrote unto me: It is good for a man not to touch a woman. [2] Nevertheless, to avoid fornication, let every man have his own wife, and let every woman have her own husband . . . [9] But if they cannot contain, let them marry: for it is better to marry than to burn.

1 Corinthians 7:36: But if any man think that he behaveth himself uncomely toward his virgin, if she pass the flower of her age, and need so require, let him do what he will, he sinneth not: let them marry.

1 Corinthians 10:8: Neither let us commit fornication, as some of them committed, and fell in one day three and twenty thousand.

2 Corinthians 12:21: And lest, when I come again, my God will humble me among you, and that I shall bewail many which have sinned already, and have not repented of the uncleanness and fornication and lasciviousness which they have committed.

Galatians 5:19: Now the works of the flesh are manifest, which are these; Adultery, fornication, uncleanness, lasciviousness,

Ephesians 5:3-5: But fornication, and all uncleanness, or covetousness, let it not be once named among you, as becometh saints; [4] Neither filthiness, nor foolish talking, nor jesting, which are not convenient: but rather giving of thanks. [5] For this ye know, that no whoremonger, nor unclean person, nor covetous man, who is an idolater, hath any inheritance in the kingdom of Christ and of God.

Colossians 3:5: Mortify therefore your members which are upon the earth; fornication, uncleanness, inordinate affection, evil concupiscence, and covetousness, which is idolatry:

1 Timothy 1:10: For whoremongers, for them that defile themselves with mankind, for menstealers, for liars, for perjured persons, and if there be any other thing that is contrary to sound doctrine;

Jude 7: Even as Sodom and Gomorrha, and the cities about them in like manner, giving themselves over to fornication, and going after strange flesh, are set forth for an example, suffering the vengeance of eternal fire.

Revelation 9:21: Neither repented they of their murders, nor of their sorceries, nor of their fornication, nor of their thefts.

Revelation 21:8: But the fearful, and unbelieving, and the abominable, and murderers, and whoremongers, and sorcerers, and idolaters, and all liars, shall have their part in the lake which burneth with fire and brimstone: which is the second death.

Revelation 22:15: For without are dogs, and sorcerers, and whoremongers, and murderers, and idolaters, and whosoever loveth and maketh a lie.

Annulment is not Catholic divorce

An annulment is not a "Catholic divorce." It's a declaration by the Church that a valid sacramental marriage was never present (because several necessary conditions were not met; for example, insufficiently free will, truthfulness of both parties, mental health, deliberate decision not to bear children, etc.). A similar distinction is found in civil law in many countries. The Old Testament dichotomy between a concubine and a wife is similar to the distinction between civil and sacramental marriage:

Genesis 21:10, 14: Wherefore she said unto Abraham, Cast out this bondwoman and her son: for the son of this bondwoman shall not be heir with my son, even with Isaac . . . [14] And Abraham rose up early in the morning, and took bread, and a bottle of water, and gave it unto Hagar, putting it on her shoulder, and the child, and sent her away: and she departed, and wandered in the wilderness of Beer-sheba.

Judges 8:31: And his concubine that was in Shechem, she also bare him a son, whose name he called Abimelech.

Likewise, in Ezra, we read that many Israelites "sent away" the "foreign women" they had married, not simply because they were foreigners, but because they caused them to become corrupted by false religions and idolatry. This was essentially an annulment, as opposed to a divorce:

Ezra 9:14: Should we again break thy commandments, and join in affinity with the people of these abominations? wouldest not thou be angry with us till thou hadst consumed us, so that there should be no remnant nor escaping? (cf. 9:1-2)

Ezra 10:2-3, 10-14, 19: And Shechaniah the son of Jehiel, one of the sons of Elam, answered and said unto Ezra, We have trespassed against our God, and have taken strange wives of the people of the land: yet now there is hope in Israel concerning this thing. [3] Now therefore let us make a covenant with our God to put away all the wives, and such as are born of them, according to the counsel of my lord, and of those that tremble at the commandment of our God; and let it be done according to the law . . . [10] And Ezra the priest stood up, and said unto them, Ye have transgressed, and have taken strange wives, to increase the trespass of Israel. [11] Now therefore make confession unto the LORD God of your fathers, and do his pleasure: and separate yourselves from the people of the land, and from the strange wives. [12] Then all the congregation answered and said with a loud voice, As thou hast said, so must we do. [13] But the people are many, and it is a time of much rain, and we are not able to stand without, neither is this a work of one day or two: for we are many that have transgressed in this thing. [14] Let now our rulers of all the congregation stand, and let all them which have taken strange wives in our cities come at appointed times, and with them the elders of every city, and the judges thereof, until the fierce wrath of our God for this matter be turned from us . . . [19] And they gave their hands that they would put away their wives; and being guilty, they offered a ram of the flock for their trespass.

Nehemiah 13:26-27: Did not Solomon king of Israel sin by these things? yet among many nations was there no king like him, who was beloved of his God, and God made him king over all Israel: nevertheless even him did outlandish women cause to sin. [27] Shall we then hearken unto you to do all this great evil, to transgress against our God in marrying strange wives?

Matthew 5:32: But I say unto you, That whosoever shall put away his wife, saving for the cause of fornication, causeth her to commit adultery:

and whosoever shall marry her that is divorced committeth adultery. (RSV: "on the ground of unchastity")

Matthew 19:9: And I say unto you, Whosoever shall put away his wife, except it be for fornication, and shall marry another, committeth adultery: and whoso marrieth her which is put away doth commit adultery. (RSV: "And I say to you: whoever divorces his wife, except for unchastity, and marries another, commits adultery")

The preceding two verses also apply to annulment situations, insofar as it is determined that a marriage never existed, and it was a state of immoral fornication instead; thus making it a situation having nothing to do with divorce, since no true sacramental marriage is involved. One can even become "one flesh" with a prostitute (1 Cor. 6:16), but obviously that does not constitute a marriage, let alone a sacramental one.

1 Corinthians 7:15: But if the unbelieving depart, let him depart. A brother or a sister is not under bondage in such cases: but God hath called us to peace.

The "Pauline privilege" is an example of a situation that precisely fits a certain type of annulment (and the Church has always accepted it because it is so clearly taught in Holy Scripture, here).

Homosexual acts are not permissible

Genesis 19:4-7: But before they lay down, the men of the city, even the men of Sodom, compassed the house round, both old and young, all the people from every quarter: [5] And they called unto Lot, and said unto him, Where are the men which came in to thee this night? bring them out unto us, that we may know them.

[6] And Lot went out at the door unto them, and shut the door after him, [7] And said, I pray you, brethren, do not so wickedly.

Leviticus 18:20-30: Moreover thou shalt not lie carnally with thy neighbour's wife, to defile thyself with her. [21] And thou shalt not let any of thy seed pass through the fire to Molech, neither shalt thou profane the name of thy God: I am the LORD.

[22] Thou shalt not lie with mankind, as with womankind: it is abomination. [23] Neither shalt thou lie with any beast to defile thyself therewith: neither shall any woman stand before a beast to lie down thereto: it is confusion. [24] Defile not ye yourselves in any of these things: for in all these the nations are defiled which I cast out before you: [25] And the land is defiled: therefore I do visit the iniquity thereof upon it, and the land itself vomiteth out her inhabitants. [26] Ye shall therefore keep my statutes and my judgments, and shall not commit any of these abominations; neither any of your own nation, nor any stranger that sojourneth among you: [27] (For all these abominations have the men of the land done, which were before you, and the land is defiled;) [28] That the land spue not you

out also, when ye defile it, as it spued out the nations that were before you.
[29] For whosoever shall commit any of these abominations, even the souls
that commit them shall be cut off from among their people. [30] Therefore
shall ye keep mine ordinance, that ye commit not any one of these abominable customs, which were committed before you, and that ye defile not
yourselves therein: I am the LORD your God.

Leviticus 20:13: If a man also lie with mankind, as he lieth with a
woman, both of them have committed an abomination: they shall surely
be put to death; their blood shall be upon them.

Deuteronomy 23:17: There shall be no whore of the daughters of Israel, nor a sodomite of the sons of Israel.

Judges 19:22-23: Now as they were making their hearts merry, behold,
the men of the city, certain sons of Belial, beset the house round about, and
beat at the door, and spake to the master of the house, the old man, saying,
Bring forth the man that came into thine house, that we may know him.
[23] And the man, the master of the house, went out unto them, Nay, my
brethren, nay, I pray you, do not so wickedly; seeing that this man is come
into mine house, do not this folly.

1 Kings 14:24: And there were also sodomites in the land: and they
did according to all the abominations of the nations which the LORD cast
out before the children of Israel.

1 Kings 15:11-12: And Asa did that which was right in the eyes of
the LORD, as did David his father. [12] And he took away the sodomites
out of the land, and removed all the idols that his fathers had made. (cf. 2
Kings 23:7)

1 Kings 22:42-46: Jehoshaphat was thirty and five years old when he
began to reign; and he reigned twenty and five years in Jerusalem. And his
mother's name was Azubah the daughter of Shilhi. [43] And he walked in
all the ways of Asa his father; he turned not aside from it, doing that which

was right in the eyes of the LORD: nevertheless the high places were not taken away; for the people offered and burnt incense yet in the high places.

[44] And Jehoshaphat made peace with the king of Israel.

[45] Now the rest of the acts of Jehoshaphat, and his might that he shewed, and how he warred, are they not written in the book of the chronicles of the kings of Judah? [46] And the remnant of the sodomites, which remained in the days of his father Asa, he took out of the land.

Romans 1:24-27: Wherefore God also gave them up to uncleanness through the lusts of their own hearts, to dishonour their own bodies between themselves: [25] Who changed the truth of God into a lie, and worshipped and served the creature more than the Creator, who is blessed for ever. Amen. [26] For this cause God gave them up unto vile affections: for even their women did change the natural use into that which is against nature: [27] And likewise also the men, leaving the natural use of the woman, burned in their lust one toward another; men with men working that which is unseemly, and receiving in themselves that recompence of their error which was meet.

1 Timothy 1:8-11: But we know that the law is good, if a man use it lawfully; [9] Knowing this, that the law is not made for a righteous man, but for the lawless and disobedient, for the ungodly and for sinners, for unholy and profane, for murderers of fathers and murderers of mothers, for manslayers, [10] For whoremongers, for them that defile themselves with mankind, for menstealers, for liars, for perjured persons, and if there be any other thing that is contrary to sound doctrine; [11] According to the glorious gospel of the blessed God, which was committed to my trust.

2 Peter 2:4-8: For if God spared not the angels that sinned, but cast them down to hell, and delivered them into chains of darkness, to be reserved unto judgment; [5] And spared not the old world, but saved Noah the eighth person, a preacher of righteousness, bringing in the flood upon the world of the ungodly; [6] And turning the cities of Sodom and

Gomorrha into ashes condemned them with an overthrow, making them an ensample unto those that after should live ungodly;

[7] And delivered just Lot, vexed with the filthy conversation of the wicked: [8] (For that righteous man dwelling among them, in seeing and hearing, vexed his righteous soul from day to day with their unlawful deeds;)

Jude 7: Even as Sodom and Gomorrha, and the cities about them in like manner, giving themselves over to fornication, and going after strange flesh, are set forth for an example, suffering the vengeance of eternal fire.

God doesn't change. If he states that something is sinful and never permissible, then that prohibition applies at all times. Secondly, it isn't true that the Bible condemns only homosexual rape and not such acts by mutual consent (as is often argued today). Most of the passages above (more than enough!) condemn consensual homosexual acts. Jude 7 mentions "unnatural lust" and 2 Peter 2:4-10 states similarly. Therefore, this objection collapses.

As for the desire itself, Catholics don't believe it is inherently sinful (short of an excessive attention amounting to lust), as long as it isn't acted upon (Catechism of the Catholic Church, nos. 2358-2359), just as heterosexual lust, fornication, and adultery must be rejected in the will, by God's grace, in order to avoid sin. Everyone has more than enough temptations to resist and overcome.

St. Paul in Romans 1 makes an explicit argument against homosexuality, as an unnatural practice; he also presents a similar argument in 1 Corinthians 6:12-20, by stating that excessive appetite for sex (and also food) amounts to being "enslaved" (6:12, RSV). There is a created reality and natural order beyond mere physical pleasure, which must not be violated. Certain things are wrong by their very nature. Sex outside of marriage — whether heterosexual or homosexual — belongs to that category (6:18-20). Paul casually assumes that sodomy is intrinsically wrong in 1 Timothy 1:8-11, as he does in Romans 1:24-27 (RSV): "dishonorable passions," "unnatural [relations]," "men committing shameless acts with men," etc.

There is also indirect indication of Jesus' acceptance of the traditional Jewish prohibition of homosexual acts, or sodomy, in his approval of the judgment of

Sodom (Matt. 10:15; 11:23-24; Luke 10:12; 17:29). We know what Jesus thought of the Mosaic Law:

Matthew 5:17-19: Think not that I am come to destroy the law, or the prophets: I am not come to destroy, but to fulfil. [18] For verily I say unto you, Till heaven and earth pass, one jot or one tittle shall in no wise pass from the law, till all be fulfilled. [19] Whosoever therefore shall break one of these least commandments, and shall teach men so, he shall be called the least in the kingdom of heaven: but whosoever shall do and teach them, the same shall be called great in the kingdom of heaven. (cf. Matt. 7:12; 22:40; Luke 16:17)

Matthew 23:2-3: Saying, The scribes and the Pharisees sit in Moses' seat: [3] All therefore whatsoever they bid you observe, that observe and do; but do not ye after their works: for they say, and do not. (cf. Matt. 23:23)

Jesus observed the Law in its entirety. He worshiped in synagogues and the Temple; he observed the Jewish feasts (the Last Supper was a Passover dinner: Matt. 26:17-19; Mark 14:12-16; Luke 22:7-15). He casually made reference to the authority of Moses over his own disciples (Matt. 8:4; Mark 1:44; 7:8-13; Luke 16:31; 24:44; John 5:46; 7:19-23). There is no indication that he disputed any of these received laws. Therefore, he accepted — as part of the whole — the injunctions against homosexual acts.

Contraception is not permissible

Genesis 38:8-10: And Judah said unto Onan, Go in unto thy brother's wife, and marry her, and raise up seed to thy brother. [9] And Onan knew that the seed should not be his; and it came to pass, when he went in unto his brother's wife, that he spilled it on the ground, lest that he should give seed to his brother. [10] And the thing which he did displeased the LORD: wherefore he slew him also.

This involved what is known as the "levirate law": the duty to produce off-spring with the wife of a dead brother. But this is not why God killed Onan, since the penalty for that was public humiliation and shunning, not death (Deut. 25:5-10). Context also supports this interpretation, since immediately after this (Gen. 38:11-26), is the story of Onan's father, Judah, refusing to enforce the law and allow his other son, Shelah, to produce a child with Tamar, his daughter-in-law. He was afraid that Shelah would be killed like Onan and his other wicked son, Er (38:7, 11). Judah acknowledges his sin in 38:26 (RSV): "She is more righteous than I, inasmuch as I did not give her to my son Shelah." He wasn't killed, so it is unreasonable to contend that Onan was judged and killed by God for the very same sin that Judah committed (in the same passage). Onan was judged for con-traception (sex with the deliberate intent to prevent procreation unnaturally).

There are a host of other biblical passages which exalt fertility and the blessing of many children, and the curse of none. Married couples are to "be fruitful and multiply"; this is a blessing:

Genesis 1:28: And God blessed them, and God said unto them, Be fruitful, and multiply, and replenish the earth, and subdue it: and have dominion over the fish of the sea, and over the fowl of the air, and over every living thing that moveth upon the earth. (cf. 9:1, 7)

Genesis 28:3: And God Almighty bless thee, and make thee fruitful, and multiply thee, that thou mayest be a multitude of people;

Genesis 35:11: And God said unto him, I am God Almighty: be fruitful and multiply; a nation and a company of nations shall be of thee, and kings shall come out of thy loins; (cf. Dan. 3:35-36)

Deuteronomy 7:13-14: And he will love thee, and bless thee, and multiply thee: he will also bless the fruit of thy womb, and the fruit of thy land, thy corn, and thy wine, and thine oil, the increase of thy kine, and the flocks of thy sheep, in the land which he sware unto thy fathers to give thee. [14] Thou shalt be blessed above all people: there shall not be male or female barren among you, or among your cattle.

Psalm 107:38: He blesseth them also, so that they are multiplied greatly; and suffereth not their cattle to decrease . . . (cf. Isa. 48:18-19; Jer. 29:6; 30:19-20; 33:22; Ezek. 36:10-12; Bar. 2:34)

Psalm 115:14: The LORD shall increase you more and more, you and your children. (cf. 105:24)

Psalm 128:3-4: Thy wife shall be as a fruitful vine by the sides of thine house: thy children like olive plants round about thy table. [4] Behold, that thus shall the man be blessed that feareth the LORD.

Proverbs 17:6: Children's children are the crown of old men; and the glory of children are their fathers. (cf. 11:30; Sir. 44:13, 21)

Barrenness is contrary to blessing and "glory":

Exodus 23:25-26: And ye shall serve the LORD your God, and he shall bless thy bread, and thy water; and I will take sickness away from the midst of thee. [26] There shall nothing cast their young, nor be barren, in thy land: the number of thy days I will fulfil.

Jeremiah 18:21: Therefore deliver up their children to the famine, and pour out their blood by the force of the sword; and let their wives be bereaved of their children, and be widows; and let their men be put to death; let their young men be slain by the sword in battle.

Hosea 9:11: As for Ephraim, their glory shall fly away like a bird, from the birth, and from the womb, and from the conception. (RSV: "E'phraim's glory shall fly away like a bird — no birth, no pregnancy, no conception!")

Procreation is central to marriage:

Malachi 2:14-15: Yet ye say, Wherefore? Because the LORD hath been witness between thee and the wife of thy youth, against whom thou hast dealt treacherously: yet is she thy companion, and the wife of thy covenant. [15] And did not he make one? Yet had he the residue of the spirit. And wherefore one? That he might seek a godly seed. Therefore take heed to your spirit, and let none deal treacherously against the wife of his youth.

Childbearing is so sacred that women are even said to be "saved" by it:

1 Timothy 2:15: Notwithstanding she shall be saved in childbearing, if they continue in faith and charity and holiness with sobriety.

It is God who opens and closes wombs and causes a conception to occur:

Genesis 20:17-18: So Abraham prayed unto God: and God healed Abimelech, and his wife, and his maidservants; and they bare children. [18] For the LORD had fast closed up all the wombs of the house of Abimelech, because of Sarah Abraham's wife.

Genesis 29:31: And when the LORD saw that Leah was hated, he opened her womb: but Rachel was barren.

Genesis 30:2, 22-24: And Jacob's anger was kindled against Rachel: and he said, Am I in God's stead, who hath withheld from thee the fruit of the womb? . . . [22] And God remembered Rachel, and God hearkened to her, and opened her womb. [23] And she conceived, and bare a son; and said, God hath taken away my reproach: [24] And she called his name Joseph; and said, The LORD shall add to me another son.

Exodus 1:21: And it came to pass, because the midwives feared God, that he made them houses.

Joshua 24:3: And I took your father Abraham from the other side of the flood, and led him throughout all the land of Canaan, and multiplied his seed, and gave him Isaac.

Ruth 4:13: So Boaz took Ruth, and she was his wife: and when he went in unto her, the LORD gave her conception, and she bare a son.

1 Samuel 1:5: But unto Hannah he gave a worthy portion; for he loved Hannah: but the LORD had shut up her womb.

Job 10:8, 11: Thine hands have made me and fashioned me together round about; yet thou dost destroy me . . . [11] Thou hast clothed me with skin and flesh, and hast fenced me with bones and sinews. (cf. 12:10)

Job 31:15: Did not he that made me in the womb make him? and did not one fashion us in the womb?

Psalm 113:9: He maketh the barren woman to keep house, and to be a joyful mother of children. Praise ye the LORD.

Ecclesiastes 11:5: As thou knowest not what is the way of the spirit, nor how the bones do grow in the womb of her that is with child: even so thou knowest not the works of God who maketh all.

Isaiah 44:2: Thus saith the LORD that made thee, and formed thee from the womb, which will help thee; Fear not, O Jacob, my servant; and thou, Jesurun, whom I have chosen. (cf. 44:24; 54:1-3; Ezek. 36:37; 2 Macc. 7:22-23)

Children are a gift from God and a blessing:

Genesis 17:16, 20: And I will bless her, and give thee a son also of her: yea, I will bless her, and she shall be a mother of nations; kings of people shall be of her . . . [20] And as for Ishmael, I have heard thee: Behold, I have blessed him, and will make him fruitful, and will multiply him exceedingly; twelve princes shall he beget, and I will make him a great nation. (cf. Deut. 30:9,15-16; Isa. 51:2)

Genesis 29:32-33: And Leah conceived, and bare a son, and she called his name Reuben: for she said, Surely the LORD hath looked upon my affliction; now therefore my husband will love me. [33] And she conceived again, and bare a son; and said, Because the LORD hath heard that I was hated, he hath therefore given me this son also: and she called his name Simeon.

Genesis 33:5: And he lifted up his eyes, and saw the women and the children; and said, Who are those with thee? And he said, The children which God hath graciously given thy servant.

1 Chronicles 25:5: All these were the sons of Heman the king's seer in the words of God, to lift up the horn. And God gave to Heman fourteen sons and three daughters.

Psalm 127:3-5: Lo, children are an heritage of the LORD: and the fruit of the womb is his reward. [4] As arrows are in the hand of a mighty man; so are children of the youth. [5] Happy is the man that hath his quiver full of them: they shall not be ashamed, but they shall speak with the enemies in the gate. (cf. 72:16; 113:9)

Tobit 4:12: Beware of all whoredom, my son, and chiefly take a wife of the seed of thy fathers, and take not a strange woman to wife, which is not of thy father's tribe: for we are the children of the prophets, Noe, Abraham, Isaac, and Jacob: remember, my son, that our fathers from the beginning, even that they all married wives of their own kindred, and were blessed in their children, and their seed shall inherit the land. (cf. Sir. 25:7)

Chapter Fifteen

Abortion

The child in the womb is fully a person

Genesis 16:11: And the angel of the LORD said unto her, Behold, thou art with child, and shalt bear a son, and shalt call his name Ishmael; because the LORD hath heard thy affliction.

Genesis 19:36: Thus were both the daughters of Lot with child by their father.

Genesis 25:21-22: And Isaac intreated the LORD for his wife, because she was barren: and the LORD was intreated of him, and Rebekah his wife conceived. [22] And the children struggled together within her; and she said, If it be so, why am I thus? And she went to inquire of the LORD.

Genesis 38:24: And it came to pass about three months after, that it was told Judah, saying, Tamar thy daughter in law hath played the harlot; and also, behold, she is with child by whoredom. And Judah said, Bring her forth, and let her be burnt.

Numbers 5:28: And if the woman be not defiled, but be clean; then she shall be free, and shall conceive seed. (RSV: "she shall be free and shall conceive children")

Judges 16:17: That he told her all his heart, and said unto her. There hath not come a rasor upon mine head; for I have been a Nazarite unto God from my mother's womb: if I be shaven, then my strength will go from me, and I shall become weak, and be like any other man.

Ruth 1:11: And Naomi said, Turn again, my daughters: why will ye go with me? are there yet any more sons in my womb, that they may be your husbands?

2 Samuel 11:5: And the woman conceived, and sent and told David, and said, I am with child. (cf. 2 Kings 8:12; 15:16; Eccles. 11:5; Amos 1:13)

2 Kings 19:3: And they said unto him, Thus saith Hezekiah, This day is a day of trouble, and of rebuke, and blasphemy: for the children are come to the birth, and there is not strength to bring forth.

Job 3:3: Let the day perish wherein I was born, and the night in which it was said, There is a man child conceived.

Job 3:16: Or as an hidden untimely birth I had not been; as infants which never saw light.

Job 31:18: (For from my youth he was brought up with me, as with a father, and I have guided her from my mother's womb;)

Psalm 51:5: Behold, I was shapen in iniquity; and in sin did my mother conceive me.

Psalm 102:18: This shall be written for the generation to come: and the people which shall be created shall praise the LORD. (RSV: "a people yet unborn")

Psalm 139:13-16: For thou hast possessed my reins: thou hast covered me in my mother's womb. [14] I will praise thee; for I am fearfully and wonderfully made: marvellous are thy works; and that my soul knoweth right well. [15] My substance was not hid from thee, when I was made in secret, and curiously wrought in the lowest parts of the earth. [16] Thine eyes did see my substance, yet being unperfect; and in thy book all my members were written, which in continuance were fashioned, when as yet there was none of them.

Song of Solomon 8:2: I would lead thee, and bring thee into my mother's house, who would instruct me: I would cause thee to drink of spiced wine of the juice of my pomegranate. (RSV: "the chamber of her that conceived me")

Isaiah 49:1, 5: Listen, O isles, unto me; and hearken, ye people, from far; The LORD hath called me from the womb; from the bowels of my mother hath he made mention of my name . . . [5] . . . the LORD that formed me from the womb to be his servant . . . (cf. 44:2, 24)

Jeremiah 1:5: Before I formed thee in the belly I knew thee; and before thou camest forth out of the womb I sanctified thee, and I ordained thee a prophet unto the nations.

Hosea 12:3: He took his brother by the heel in the womb . . .

Tobit 4:4: Remember, my son, that she saw many dangers for thee, when thou wast in her womb . . .

Wisdom 7:1: I myself also am a mortal man, like to all, and the offspring of him that was first made of the earth, (RSV: "descendant of the first-formed child of earth; and in the womb of a mother I was molded into flesh,")

Sirach 49:7: . . . who nevertheless was a prophet, sanctified in his mother's womb . . .

2 Maccabees 7:22-23: I cannot tell how ye came into my womb: for I neither gave you breath nor life, neither was it I that formed the members of every one of you; [23] But doubtless the Creator of the world, who formed the generation of man, and found out the beginning of all things, will also of his own mercy give you breath and life again, as ye now regard not your own selves for his laws' sake.

2 Maccabees 7:27: . . . O my son, have pity upon me that bare thee nine months in my womb . . . (RSV: "I carried you nine months in my womb")

Matthew 1:18: Now the birth of Jesus Christ was on this wise: When as his mother Mary was espoused to Joseph, before they came together, she was found with child of the Holy Ghost.

Matthew 18:10: Take heed that ye despise not one of these little ones; for I say unto you, That in heaven their angels do always behold the face of my Father which is in heaven.

Matthew 24:19: And woe unto them that are with child, and to them that give suck in those days! (cf. Mark 13:17)

Matthew 25:40: And the King shall answer and say unto them, Verily I say unto you, Inasmuch as ye have done it unto one of the least of these my brethren, ye have done it unto me.

Luke 1:15: For he shall be great in the sight of the Lord, and shall drink neither wine nor strong drink; and he shall be filled with the Holy Ghost, even from his mother's womb.

Luke 1:35-36: And the angel answered and said unto her, The Holy Ghost shall come upon thee, and the power of the Highest shall over-shadow thee: therefore also that holy thing which shall be born of thee shall be called the Son of God. [36] And, behold, thy cousin Elisabeth, she hath also conceived a son in her old age: and this is the sixth month with her, who was called barren.

Luke 1:44: For, lo, as soon as the voice of thy salutation sounded in mine ears, the babe leaped in my womb for joy.

Luke 2:5: To be taxed with Mary his espoused wife, being great with child. (RSV: "Mary, his betrothed, who was with child")

Luke 2:21: And when eight days were accomplished for the circumcising of the child, his name was called JESUS, which was so named of the angel before he was conceived in the womb.

Romans 9:10: And not only this; but when Rebecca also had conceived by one, even by our father Isaac; (RSV: "Rebecca had conceived children")

Galatians 1:15: But when it pleased God, who separated me from my mother's womb, and called me by his grace,

Killing the innocent is forbidden

Exodus 21:22: If men strive, and hurt a woman with child, so that her fruit depart from her, and yet no mischief follow: he shall be surely punished, according as the woman's husband will lay upon him; and he shall pay as the judges determine.

Exodus 23:7: . . . the innocent and righteous slay thou not: for I will not justify the wicked.

Numbers 35:30: Whoso killeth any person, the murderer shall be put to death by the mouth of witnesses: but one witness shall not testify against any person to cause him to die.

Deuteronomy 19:13: Thine eye shall not pity him, but thou shalt put away the guilt of innocent blood from Israel, that it may go well with thee. (cf. 19:10; 21:8-9)

Deuteronomy 27:25: Cursed be he that taketh reward to slay an innocent person . . .

2 Kings 14:6: But the children of the murderers he slew not: according unto that which is written in the book of the law of Moses, wherein the LORD commanded, saying, The fathers shall not be put to death for the children, nor the children be put to death for the fathers; but every man shall be put to death for his own sin. (cf. Deut. 24:16)

2 Kings 21:16: Moreover Manasseh shed innocent blood very much, till he had filled Jerusalem from one end to another; beside his sin wherewith he made Judah to sin, in doing that which was evil in the sight of the LORD.

2 Kings 24:4: And also for the innocent blood that he shed: for he filled Jerusalem with innocent blood; which the LORD would not pardon.

Jeremiah 7:6-7: If ye oppress not the stranger, the fatherless, and the widow, and shed not innocent blood in this place, neither walk after other gods to your hurt: [7] Then will I cause you to dwell in this place, in the land that I gave to your fathers, for ever and ever. (cf. 22:3, 17)

Joel 3:19: Egypt shall be a desolation, and Edom shall be a desolate wilderness, for the violence against the children of Judah, because they have shed innocent blood in their land.

1 Maccabees 2:37: But said, Let us die all in our innocency: heaven and earth will testify for us, that ye put us to death wrongfully.

Child sacrifice is an abomination

Leviticus 18:21: And thou shalt not let any of thy seed pass through the fire to Molech, neither shalt thou profane the name of thy God: I am the LORD. (RSV: "You shall not give any of your children to devote them by fire to Molech")

Leviticus 20:2-3: Again, thou shalt say to the children of Israel, Whosoever he be of the children of Israel, or of the strangers that sojourn in Israel, that giveth any of his seed unto Molech; he shall surely be put to death: the people of the land shall stone him with stones. [3] And I will set my face against that man, and will cut him off from among his people; because he hath given of his seed unto Molech, to defile my sanctuary, and to profane my holy name. (RSV: "who gives any of his children to Molech")

Deuteronomy 12:31: . . . for every abomination to the LORD, which he hateth, have they done unto their gods; for even their sons and their daughters they have burnt in the fire to their gods.

2 Kings 16:2-3: Twenty years old was Ahaz when he began to reign, and reigned sixteen years in Jerusalem, and did not that which was right in the sight of the LORD his God, like David his father. [3] But he walked in the way of the kings of Israel, yea, and made his son to pass through the fire, according to the abominations of the heathen, whom the LORD cast out from before the children of Israel. (RSV: "He even burned his son as an offering")

2 Kings 17:17-18: And they caused their sons and their daughters to pass through the fire, and used divination and enchantments, and sold themselves to do evil in the sight of the LORD, to provoke him to anger. [18] Therefore the LORD was very angry with Israel, and removed them out of his sight: there was none left but the tribe of Judah only. (RSV: "And they burned their sons and their daughters as offerings")

2 Kings 23:10: And he defiled Topheth, which is in the valley of the children of Hinnom, that no man might make his son or his daughter to pass through the fire to Molech. (RSV: "that no one might burn his son or his daughter as an offering to Molech")

2 Chronicles 28:3: Moreover he burnt incense in the valley of the son of Hinnom, and burnt his children in the fire, after the abominations of the heathen whom the LORD had cast out before the children of Israel.

2 Chronicles 33:6: And he caused his children to pass through the fire in the valley of the son of Hinnom: also he observed times, and used enchantments, and used witchcraft, and dealt with a familiar spirit, and with wizards: he wrought much evil in the sight of the LORD, to provoke him to anger. (RSV: "And he burned his sons as an offering")

Psalm 106:36-39: And they served their idols: which were a snare unto them. [37] Yea, they sacrificed their sons and their daughters unto devils, [38] And shed innocent blood, even the blood of their sons and of their daughters, whom they sacrificed unto the idols of Canaan: and the land was polluted with blood. [39] Thus were they defiled with their own works, and went a whoring with their own inventions.

Jeremiah 7:31-32: And they have built the high places of Tophet, which is in the valley of the son of Hinnom, to burn their sons and their daughters in the fire; which I commanded them not, neither came it into my heart. [32] Therefore, behold, the days come, saith the LORD, that it shall no more be called Tophet, nor the valley of the son of Hinnom, but the valley of slaughter: for they shall bury in Tophet, till there be no place.

Jeremiah 19:5: They have built also the high places of Baal, to burn their sons with fire for burnt offerings unto Baal, which I commanded not, nor spake it, neither came it into my mind:

Jeremiah 32:35: And they built the high places of Baal, which are in the valley of the son of Hinnom, to cause their sons and their daughters to pass through the fire unto Molech; which I commanded them not, neither came it into my mind, that they should do this abomination, to cause Judah to sin. (RSV: "to offer up their sons and daughters to Molech")

Ezekiel 16:20-21: Moreover thou hast taken thy sons and thy daughters, whom thou hast borne unto me, and these hast thou sacrificed unto them to be devoured. Is this of thy whoredoms a small matter, [21] That thou hast slain my children, and delivered them to cause them to pass through the fire for them? (RSV: "you slaughtered my children and delivered them up as an offering by fire to them?")

Ezekiel 20:31: For when ye offer your gifts, when ye make your sons to pass through the fire, ye pollute yourselves with all your idols, even unto this day . . . (RSV: When you offer your gifts and sacrifice your sons by fire, you defile yourselves with all your idols to this day")

Ezekiel 23:37-39: That they have committed adultery, and blood is in their hands, and with their idols have they committed adultery, and have also caused their sons, whom they bare unto me, to pass for them through the fire, to devour them. [38] Moreover this they have done unto me: they have defiled my sanctuary in the same day, and have profaned my sabbaths.

[39] For when they had slain their children to their idols, then they came the same day into my sanctuary to profane it; and, lo, thus have they done in the midst of mine house. (RSV: "they have even offered up to them for food the sons whom they had borne to me . . . they had slaughtered their children in sacrifice to their idols . . ."

Wisdom 12:3-6: For it was thy will to destroy by the hands of our fathers both those old inhabitants of thy holy land, [4] Whom thou hatedst for doing most odious works of witchcrafts, and wicked sacrifices; [5] And also those merciless murderers of children, and devourers of man's flesh, and the feasts of blood,

[6] With their priests out of the midst of their idolatrous crew, and the parents, that killed with their own hands souls destitute of help: (RSV: "merciless slaughter of children, and their sacrificial feasting on human flesh and blood. These initiates from the midst of a heathen cult, these parents who murder helpless lives, thou didst will to destroy by the hands of our fathers,")

It is sinful to perform or
even to support abortion

Exodus 1:15-17: And the king of Egypt spake to the Hebrew midwives, of which the name of the one was Shiphrah, and the name of the other Puah: [16] And he said, When ye do the office of a midwife to the Hebrew women, and see them upon the stools; if it be a son, then ye shall kill him: but if it be a daughter, then she shall live. [17] But the midwives feared God, and did not as the king of Egypt commanded them, but saved the men children alive.

2 Kings 8:12: And Hazael said, Why weepeth my lord? And he answered, Because I know the evil that thou wilt do unto the children of Israel: their strong holds wilt thou set on fire, and their young men wilt thou slay with the sword, and wilt dash their children, and rip up their women with child.

2 Kings 15:16: Then Menahem smote Tiphsah, and all that were therein, and the coasts thereof from Tirzah: because they opened not to him, therefore he smote it; and all the women therein that were with child he ripped up.

Psalm 5:6: Thou shalt destroy them that speak leasing: the LORD will abhor the bloody and deceitful man.

Psalm 10:2-11: The wicked in his pride doth persecute the poor: let them be taken in the devices that they have imagined. [3] For the wicked boasteth of his heart's desire, and blesseth the covetous, whom the LORD abhorreth. [4] The wicked, through the pride of his countenance, will not seek after God: God is not in all his thoughts. [5] His ways are always grievous; thy judgments are far above out of his sight: as for all his enemies, he puffeth at them. [6] He hath said in his heart, I shall not be moved: for I shall never be in adversity. [7] His mouth is full of cursing and deceit and fraud: under his tongue is mischief and vanity. [8] He sitteth in the lurking places of the villages: in the secret places doth he murder the innocent: his eyes are privily set against the poor. [9] He lieth in wait secretly as a lion in his den: he lieth in wait to catch the poor: he doth catch the poor, when he draweth him into his net. [10] He croucheth, and humbleth himself, that the poor may fall by his strong ones. [11] He hath said in his heart, God hath forgotten: he hideth his face; he will never see it.

Psalm 94:20-21: Shall the throne of iniquity have fellowship with thee, which frameth mischief by a law? [21] They gather themselves together against the soul of the righteous, and condemn the innocent blood. (RSV: "Can wicked rulers be allied with thee, who frame mischief by statute? They band together against the life of the righteous, and condemn the innocent to death.")

Proverbs 1:10-11: My son, if sinners entice thee, consent thou not. [11] If they say, Come with us, let us lay wait for blood, let us lurk privily for the innocent without cause: (RSV: "let us lie in wait for blood, let us wantonly ambush the innocent;")

Proverbs 6:16-19: These six things doth the LORD hate: yea, seven are an abomination unto him: [17] A proud look, a lying tongue, and hands that shed innocent blood, [18] An heart that deviseth wicked imaginations, feet that be swift in running to mischief, [19] A false witness that speaketh lies, and he that soweth discord among brethren.

Proverbs 29:10: The bloodthirsty hate the upright: but the just seek his soul.

Isaiah 13:18: Their bows also shall dash the young men to pieces; and they shall have no pity on the fruit of the womb; their eye shall not spare children.

Isaiah 57:4-5: . . . are ye not children of transgression, a seed of falsehood, [5] Enflaming yourselves with idols under every green tree, slaying the children in the valleys under the clifts of the rocks?

Isaiah 59:7: Their feet run to evil, and they make hast to shed innocent blood: their thoughts are thoughts of iniquity; wasting and destruction are in their paths.

Hosea 4:2: By swearing, and lying, and killing, and stealing, and committing adultery, they break out, and blood toucheth blood.

Amos 1:13: Thus saith the LORD; For three transgressions of the children of Ammon, and for four, I will not turn away the punishment thereof; because they have ripped up the women with child of Gilead, that they might enlarge their border:

Wisdom 1:12-14: Seek not death in the error of your life: and pull not upon yourselves destruction with the works of your hands. [13] For God made not death: neither hath he pleasure in the destruction of the living. [14] For he created all things, that they might have their being: and the generations of the world were healthful; and there is no poison of destruction in them, nor the kingdom of death upon the earth:

Wisdom 14:22-26: Moreover this was not enough for them, that they erred in the knowledge of God; but whereas they lived in the great war of ignorance, those so great plagues called they peace. [23] For whilst they slew their children in sacrifices, or used secret ceremonies, or made revellings of strange rites; [24] They kept neither lives nor marriages any longer undefiled: but either one slew another traiterously, or grieved him by adultery. [25] So that there reigned in all men without exception blood, manslaughter, theft, and dissimulation, corruption, unfaithfulness, tumults, perjury, [26] Disquieting of good men, forgetfulness of good turns, defiling of souls, changing of kind, disorder in marriages, adultery, and shameless uncleanness.

Sirach 8:7: Rejoice not over thy greatest enemy being dead, but remember that we die all. (RSV: "Do not rejoice over any one's death;")

1 John 3:15: Whosoever hateth his brother is a murderer: and ye know that no murderer hath eternal life abiding in him.

Revelation 9:21: Neither repented they of their murders, nor of their sorceries, nor of their fornication, nor of their thefts.

Revelation 12:4: . . . and the dragon stood before the woman which was ready to be delivered, for to devour her child as soon as it was born.

Revelation 21:8: But the fearful, and unbelieving, and the abominable, and murderers, and whoremongers, and sorcerers, and idolaters, and all liars, shall have their part in the lake which burneth with fire and brimstone: which is the second death.

We must rescue children being led to slaughter

Psalm 82:2-4: How long will ye judge unjustly, and accept the persons of the wicked? Selah. [3] Defend the poor and fatherless: do justice to the afflicted and needy. [4] Deliver the poor and needy: rid them out of the hand of the wicked.

Proverbs 24:10-12: If thou faint in the day of adversity, thy strength is small. [11] If thou forbear to deliver them that are drawn unto death, and those that are ready to be slain; [12] If thou sayest, Behold, we knew it not; doth not he that pondereth the heart consider it? and he that keepeth thy soul, doth not he know it? and shall not he render to every man according to his works?

Proverbs 31:8: Open thy mouth for the dumb in the cause of all such as are appointed to destruction.

Jeremiah 22:3: Thus saith the LORD; Execute ye judgment and righteousness, and deliver the spoiled out of the hand of the oppressor: and do no wrong, do no violence to the stranger, the fatherless, nor the widow, neither shed innocent blood in this place. (cf. Tob. 1:17)

Dave Armstrong

Dave Armstrong is a Catholic writer, apologist, and evangelist who has been actively proclaiming and defending Christianity for more than twenty years. Formerly a campus missionary, as a Protestant, Armstrong was received into the Catholic Church in 1991 by the late, well-known catechist and theologian Fr. John A. Hardon, S.J. Armstrong's conversion story appeared in the best-selling book *Surprised by Truth*, and his articles have been published in a number of Catholic periodicals, including *The Catholic Answer, This Rock, Envoy, Hands On Apologetics, The Coming Home Journal*, and *The Latin Mass*. His apologetic and writing apostolate was the subject of a feature article in the May 2002 issue of *Envoy*. Armstrong is the author of the books A *Biblical Defense of Catholicism* and *More Biblical Evidence for Catholicism* and of forty-four apologetics articles in *The Catholic Answer Bible*. His website, Biblical Evidence for Catholicism (www.biblicalcatholic.com), online since March 1997, received the 1998 Catholic Website of the Year award from *Envoy*, which also nominated Armstrong himself for Best New Evangelist. Armstrong and his wife, Judy, and their four children live near Detroit, Michigan.